PART 1

الجملة العربية

# THE ARABIC SENTENCE

## PART 1
## EXPLORING THE FOUNDATION OF GRAMMAR

IDEAL FOR
KS3/KS4 ARABIC
PART TIME/ FULL TIME
ARABIC PROGRAMMES

WRITTEN BY
U.A.ABDUL AZIZ

Published by Maktabatul-Hibr limited,

www.maktabatul-hibr.co.uk



First published in 2020

Author Uwais Abdul Aziz
Editing Mufti Irfan Nadawi
Zahra Abdul Aziz
Maryam Abba

Cover design and type setting
Muhammad Yasin Sattar



British Library Cataloguing in Publication Data

A catalogue record for this book is available from the British Library

10 9 8 7 6 5 4 3 2 1

ISBN 978-1-9999760-1-9



Correspondence to the author or publisher may be sent to info@maktabatul-hibr.co.uk

# Contents

# Introduction

When it comes to learning Arabic, the defining factor of mastering grammar and its subtleties seems to be an overwhelming task for majority of learners. Many of which feel a sense of incompatibility with the grammatical rules that govern sentences, whilst others are unable to relate with the intricacies that manifest within grammar and consider them alien and remote.

For English native speakers that have not delved into the science of grammar; or during their elementary schooling were provided with an adequate amount of knowledge for purposes of reading and writing, learning a language that depends wholly on syntax and morphological formations can seem daunting. The vast majority of English speakers have become well adapted with the English language through the means of speaking and listening, that at most circumstances, utterances can be produced and spoken without any recollection to the grammar that strings the sentences together.

Another pitfall that is placed before the native speaker of English when learning Arabic, is that over the last eight hundred years most of the inflectional morphology of English has been shed and all of its case markings have been abandoned. As a result, modern English relies almost entirely on sequencing and positioning of words in order to mark formational functions. Arabic, on the other hand, maintains its case markings via demarcation of words and has thorough morphological implications in the derivations of words. This style of preservation can be somewhat intimidating for those that may not be accustomed and familiar with the grammatical process of sentence formation.

Despite the differences between these two languages, there are many similarities that can assist in learning what seems to be an unattainable language. The construction of the English language was a culmination of different languages; languages that shared resemblances to that of Arabic, whether it be in case marking like Latin or gender differentiation like French. All of these factors were inherited by the English language and can be used to better a student's understanding of how grammar plays a vital role in depicting an intended meaning via words.

Studying the Arabic language as a student posed many abnormalities with what I currently knew. The books that were read and studied provided much information, however I was still unable to get a firm grasp of the language. The science of grammar was split into two aspects – syntax and morphology. This can seem problematic as both aspects are integral when forming a sentence and dividing them made it seem as though they were two separate entities.

The resources that were covered for both topics were like manuals that provided relevant information that could be stored, but not appropriately clear on how they could be applied. In relation to this, the chapters that were discussed did not always link with other chapters and therefore understanding the formation of sentences was at times ambiguous. The concept of how sentences were formed with different elements, due to a lack of my own knowledge, was another area which caused problems for myself. During my years of study, I read a range of grammar books that would cultivate my knowledge of this science and practicing what I had learnt enabled me to gain a reasonable awareness of the Arabic language.

After studying, I was fortunate to teach the Arabic language to a group of individuals. However, the group of students that were assigned to me were Key Stage Three students; their ages ranged between eleven and twelve. This seemed like a gargantuan task. A language so elaborate and detailed that possessed concepts and principles that may estrange common individuals was to be taught to these youngsters. I commenced with explaining the basic premise and ideology of language in a way that was not too convoluted. In order to expand and unravel the strenuous grammatical theories, I studied extensively furthering my knowledge and finding a way of combining common features between Arabic and their native language; English. I would like to thank these individuals for their passion and inquisitiveness that propelled me to begin this book. It was their motivation and relentlessness to learn this majestic language that spurred me to create activities and tasks that would assist them in making Arabic enjoyable as well as achievable.

This was the perfect opportunity to create a book, a book that would allow students from a young age as well as adults to learn Arabic in an organised way focusing on grammar and sentence structure. This book is intended for those English native speakers who would like to learn Modern Standard Arabic. It must be noted however, that basic prior knowledge of Arabic letters and reading of Arabic words is needed.

Hereunder are reasons that are preliminary factors that differentiate this book from other Arabic text books and will allow readers to comprehend the infrastructure of its composition.

1. Organisation - This book has been organised in a way that explores the foundation of sentences. Starting with the main components of a sentence and working its way up to more difficult conjugations of verbs and phrases. The main focus within this first part is understanding the function of nouns

and how they interact with other nouns. Within each chapter, relevant features that are specific to the topic are included allowing students the ability to ascertain the information they need.

2. Repetition of topics - Each new chapter includes a section in which the previous topics and their grammatical compositions are reiterated. This repetition will allow students to recognise how sentences can be affected by the rules previously discussed. This also is an excellent method in reinforcing and revising previous lessons without re-reading and tedious homework.

3. Understanding the English grammar - Every chapter begins with a clear explanation of its grammar from the English perspective. By familiarising oneself with the grammatical function of a word, the Arabic formation of a sentence will become more understandable. Students will have a clearer view of how Arabic and English are similar in their grammatical methodology. This book also uses English grammatical terminologies when forming sentences for the ease of its readers.

4. Examples - When a rule is being discussed, sufficient examples are provided. These examples are not only in Arabic, but, where English grammar is introduced examples are also used. The examples that are provided are relevant and progress from an easy level to a more complex approach. Examples are broken down to show each part of the sentence and its functional behaviour.

5. Sentence parsing - This is a method of breaking down sentences to understand the behavioural functions of a word and its role with other words in a sentence. In English, tree diagrams are often used to analyse the relationship of words in a sentence; the same method is used for Arabic sentences.

6. Activities and tasks - For each topic and chapter there are plenty of different tasks for students to complete. Tasks and activities that support and assist students who may wish to learn by themselves without a teacher. An example is provided for each task and there are varied exercises to target certain areas in mastering Arabic.

7. Revision notes and exams - This book provides simple revision notes that will help students remember the topics they have studied. In addition to that,

there are practice exams that will allow readers to test their knowledge of how well they have acquainted themselves with the Arabic language.

8. Tables and graphs - There are many useful tables and graphs within this book that will provide information that a student may needs in forming a sentence. These tables and graphs will simplify the more difficult aspects of learning and remembering certain words.

9. Colour coded rules - This book is filled with a systematic colour coded method that will assist students in their learning of the Arabic language. As mentioned previously, case markings are an important aspect within Arabic, therefore special attention has been placed on the demarcation of Arabic words with a specified colour.

10. Specific vocabulary - When it comes to learning any new language, vocabulary is the most important aspect for creating sentences. However, in this book the vocabulary has been limited in order for students to concentrate more on the grammar. Vocabulary is provided for every task and the same vocabulary is used in each example. For a student to progress further in their abilities of learning the Arabic language a multilingual/bilingual dictionary will be of great benefit. The vocabulary used within this book is very basic and easy to remember. Students should try to learn the vocabulary used in this book; in addition to this, a list of vocabulary has been attached to the end of this book.

Inclusive within this book, there is also a glossary of English terminologies with their Arabic equivalent for teachers as well as students. This glossary is useful for teachers who have studied the language with Arabic terminologies and find it difficult to associate them with English when teaching this book. Students, who are currently studying Arabic, may also benefit from them as it will provide them with clarity in defining certain terminologies within their studies.

I hope, through this book and the series of books that follow, students gain the necessary education and ability to comprehend the formation of Arabic. Thus, allowing them to dive into the monumental ocean of unsurmountable literature and incomparable poetry, in which verses and eloquence of rhetoric styles cannot be appreciated by means of mere translation.

My gratitude has no bounds and I am indebted to all those who have contributed in making this aspiration of mine a reality.

Uwais Arif Abdul Aziz

# Grammatical Terms

**Sentence** – الجملة

A statement, question or command that usually has a verb and a subject, and may be a **simple** sentence (consisting of one clause), a **compound** sentence (two simple sentences joined together) or a **complex** sentence (consisting of two or more clause).

**Noun** – اسم

A word which refers to a person, thing, places or abstract idea; such as feelings and qualities.

**Verb** – فعل

A word used with a subject to say what someone or something does, or what happens to them.

**Preposition** – حرف الجر/ ظرف

A word suggesting a relationship of time or place that normally appears in front of a noun.

**Subject** – المبتدأ

A noun in a clause that refers to the person or thing who does the action expressed by the verb.

**Predicate** – الخبر

The part of a sentence or clause containing a verb, which gives information about the subject.

**Definite article** – المعرفة

An article that specifies a noun.

**Indefinite article** – النكرة

An article that generalises a noun.

**Nominal sentence** – الجملة الاسمية

A nonverbal sentence that contains a nominal predicate, an adjectival predicate, an adverbial predicate or even a prepositional predicate.

**Verbal sentence** – الجملة الفعلية

A sentence that carries out an action to its related subject, and forms the main part of the predicate.

**Masculine** – المذكر

Denoting a gender of nouns and adjectives, conventionally regarded as male.

**Feminine** – المؤنث

Denoting a gender of nouns and adjectives, conventionally regarded as female.

**Dual** – التثنية

A form referring to exactly two people or things.

**Plural** – الجمع

A form used to refer to more than one person or thing.

**Case/state** – حالة

An inflectional distinction in nouns and pronouns related to their grammatical functions.

**Nominative** – حالة الرفع/ مرفوع

The inflection of nouns and pronouns in the nominative case, denoting a case that is used to identify the subject of a finite verb.

**Accusative** – حالة النصب/ منصوب

The inflection of nouns and pronouns in the accusative case, denoting a case that is used to identify the direct object of a finite verb, and for certain other purposes.

**Genitive** – حالة الجر/ مجرور

The inflection of nouns and pronouns in the accusative case, denoting a case used to indicate a relation of ownership and association.

**Irregular plural** – جمع التكسير

A noun that does not follow the normal rules of pluralisation.

**Diptotes** – غير منصرف/ الممنوع من الصرف

A noun that is restricted to two cases as a result of etymological causes relating to the origin and historical development of words.

**Plural non-intellectual** – جمع غير عاقل

The plural form of a word that has no humanly characteristics or traits.

**Prepositional phrase** – مجرور

A phrase that includes a preposition.

**Acting predicate** – شبه الجملة

A prepositional predicate that conveys some elements of information regarding the subject.

**Adverbial** – ظرف

A word or phrase used to modify meaning to give the reader more information

**Coordinating conjunction** – حرف عطف

A word linking two clauses or groups of words together.

**Advanced predicate** – خبر مقدم

A prepositional phrase that is brought ahead of its subject in contrary to its grammatical sequence.

**Deferred subject** – مبتدأ مؤخر

An indefinite noun that is brought after a prepositional phrase in contrary to its grammatical sequence.

**Pronouns** – ضمائر

A word that can replace a noun when the noun itself is not named directly.

**Third person** – غائب

Refers to a person that is being talked about.

**Second person** – حاضر

Refers to a person that is being spoken too.

**First person** – متكلم

Refers to the person speaking or writing.

**Personal pronoun** – الضمير المنفصل

A group of pronouns that are used to refer to the people or things that are being discussed.

**Possessive pronoun** – الضمير المتصل

A group of pronouns that are used to indicate possession.

**Possession** –مضاف

A word that is definite as a result of being in possession.

**Possessor** – مضاف اليه

A word that enables possession or ownership to another noun.

**Indeclinable** – مبني

A word that bears no inflectional change.

**Declinable** – معرب

A word that can alter in case/state.

**Diacritical marks** – اعراب

Various marks that are located above and below a letter specifying the grammatical function of words in a sentence.

**Demonstrative pronoun** – اسم الاشارة

A pronoun that is used to indicate the location or proximity of a specific thing.

**Demonstrative adjective** – مشار اليه

The noun which is modified by a demonstrative pronoun.

**Negative particle** – ما المشبهة بليس

A particle used to indicate the absence or opposite of something in a sentence.

**Interrogative pronoun** – اسم الاستفهام

A pronoun that is used to interrogate or ask questions.

# 01

The Arabic Sentence

# The Arabic Letters

# The Arabic Sentence
# The Arabic Letters

The Arabic alphabet:

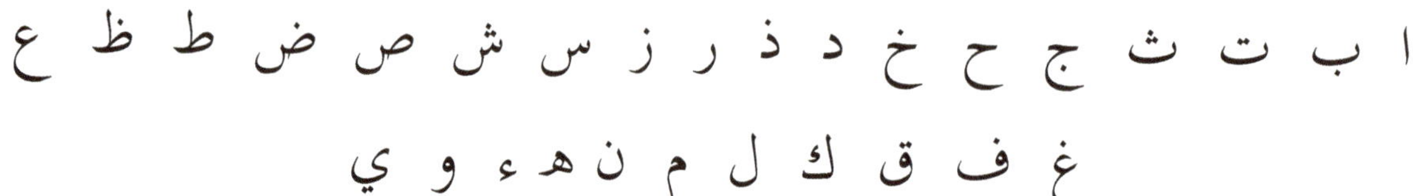


The short vowels are:

Dhamma: ◌ُ سُ

Fatha: ◌َ بَ

Kasra: ◌ِ اِ

The long vowels are:

Waaw al-Madd: When a Dhamma is followed by a Waaw Saakin. فُوْ

Alif al-Madd: When a Fatha is followed by an Alif. تَا

Yaa al-Madd: When a Kasra is followed by a Yaa Saakin. بِي

Tanween:

Dhammataan: ◌ٌ لٌ

Fathataan: ◌ً وًا

- Fathataan is usually supported by an Alif

Kasrataan: ◌ٍ تٍ

Joining letters

Arabic words are usually written by joining letters together; Most letters are able to be joined on either side. The shape of each letter changes according to its position.

The unjoined letters

There are six letters that do not join to the letter which appears after them. However, they can be joined to letters which appear before them.

They are:

ا د ذ و ر ز

For example:

Unjoined letters

اب ذب زف ول رم دج

The six unjoined letters can not be written together with the letters that follow them.

Joined

با بذ فز لو مر جد

The six unjoined letters can be attached to the words that precede them in writing.

The rest of the letters apart from the unjoined letters will join to the letters that come before and after them.

For example:

| جلس | ج ل س | جمع | ج م ع | حشر | ح ش ر |
|---|---|---|---|---|---|
| نعس | ن ع س | لصق | ل ص ق | غسل | غ س ل |
| جمجمة | ج م ج م ة | مسجد | م س ج د | ربط | ر ب ط |

a) Join the following letters and underline the unjoined letters.

| | ث ع ب ا ن | | ب ط ي خ | | ظ ف ر |
|---|---|---|---|---|---|
| | ض ف د ع ة | | ن ظ ر | | ص ف ا ر ة |
| | ب ص ل | | م ش م ش | | ق م ي ص |
| | ا ن ا ن ا س | | س م ك ة | | س ن ج ا ب |
| | ك ر س ي | | ت ي ن | | م ه ر |
| | ع ن ك ب و ت | | ب ر ق و ق | | ح ق ي ب ة |

b) Join the following letters and underline the long vowels.

| | ش ب ا ك | | ب ا ب | | ح ص ا ن |
|---|---|---|---|---|---|
| | ت م س ا ح | | ط ي و ر | | ف ي ل |
| | ر ي ش ة | | ح و ت | | خ ر ي ط ة |

c) Write the letters of the following words. E.g.

| م س ل م | **مسلم** |
|---|---|

| | ستر | | شجرة | | البيت |
|---|---|---|---|---|---|
| | حجاج | | اسنان | | لسان |
| | الزرافة | | مسلمات | | قهوة |

# The Arabic Sentence
# Subject & Predicate

Simple sentences (main clauses), also known as independent sentences, are constructed by having a **subject** and a ***predicate***.

**Subject:** the noun which is being discussed.
E.g. The **man**
The **woman**
The **trees**

***Predicate:*** any relevant information regarding the subject.
E.g. The man ***is tall.***
The woman ***is clever.***
The trees ***are beautiful.***

## 1. Can you identify the subject and predicate from the following sentences?

*E.g. The girl is crying.*

**Subject:** *The girl*
***Predicate:*** *crying*

*The gardens are beautiful.*

**Subject:**
***Predicate:***

*The stone is hard.*

**Subject:**
***Predicate:***

*The children are playing.*

**Subject:**
***Predicate:***

*The car is fast.*

**Subject:**
***Predicate:***

*The boys are sleeping.*

**Subject:**
***Predicate:***

Just like in English, an Arabic sentence also consists of a **subject** and a ***predicate.***

- In English, the subject is made definite by adding the article **'The'** before the subject.
- In Arabic, the subject is made definite by adding the article اَلْ before the noun and a singular vowel at the end of it.

E.g. وَلَدٌ → اَلْوَلَدُ

رَجُلًا → اَلرَّجُلَ

كِتَابٍ → اَلْكِتَابِ

- In English, sentences are made complete by the words 'is' or 'are' before the predicate.

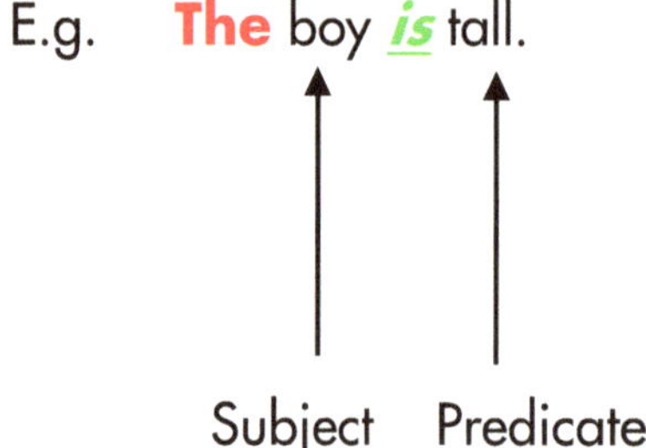


- In Arabic sentences are completed by the symbol of the Dhammatan (ٌ) at the end of the predicate, which expresses the 'is' and 'are' in the Arabic sentence.

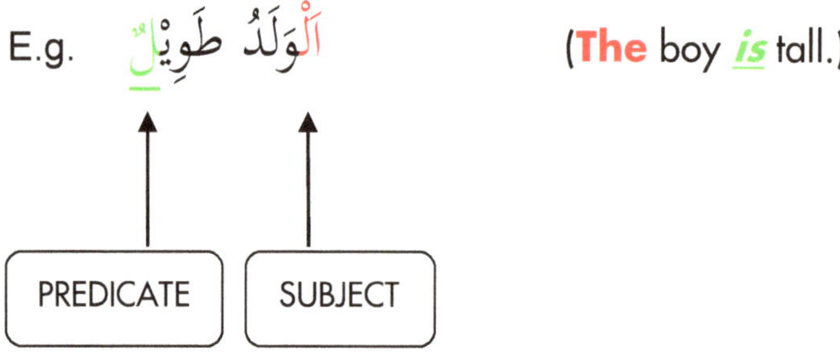

Remember:

- In Arabic there are two types of sentence formation:
    1. Nominal sentences – containing nouns
    2. Verbal sentences – containing a verb

- Arabic starts from right to left whereas English is left to right. In Arabic the subject normally comes first in a nominal sentence

- The subject and predicate in Arabic will always be in the nominative state, which means the end of the words will have a Dhamma (ُ) or Dhammataan (ٌ)

- A Tanween no longer remains on a word which has the article اَلْ

## 1. Make the indefinite words definite by adding the article اَلْ

The first one is done for you.

*** DON'T FORGET TO CHANGE THE DHAMMATAAN IN TO A SINGULAR DHAMMA***

| | Indefinite | | Definite | |
|---|---|---|---|---|
| a. | طَبِيْبٌ | (A doctor) | اَلطَّبِيْبُ | (The doctor) |
| b. | بَيْتٌ | (A house) | ----------- | (The house) |
| c. | مُعَلِّمٌ | (A teacher ) | ----------- | (The teacher) |
| d. | طَالِبٌ | (A student) | ----------- | (The student) |
| e. | اِبْنٌ | (A son) | ----------- | (The son) |

2. Make the definite words indefinite by removing the particle اَلْ and adding the Dhammataan.

| | Definite | | Indefinite | |
|---|---|---|---|---|
| a. | اَلْأَبُ | (The father) | أَبٌ | (A father) |
| b. | اَلتَّاجِرُ | (The merchant) | ----------- | (A merchant) |
| c. | اَلْبَابُ | (The door) | ----------- | (A door) |
| d. | اَلْوَلَدُ | (The boy) | ----------- | (A boy) |
| e. | اَلْأَمِيْرُ | (The governor) | ----------- | (A governor) |

3. Can you identify the subject and predicate from these Arabic sentences?

| اَلْبَيْتُ كَبِيْرٌ | |
|---|---|
| Subject: | اَلْبَيْتُ |
| Predicate: | كَبِيْرٌ |

| اَلرَّجُلُ صَادِقٌ | |
|---|---|
| Subject: | |
| Predicate: | |

| اَلْأَبُ رَحِيْمٌ | |
|---|---|
| Subject: | |
| *Predicate:* | |

| اَلْبَابُ شَدِيْدٌ | |
|---|---|
| Subject: | |
| *Predicate:* | |

| اَلتَّاجِرُ جَالِسٌ | |
|---|---|
| Subject: | |
| *Predicate:* | |

| اَلْمُعَلِّمُ ذَكِيٌّ | |
|---|---|
| Subject: | |
| *Predicate:* | |

| اَلطَّالِبُ مُجْتَهِدٌ | |
|---|---|
| Subject: | |
| *Predicate:* | |

4. Using the word from the table can you make 5 sentences of your own in Arabic?

| Nouns | | Adjectives | |
|---|---|---|---|
| اَلْوَلَدُ | اَلطَّبِيْبُ | مُجْتَهِدٌ | طَوِيْلٌ |
| The boy | The doctor | Hardworking | Tall |
| اَلرَّجُلُ | اَلْأَبُ | رَحِيْمٌ | صَغِيْرٌ |
| The man | The Father | Merciful | Small |
| اَلْمُعَلِّمُ | اَلطَّالِبُ | جَالِسٌ | ذَكِيٌّ |
| The teacher | The student | Sitting | Clever |

(i

(ii

(iii

(iv

(v

5. Translate the following Arabic sentences in to English filling in the missing gaps with the correct words.

اَلطَّبِيْبُ رَحِيْمٌ

i) The ____________________ is merciful.

اَلرَّجُلُ جَالِسٌ

ii) The man is ____________________

اَلْأَبُ مُجْتَهِدٌ

iii) ____________________ is hardworking.

اَلطَّالِبُ ذَكِيٌّ

iv) The student ____________________

اَلْوَلَدُ صَغِيْرٌ

v) ________________________________

اَلطَّبِيْبُ طَوِيْلٌ

vi) ________________________________

# 02

The Arabic Sentence

# Compound sentences

# The Arabic Sentence
# Compound Sentences

In English, a compound sentence is constructed by joining two or more simple sentences together; this can be done by using a coordinating conjunction, i.e. and

For instance,

*The student is sitting and the teacher is standing.*

Simple sentence 1- *The student is sitting.*

Coordinating conjunction - and

Simple sentence 2- *The teacher is standing.*

- In Arabic we join two simple sentences together by adding the conjunction وَ (And) before the second simple sentence.

- The conjunction وَ does not change the grammatical rules which have been mentioned previously in regards to a subject and its predicate.

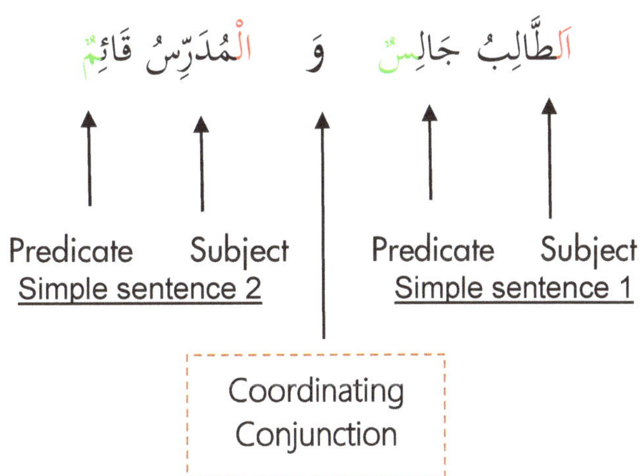

1. Using the words from the table below, change the English compound sentences in to Arabic.

*** DON'T FORGET THE وَ ***

| Nouns | | Adjectives | |
|---|---|---|---|
| اَلْوَلَدُ | اَلطَّبِيْبُ | مُجْتَهِدٌ | طَوِيْلٌ |
| The boy | The doctor | Hardworking | Tall |
| اَلرَّجُلُ | اَلْأَبُ | رَحِيْمٌ | صَغِيْرٌ |
| The man | The Father | Merciful | Small |
| اَلْمُعَلِّمُ | اَلطَّالِبُ | كَسْلَانٌ | ذَكِيٌّ |
| The teacher | The student | Lazy | Clever |

a. The boy is small <u>and</u> the man is tall.

---

b. The teacher is merciful <u>and</u> the student is clever.

---

c. The doctor is hardworking <u>and</u> the father is lazy.

---

d. The student is lazy <u>and</u> the boy is clever.

---

# 03

# Masculine & Feminine

The Arabic Sentence

# The Arabic Sentence
# Masculine and Feminine

In English there is very little or no distinction in gender. For instance, if you were to say;

*"The doctor is clever."*

There is no way to tell whether the doctor is a male doctor or a female doctor. There are some words in the English language which can take a feminine form for instance, actress, heiress and princess.

However, Arabic is different as there are clear ways of identifying whether a word is masculine or feminine. If the following rules occur on a word, then they will be considered feminine:

- If a word in Arabic has the feminine ة (TAA MARBUTA) at the end of a word it will be considered feminine. For instance,

اَلطَّبِيْبَةُ
اَلْمُعَلِّمَةُ
صَغِيْرَةٌ

- If the word is specific to the name of a woman or to a description or quality specific for women, then the word will be feminine.
  E.g.

Zainab – زَيْنَبُ

Maryam – مَرْيَمُ

Mother – أُمٌّ

The girl – اَلْبِنْتُ

- If a word in Arabic has an ALIF MAQSURAH (ىٰ) at the end, it will be considered feminine.
  E.g.

حُسْنَىٰ
صُغْرَىٰ
سَلْمَىٰ

- If a word in Arabic has an ALIF MAMDOODA (اء) at the end of a word, it will be considered feminine. E.g.

- There are some words which the Arab speaking people have considered as feminine in speech, despite not having any clear reasons for them to be so. Mentioned hereunder are a few;

i) Names of cities. E.g.
Egypt – مِصْرٌ
Makah – مَكَّةُ
Shaam –اَلشَّامُ

ii) Body parts which come in pairs. E.g.
Eyes -عَيْنٌ
Ears- أُذُنٌ
Feet - قَدَمٌ

iii) Elements of nature. E.g.
Wind – رِيْحٌ
Fire – نَارٌ
Earth – اَرْضٌ
Sky - سَمَاءٌ

iv) Miscellaneous words which are feminine:

| English | Arabic | English | Arabic |
|---|---|---|---|
| War | حَرْبٌ | Wine | خَمْرٌ |
| House | دَارٌ | Market | سُوْقٌ |
| Ship | فَلَكٌ | Sun | شَمْسٌ |
| Knife | سِكِّيْنٌ | Soul | نَفْسٌ |

## Making a masculine word feminine

- To make a masculine word feminine in Arabic, the last letter of the word will be changed to a Fatha and the letter ة will be added to the end. E.g.

| | | | | |
|---|---|---|---|---|
| اَلطَّالِبُ | + | ة | = | اَلطَّالِبَةُ |
| The male student | + | the symbol for femininity | = | The female student |

اَلْمُعَلِّمُ + ة = اَلْمُعَلِّمَةُ

رَحِيْمٌ = رَحِيْمَةٌ

1. Can you make the following masculine words in to the feminine state? The first one is done for you.

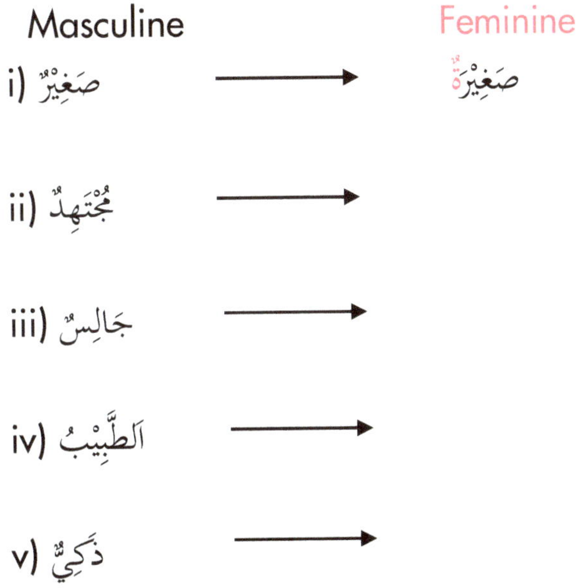


2. Put the letter M for the words which are masculine and the letter F for the words which are feminine.

| Arabic Words | M / F |
|---|---|
| مُحَمَّدٌ | |
| فَاطِمَةُ | |
| دَارٌ | |
| اَلْمَلِكَةُ | |
| اَلسِّكِّيْنُ | |
| اَلْوَلَدُ | |

| Arabic words | M / F |
|---|---|
| قَدَمٌ | |
| مِصْرُ | |
| اَلطَّوِيْلُ | |
| أُمٌّ | |
| اَلْأَرْضُ | |
| زَهْرَاءُ | |

## Subject and predicate agreement

- In Arabic the predicate will follow the subject in masculinity and femininity. Therefore, if the subject is masculine the predicate will be masculine. If the subject is feminine the predicate will also be feminine. E.g.

The (female) teacher is clever – اَلْمُعَلِّمَةُ ذَكِيَّةٌ

The female teacher -

اَلْمُعَلِّمُ + ة = اَلْمُعَلِّمَةُ

is clever -

ذَكِيٌّ + ة = ذَكِيَّةٌ

- If any of the rules of femininity are present in a word, then there is no need to add the letter ة to make it feminine.
- اَلْبِنْتُ (The girl) or أُمٌّ (A mother) are already specific to the feminine form, therefore the ة is not needed.

### 1. Can you change the following sentences in to the feminine state?

The first one is done for you.

اَلْمُهَنْدِسُ كَبِيْرٌ ---- اَلْمُهَنْدِسَةُ كَبِيْرَةٌ

اَلْمَلِكُ عَادِلٌ ----------------------------------------

اَلطَّالِبُ صَادِقٌ ----------------------------------------

اَلْمُدِيْرُ شَدِيْدٌ ----------------------------------------

اَلْعَالِمُ مَاهِرٌ وَ الطَّبِيْبُ مُجْتَهِدٌ ----------------------------------------

2. Using the words from the table below can you make 5 sentences of your own in Arabic?

| Nouns | | Adjectives | |
|---|---|---|---|
| اَلسَّيَّارَةُ | اَلْبِنْتُ | كَسْلَانٌ | مَفْتُوْحٌ |
| The Car | The Girl | Lazy | Open |
| اَلْمَدْرَسَةُ | اَلْجَدَّةُ | شَدِيْدٌ | سَرِيْعٌ |
| The School | The Grandmother | Stong | Fast |
| اَلْمَرْاَةُ | اَلْمُمَرِّضَةُ | قَائِمٌ | نَائِمٌ |
| The Woman | The nurse | Standing | Sleeping |

*** Remember the predicate has to follow the subject in **gender** ***

(i

---

(ii

---

(iii

---

(iv

---

(v

---

# 04

The Arabic Sentence

# Dual and Plural

# The Arabic Sentence
# Dual & Plural

In English, the predicate will agree with the subject in its amount of being singular or plural. This can be achieved by replacing the term 'is' with the plural form 'are'.

E.g. Singular: The boy is playing. The girl is tall.

Plural: The boys are playing. The girls are tall.

Likewise, in Arabic the predicate will agree with the subject in amount. The difference in Arabic is that the subject and predicate will be altered and reconstructed to form the dual and plural form.

Before moving on to the dual and plural formation in Arabic, we need to understand the cases of a word in Arabic grammar.

## The three cases of Arabic grammar

- There are three states in which a word will be categorised in to depending on the grammatical position of the word in Arabic.

  For instance,
  In Arabic the subject and predicate are in the nominative state.

  In Arabic an object of a verb will be in an accusative state.

  And in Arabic the noun after a preposition will be in the genitive state.

- Knowing the states/cases for a word in a sentence requires learning the Arabic grammar. However, there are some indications that enables us to identify which state a word would fall into.

- If the last letter of a word has a Dhamma (ُ◌) or a Dhammatan (ٌ◌) then it will be in the nominative state.

اَلْوَلَدُ قَائِمٌ

- If the last letter of a word has a Fatha (َ◌) or a Fathataan (ً◌) then it will be in the accusative state.

كَانَ اَلْوَلَدُ نَائِمًا

- If the last letter of a word has a Kasra (ِ◌) or a Kasrataan (ٍ◌) then it will be in the genitive state.

فِي اَلْبَيْتِ

*What's with all these cases?*

The English language is classified with cases. This classification depends on the function of the word within the sentence; for instance, a subject in a sentence will always be in the nominative case. However, the different cases that are present have no visible changes to the sounding or structure of the word. **In Arabic we see and hear the different vowel endings of words to identify what role the word plays in a sentence.** To understand what role a word plays in English; whether a word is a subject or an object, we can look at the sequence of the sentence and figure out its role. Arabic does not follow the ruling of sequencing as such, rather learning the case endings will give a clear meaning to the sentence. This will be explained further when discussing verbal sentences.

1. For the following words put the letter 'N' if the word is in the nominative state, the letter 'A' for the accusative state and the letter 'G' for the genitive state.

| | | |
|---|---|---|
| - بَيْتٍ | - لَاعِبٌ | - اَلشُّبَّاكَ |
| - مُسْلِمًا | - اَلسَّمَكِ | - تَاجِرٌ |
| - شَمْسٌ | - قَمَرٍ | - اَلْاَرْضَ |
| - اَلْفَرْحَ | - اَلسِّكِّيْنُ | - طَاوِلَةٍ |
| - اَلنِّسَاءَ | - رِجَالٌ | - ذَاهِبٍ |

## The dual form

The English language stipulates words to be singular or plural, the dual form of words is not found in the language. For instance:

Singular - The child is playing.

Plural - The children are playing.

The above sentence *"The children are playing"* could refer to **two** children or more.

- In Arabic we create the dual form of a word, whether masculine or feminine, by altering the end of a singular word and attaching the letters ◌َانِ to the end of the word. The above rule will be applied to words that are in the nominative state.

  E.g.

  اَلْوَلَدُ ← اَلْوَلَد ← اَلْوَلَدَا ← اَلْوَلَدَانِ (The two boys)

  مُعَلِّمَةٌ ← مُعَلِّمَة ← مُعَلِّمَتَا ← مُعَلِّمَتَانِ

  شَدِيْدٌ ← شَدِيْدَانِ

- When the dual form of a word, whether masculine or feminine, is either in the accusative state or the genitive state, then the following rule will apply.

  The end of the singular word will be altered and the letters ◌َ يْنِ will be joined to the end of the word.

  E.g.

  طِفْلًا ← طِفْل ← طِفْلَي ← طِفْلَيْنِ (The two children)

  اَلْقَائِمَةِ ← اَلْقَائِمَة ← اَلْقَائِمَتَيْ ← اَلْقَائِمَتَيْنِ

  جَالِسًا ← جَالِسَيْنِ

## 1. Change the following singular words in to the dual form.

### Nominative state

1) بَابٌ ........ بَابَانِ
2) اَلزَّهْرَةُ ..........
3) ذَكِيٌّ ..........
4) صَالِحٌ ..........
5) شَارِعٌ ..........

### Accusative state

1) رَجُلًا ........ رَجُلَيْنِ
2) اَلتُّفَّاحَةَ ..........
3) قَصِيْرًا ..........
4) طَالِبًا ..........
5) اَلْعَالِمَ ..........

### Genitive state

1) بَيْتٍ ........ بَيْتَيْنِ
2) اَلشَّجَرَةِ ..........
3) قَلَمٍ ..........
4) اَلْمَتْحَفِ ..........
5) غُرْفَةٍ ..........

## 2. Change the following sentences in to the dual form

| Singular | Dual |
| --- | --- |
| اَلْبَابُ قَدِيْمٌ | اَلْبَابَانِ قَدِيْمَانِ |
| اَلْمُهَنْدِسَةُ مَاهِرَةٌ | ---------------------------------------- |
| اَلْخَادِمُ ظَالِمٌ | ---------------------------------------- |
| اَلسَّرِيْرُ لَيِّنٌ | ---------------------------------------- |
| اَلْمَلِكَةُ عَادِلَةٌ | ---------------------------------------- |
| اَلطِّفْلُ كَاذِبٌ | ---------------------------------------- |
| اَلْمُؤْمِنَةُ صَادِقَةٌ | ---------------------------------------- |
| اَلْقَمِيْصُ جَدِيْدٌ | ---------------------------------------- |
| اَلصَّدِيْقُ اَمِيْنٌ | ---------------------------------------- |
| اَلشُّبَّاكُ مَفْتُوْحٌ | ---------------------------------------- |

## The plural form

The plural form in English is created by adding the letter '**s**' to the end of the word, for instance the plural of the word 'car' will be 'car**s**'.

The rules which we apply to create the plural form have a general structure and a regular method. E.g.

1, Adding the letter 's', 'es' or 'ies' to the end of a singular word.

However, there are some words that do not conform to the general rule and their plural form will be in a different form altogether. For instance, the plural of the word 'mouse' is 'mice' or the plural of 'man' being 'men'.

These irregular plurals have to be learnt and memorised by the English speaking student in order to learn the language. Irregular plurals can be created from:

1. The plural of a word has come through speech, e.g. mice.

2. The singular form of a word and the plural is the same, e.g. sheep.

- Like English, Arabic also has similar rules for creating the plural form. In Arabic, singular words that follow a rule to create their plural forms are know as ***REGULAR PLURALS.***

- Singular words that do not follow this specific rule are known as ***IRREGULAR PLURALS.*** There is no way of determining how these plurlas are formed; however, there are some patterns on which irregular plurals can take which helps in remembering them. Majority of these plural forms can be learnt by memorising them when learning any new vocabulary.

- As we have studied before, Arabic is more varied in its gender differentiation then that of English. Hence, the structure of ***REGULAR PLURALS*** will also be different for masculine and feminine words.

## The masculine ***REGULAR PLURAL*** form

- In Arabic we create the masculine ***REGULAR PLURAL*** form by altering the end of a singular word and attaching the letters ـُوْنَ to the end of the word. The above rule will be applied to words that are in the nominative state, e.g.

مُسْلِمٌ ⟶ مُسْلِمُ ⟶ مُسْلِمُوْ ⟶ مُسْلِمُوْنَ

اَلصَّالِحُ ⟶ اَلصَّالِحُ ⟶ اَلصَّالِحُوْ ⟶ اَلصَّالِحُوْنَ

صَادِقٌ ⟶ صَادِقُوْنَ

- If the masculine ***REGULAR PLURAL*** form of a word is either in the accusative state or the genitive state, then the following rule will apply; the end of the singular word will be altered and the letters ـِيْنَ will be joined to the end of the word, e.g.

مُؤْمِنًا ⟶ مُؤْمِنِ ⟶ مُؤْمِنِيْ ⟶ مُؤْمِنِيْنَ

اَلطَّالِحِ ⟶ اَلطَّالِحِ ⟶ اَلطَّالِحِيْ ⟶ اَلطَّالِحِيْنَ

سَارِقٍ ⟶ سَارِقِيْنَ

## The feminine ***REGULAR PLURAL*** form

- In Arabic, we create the feminine ***REGULAR PLURAL*** form of a word by deleting the final letter of the feminine singular word and attaching the letters ◌َاتٌ to the end of the word. The above rule will be applied to words that are in the nominative state, e.g.

تِلْمِيْذَةٌ ⟶ تِلْمِيْذَ ⟶ تِلْمِيْذَا ⟶ تِلْمِيْذَاتٌ

اَلتُّفَّاحَةُ ⟶ اَلتُّفَّاحَ ⟶ اَلتُّفَّاحَا ⟶ اَلتُّفَّاحَاتُ

بَقَرَةٌ ⟶ بَقَرَاتٌ

- If the feminine ***REGULAR PLURAL*** form for a word is either in the accusative state or the genitive state, then the following rule will apply; the final letter of the feminine singular word will be deleted and the letters ◌َاتٍ will be attached to the end of the word, e.g.

زُجَاجَةً ⟶ زُجَاجَ ⟶ زُجَاجَا ⟶ زُجَاجَاتٍ

اَلسَّاعَةِ ⟶ اَلسَّاعَ ⟶ اَلسَّاعَا ⟶ اَلسَّاعَاتِ

اَلطَّاوِلَةِ ⟶ اَلطَّاوِلَاتِ

## 1. Change the following singular words in to the plural form.

### Nominative state

1) اَلظَّالِمُ ‎ اَلظَّالِمُوْنَ
2) عَادِلٌ ‎ ................
3) مُعَلِّمٌ ‎ ................
4) اَلطَّائِرَةُ ‎ اَلطَّائِرَاتُ
5) سَيَّارَةٌ ‎ ................
6) اَلْخَاشِعَةُ ‎ ................

### Accusative state

1) مُفْلِحًا ‎ مُفْلِحِيْنَ
2) اَلْمُفْلِسَ ‎ ................
3) مُجْتَهِدًا ‎ ................
4) اَلْمُكْرَمَةَ ‎ اَلْمُكْرَمَاتِ
5) نَاجِحَةً ‎ ................
6) اَلْمَكْسُوْرَةَ ‎ ................

### Genitive state

1) دَرَجَةٍ ‎ دَرَجَاتٍ
2) اَلْبَرَكَةِ ‎ ................
3) خَائِفَةٍ ‎ ................
4) اَلْجَالِسِ ‎ ................
5) اَلْكَاذِبِ ‎ ................
6) مُهَنْدِسٍ ‎ ................

2.Using the words from the table below, make 5 regular plural sentences of your own in Arabic.

| Nouns (Plural) | | Adjectives (Singular) | |
|---|---|---|---|
| اَلْمُدَرِّسُوْنَ<br>The teachers | اَلْمُؤْمِنُوْنَ<br>The believers | صَالِحٌ<br>Pious | مُجْتَهِدٌ<br>Hardworking |
| اَلْمُهَنْدِسُوْنَ<br>The engineers | اَلْمُعَلِّمَاتُ<br>The teachers(female) | عَادِلٌ<br>Just | صَادِقَةٌ<br>Truthful |
| اَلْمُمَرِّضَاتُ<br>The nurses(female) | اَلْمُسْلِمَاتُ<br>The Muslim women | فَرِحَةٌ<br>Happy | رَحِيْمَةٌ<br>Merciful |

*** Remember the predicate has to agree in **amount** and **gender** with the subject***

(i
------------------------------------------------

(ii
------------------------------------------------

(iii
------------------------------------------------

(iv
------------------------------------------------

(v
------------------------------------------------

## The IRREGULAR PLURAL form

- As mentioned previously, there are no specific rules to IRREGULAR PLURALS. The patterns of these plurals have to be learnt by memorising them. Mentioned below are some IRREGULAR PLURALS alongside their singular version, you can see there is no clear rule in determining their pattern on which they are formed.

| Singular | *IRREGULAR PLURALS* |
|---|---|
| شَجَرَةٌ | اَشْجَارٌ |
| صَدِيْقٌ | اَصْدِقَاءُ |
| مَلِكٌ | مُلُوْكٌ |
| مَطْبَخٌ | مَطَابِخُ |
| حَسَنٌ | حِسَانٌ |
| اَمِيْنٌ | اُمَنَاءُ |
| اَلْوَلَدُ | اَلْأَوْلَادُ |
| اَلْمَرْأَةُ | اَلنِّسَاءُ |
| اَلرَّجُلُ | اَلرِّجَالُ |

❖ In Arabic, there are exemptions by which certain words, due to linguistics, cannot bear Tanween and can only come in two states; the nominative and accusative, these are known as diptotes. The ruling for this can be learnt through further reading.

## The plural form for non-intellectual beings

In Arabic, there is a specific rule regarding the plural form for non-intellectual beings. This is not found in the English language but plays a vital role in Arabic grammar; therefore, its ruling must be learnt.

- If the plural form of a word is an inanimate object, animal or being which is not a human or does not possess humanly traits and characteristics, it will be regarded as a non-intellectual being.

- If the above quality is found in the plural form of an Arabic word, then any grammar which is linked with it will go against the laws of its grammatical principle and will take the basis of being SINGULAR FEMININE.

- We have learnt previously, that a predicate will agree with its subject in two aspects; amount and gender. However, if the subject is a non-intellectual plural word then its predicate will come as SINGULAR FEMININE. E.g.

A subject predicate sentence

(The Muslims are present.)

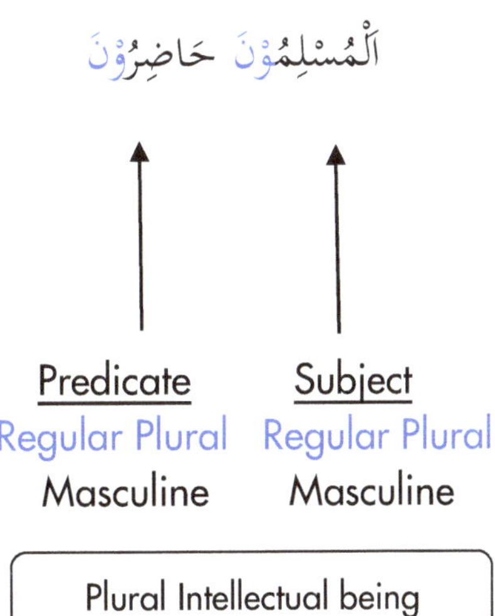

A subject predicate sentence

(The boys are sleeping.)

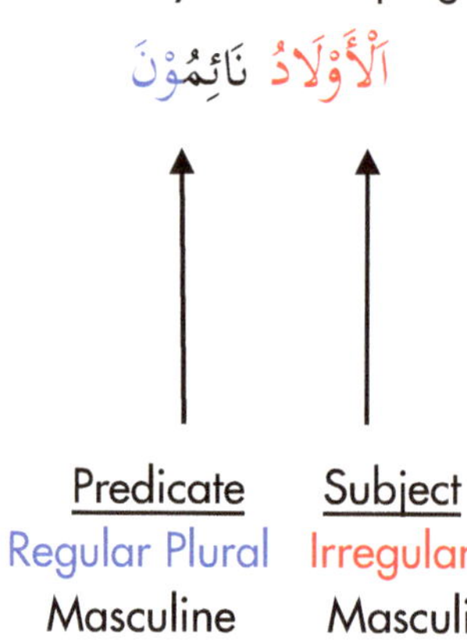


| Predicate | Subject |
|---|---|
| Regular Plural | Irregular Plural |
| Masculine | Masculine |

Plural Intellectual being

A subject predicate sentence

(The books are open.)

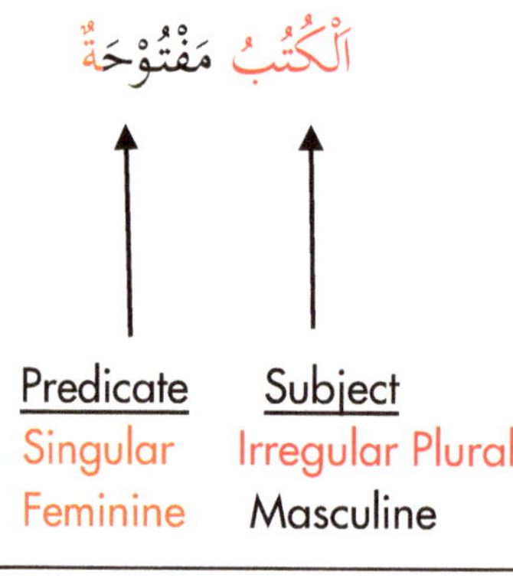


| Predicate | Subject |
|---|---|
| Singular | Irregular Plural |
| Feminine | Masculine |

Non-intellectual plural being

A subject predicate sentence

(The cows are coming.)

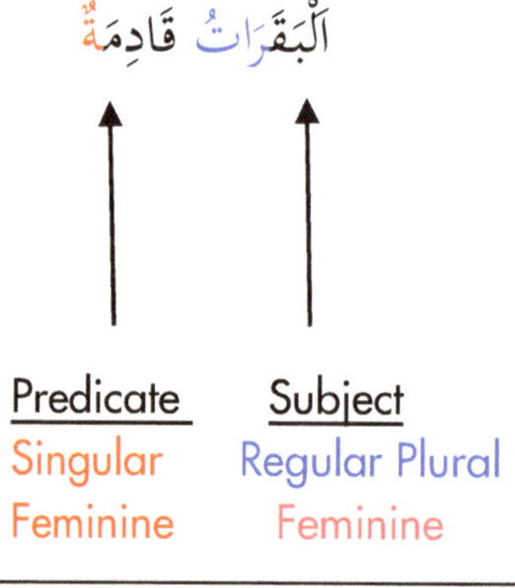


| Predicate | Subject |
|---|---|
| Singular | Regular Plural |
| Feminine | Feminine |

Non-intellectual plural being

1. Using the words below create 5 of your own plural sentences.

| English | Singular | Plural | English | Singular | Plural |
|---|---|---|---|---|---|
| Teacher | مُدَرِّسٌ | مُدَرِّسُوْنَ | Boy | وَلَدٌ | اَوْلَادٌ |
| Honest | اَمِيْنٌ | أُمَنَاءُ | Pen | قَلَمٌ | اَقْلَامٌ |
| Noble | كَرِيْمٌ | كِرَامٌ | Old | قَدِيْمٌ | قُدَمَاءُ |
| Door | بَابٌ | اَبْوَابٌ | Window | شُبَّاكٌ | شَبَابِيْكُ |
| Street | شَارِعٌ | شَوَارِعُ | Open | مَفْتُوْحٌ | مَفْتُوْحُوْنَ |
| Long | طَوِيْلٌ | طِوَالٌ | Apple | تُفَّاحَةٌ | تُفَّاحَاتٌ |
| Celver | ذَكِيٌّ | اَذْكِيَاءُ | Glass | زُجَاجَةٌ | زُجَاجَاتٌ |
| Student | طَالِبٌ | طُلَّابٌ | Woman | اِمْرَأَةٌ | نِسَاءٌ |
| Room | غُرْفَةٌ | غُرَفٌ | Tree | شَجَرَةٌ | اَشْجَارُ |
| Coming | قَادِمٌ | قُدُوْمٌ | Big | كَبِيْرٌ | كِبَارٌ |
| Good | جَيِّدٌ | جِيَادٌ | Small | صَغِيْرٌ | صِغَارٌ |
| Doctor | طَبِيْبٌ | اَطِبَّاءُ | New | جَدِيْدٌ | جُدُدٌ |

a. ......................................................................................................

b. ......................................................................................................

c. ......................................................................................................

d. ......................................................................................................

e. ......................................................................................................

## 2. Using the table, translate these following sentences in to English.

اَلْاَبْوَابُ مَفْتُوْحَةٌ

---

اَلْأَطِبَّاءُ جُدُدٌ

---

اَلْأَشْجَارُ صَغِيْرَةٌ

---

اَلنِّسَاءُ كَرِيْمَاتٌ

---

اَلشَّارِعَانِ طَوِيْلَانِ

---

اَلتُّفَّاحَتَانِ قَدِيْمَتَانِ

---

اَلْوَلَدُ اَمِيْنٌ

---

## 3. Change the sentences below in to Arabic using the grammar you have learnt.

*** Remember the predicate has to agree with the subject in **gender** and **amount*****

*** Don't forget the ruling about the non-intellectual beings***

1) The boys are new.

2) The teachers are honest.

3) The pens are new.

4) The trees are old.

5) The women are noble.

6) The girls are small.

7) The doors are big.

8) The glasses are new.

9) The apples are old.

10) The windows are closed.

# Review & Practice Test

# 05

The Arabic Sentence

# The Arabic Sentence Review

Points to remember

✓ In Arabic, the subject and predicate are by default in the nominative state.

✓ In Arabic, when a subject is made definite it cannot bear a Tanween and must have a singular vowel.

✓ A nominal sentence is made complete by adding a predicate. The predicate will bear a Tanween.

✓ Compound sentences can be created by adding the coordinating conjunction وَ (And).

✓ A predicate must agree to its subject in gender and amount.

✓ A word can be made feminine by adding a ة to the end of the word, as long as there is no other sign of femininity.

✓ In Arabic a singular word can be made into the dual and plural forms by adding the correct structural features.

| | Masculine | | Feminine | |
|---|---|---|---|---|
| | Nominative state | Accusative and Genitive state | Nominative state | Accusative and Genitive state |
| Dual | ◌َانِ | ◌َ يْنِ | تَانِ | تَيْنِ |
| Plural | ◌ُ وْنَ | ◌ِيْنَ | ◌َاتٌ | ◌َاتٍ |

✓ There are no set rules in forming an irregular plural word.

✓ In Arabic, when the subject is a non-intellectual plural word, the predicate will come in the singular feminine form.

Now see if you can complete a quick exam testing your knowledge on the rules of Arabic that you have learnt until now.

Practice Test

## SECTION A

1) In Arabic a word will come under one of the three states, how is it possible to identify whether a word is in the. . .

   i) Nominative form

   ______________________________

   ______________________________

   ii) Accusative form

   ______________________________

   ______________________________

   iii) Genitive form

   ______________________________

   ______________________________

2) i) Explain how the dual masculine word is created in Arabic for all three states.

| Nominative state | Accusative/Genitive state |
| --- | --- |
| | |
| | |
| | |

ii) Explain how the dual feminine word is created in Arabic for all three states.

| Nominative state | Accusative/Genitive state |
| --- | --- |
| | |
| | |
| | |

3) How many types of plurals are there in Arabic and explain what they mean?

4) i) How is the regular plural masculine form created in Arabic in all three states?

| Nominative state | Accusative/Genitive state |
|---|---|
| | |
| | |
| | |

ii) How is the regular plural feminine form created in Arabic in all three states?

| Nominative state | Accusative/Genitive state |
|---|---|
| | |
| | |
| | |

* * *

## SECTION B

1) Translate the following sentences in to Arabic using the words below.

The boy is sitting. ..............................
The girls are truthful. ..............................
The two merchants are lazy. ..............................
The pens are old. ..............................
The two cars are small. ..............................
The female nurses are skilful. ..............................
The female engineers are clever. ..............................
The flower is small. ..............................
The shops are near. ..............................
The books are new and the windows are old. ..............................

| English | Singular | Plural | English | Singular | Plural |
|---|---|---|---|---|---|
| Boy | وَلَدٌ | أَوْلَادٌ | Shop | سُوْقٌ | أَسْوَاقٌ |
| Girl | بِنْتٌ | بَنَاتٌ | Book | كِتَابٌ | كُتُبٌ |
| Merchant | تَاجِرٌ | تُجَّارٌ | Window | شُبَّاكٌ | شَبَابِيْكُ |
| Pen | قَلَمٌ | أَقْلَامٌ | Sitting | جَالِسٌ | جَالِسُوْنَ |
| Car | سَيَّارَةٌ | سَيَّارَاتٌ | Trurthful | صَادِقٌ | صَادِقُوْنَ |
| Nurse | مُمَرِّضٌ | مُمَرِّضُوْنَ | Lazy | كَسْلَانٌ | كُسَالَى |
| Engineer | مُهَنْدِسٌ | مُهَنْدِسُوْنَ | Old | قَدِيْمٌ | قُدَمَاءُ |
| Flower | زَهْرَةٌ | أَزْهَارٌ | Small | صَغِيْرٌ | صِغَارٌ |
| Clever | ذَكِيٌّ | أَذْكِيَاءُ | Skilful | مَاهِرٌ | مَهَرَةٌ |
| Near | قَرِيْبٌ | أَقْرِبَاءُ | New | جَدِيْدٌ | جُدُدٌ |

## SECTION C

1) Change the following sentences in to the dual form.

i) اَلْاَمِيْرُ رَحِيْمٌ ----------------------------------------------------------------

ii) اَلْاِبْنُ طَالِحٌ ----------------------------------------------------------------

iii) اَلطِّفْلَةُ صَغِيْرَةٌ ----------------------------------------------------------------

iv) اَلْمُعَلِّمُ غَنِيٌّ ----------------------------------------------------------------

v) اَلشَّجَرَةُ طَوِيْلَةٌ ----------------------------------------------------------------

2) Change the following sentences in to the plural form.

i) اَلطَّبِيْبُ مَاهِرٌ ----------------------------------------------------------------

ii) اَلْبَقَرَةُ كَسْلَانَةٌ ----------------------------------------------------------------

iii) اَلْاَخُ صَالِحٌ ----------------------------------------------------------------

iv) اَلسُّوْقُ جَدِيْدٌ ----------------------------------------------------------------

v) اَلْمُهَنْدِسَةُ كَرِيْمَةٌ ----------------------------------------------------------------

3) The following Arabic sentences are all incorrect; re-write the sentences according to the correct rules of Arabic.

| | | |
|---|---|---|
| i) | اَلْعُلْبَةُ كَبِيْرٌ<br>The box is big. | |
| ii) | اَلْوَلَدَانِ رَحِيْمٌ<br>The two boys are merciful. | |
| iii) | اَلْمُعَلِّمَاتُ ذَكِيَّةٌ<br>The female teachers are clever. | |
| iv) | اَلسِّلَالُ جَدِيْدَيْنِ<br>The Baskets are new. | |
| v) | اَلْأَبْوَابُ شَدِيْدُوْنَ<br>The doors are strong. | |

# 06

The Arabic Sentence

# Prepositions

# The Arabic Sentence
# Prepositions

Prepositions are words which connect nouns together, verbs together and both nouns and verbs together. For instance:

The boy is *in* the house. (Two nouns)
I hope *to* return safely. (Two verbs)
I hid *under* the table. (One verb and one noun)

The examples above demonstrate sentences connected by prepositions to show a time or place. Prepositions are words which do not give any meaning by themselves, but can only be understood when affixed to a noun or verb.

Prepositions in Arabic also connect nouns and verbs together. However, in Arabic there are some grammatical rules we need to follow.

- Nouns which come after a preposition in an Arabic sentence will always be in the genitive state.

(In the house)

فِي الْبَيْتِ

Noun Preposition

- The final letter of the word will be symbolised with a Kasra (ِ) or a Kasrataan (ٍ) as can be seen from the above example - تِ

- Some prepositions in Arabic are:

| Prepositions | | | | | | | |
|---|---|---|---|---|---|---|---|
| In | فِي | Under | تَحْتَ | For | لِ | With | مَعَ |
| On | عَلَى | Above | فَوْقَ | With | بِ | By/with | عِنْدَ |
| From | مِنْ | In front of | اَمَامَ | Like | كَ | | |
| To, towards | اِلَى | Behind | خَلْفَ | Behind | وَرَاءَ | | |

- Prepositions that come before a noun that is either in the dual or plural form, will also be in the genitive state.

(Dual)
On the desks.

عَلَى الطَّاوِلَتَيْنِ

(Plural)
With the teachers.

مَعَ الْمُدَرِّسِيْنَ

(Plural)
In the cars.

فِي السَّيَّارَاتِ

(Plural)
Like students.

كَطُلَّابٍ

1. Fill in the gaps by putting the correct prepositions.

1) In the car.

--------- السَّيَّارَةِ

2) On the door.

--------- الْبَابِ

3) With a pen.

--------- قَلَمٍ

4) Behind the two buses.

--------- الْحَافِلَتَيْنِ

5) Under the tables.

--------- الطَّاوِلَاتِ

6) For kings.

--------- مُلُوْكٍ

## The acting predicate

A prepositional phrase is part of a sentence which consist of a *preposition* and a **noun**, for instance: "*in* the **car**".

Prepositional phrases can also inform us regarding a subject; hence acting like a predicate. For example, if we were to add a subject "The boy" to the above prepositional phrase:

"The boy is *in* the **car.**"

The prepositional phrase gives information regarding the subject and therefore acts like a predicate.

- In Arabic, a prepositional phrase can act like a predicate, however, there will be no agreement between the prepositional phrase and the subject in **gender** and **amount**.
  E.g.

'The pens are on the desk.'

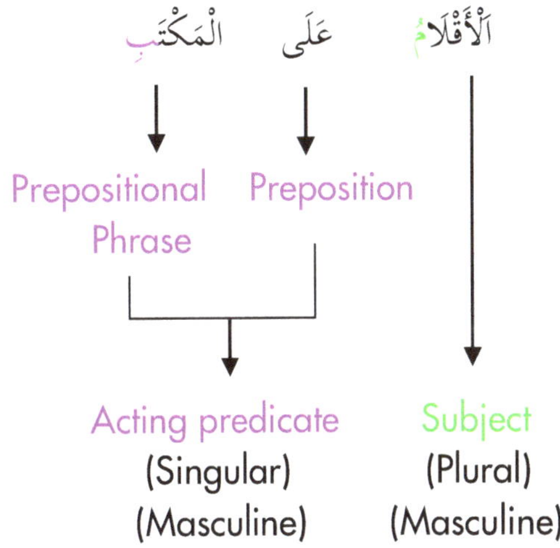


- However, if a predicate is present in the sentence, then the prepositional phrase will **not** act like a predicate rather it will provide additional information regarding the predicate itself, this is known as an **Adverbial**.

- **Adverbials** can also give additional information of a subject. The rules of subject and predicate will be in effect.
  For example,
  'The boys from the school are sitting with the teacher.'

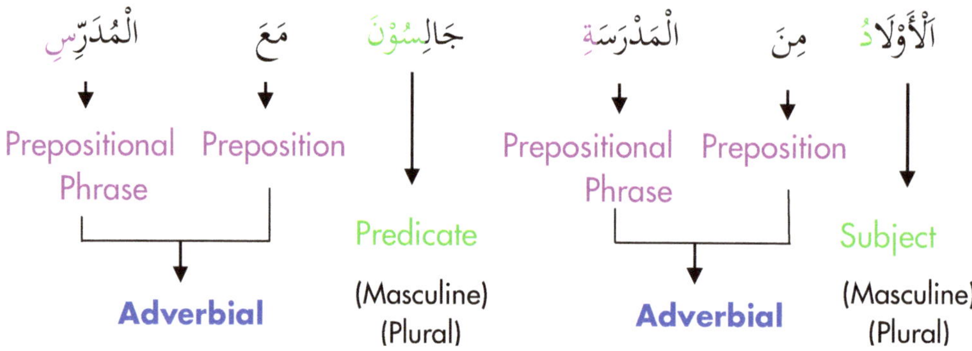


1. Underline the prepositional phrases from the following sentences and circle the prepositions in each sentence.

*** Some sentenace may have more than one prepositional phrase***

The first one is done for you.

i) The children are sleeping (in) their beds.

ii) The plate is on the table.

iii) My bag is under the desk.

iv) The school bus will depart from the school and will go to the museum.

v) Under my bed, you will find trainers that my uncle bought for me from the sportswear shop.

## 2. Fill in the gaps by putting the correct prepositions.

i) The women are <u>in</u> the house.

اَلنِّسَاءُ ....... الْبَيْتِ

ii) The masjid is <u>behind</u> the shop.

اَلْمَسْجِدُ ....... السُّوْقِ

iii) The men are sitting <u>with</u> the doctor.

اَلرِّجَالُ جَالِسُوْنَ ........ الطَّبِيْبِ

iv) The students <u>from</u> the two cities are standing <u>in front</u> of the king.

اَلطُّلَّابُ ........ الْمَدِيْنَتَيْنِ قَائِمُوْنَ ........ الْمَلِكِ

v) The bus is going <u>from</u> the museum <u>to</u> the airport <u>with</u> the students.

اَلحَافِلَةُ ذَاهِبَةٌ ...... الْمَتْحَفِ ..... الْمَطَارِ ...... الطُّلَّابِ

3.Using the words from the table, translate the sentences below in to Arabic.

| English | Singular | Plural | English | Singular | Plural |
|---|---|---|---|---|---|
| Boy | وَلَدٌ | أَوْلَادٌ | Teacher | مُعَلِّمٌ | مُعَلِّمُوْنَ |
| Pen | قَلَمٌ | أَقْلَامٌ | House | بَيْتٌ | بُيُوْتٌ |
| Office | مَكْتَبٌ | مَكَاتِبُ | Kitchen | مَطْبَخٌ | مَطَابِخُ |
| Desk | مَكْتَبٌ | مَكَاتِبُ | Door | بَابٌ | أَبْوَابٌ |
| Governors | أَمِيْرٌ | أُمَرَاءُ | Knife | سِكِّيْنٌ | سَكَاكِيْنُ |
| Apple | تُفَّاحَةٌ | تُفَّاحَاتٌ | Table | طَاوِلَةٌ | طَاوِلَاتٌ |
| Going | ذَاهِبٌ | ذَاهِبُوْنَ | Clever | ذَكِيٌّ | أَذْكِيَاءُ |
| Woman | اِمْرَأَةٌ | نِسَاءٌ | Student | طَالِبٌ | طُلَّابٌ |
| King | مَلِكٌ | مُلُوْكٌ | Room | غُرْفَةٌ | غُرَفٌ |
| Standing | قَائِمٌ | قَائِمُوْنَ | Car | سَيَّارَةٌ | سَيَّارَاتٌ |
| Sitting | جَالِسٌ | جَالِسُوْنَ | Basket | سَلَّةٌ | سِلَالٌ |
| Nurse | مُمَرِّضٌ | مُمَرِّضُوْنَ | Doctor | طَبِيْبٌ | أَطِبَّاءُ |

a. The apple is on the table.

اَلتُّفَّاحَةُ عَلَى الطَّاوِلَةِ

b. The students are going to the office.

c. The governors are sitting with the king in the house.

d. The two teachers (f) are standing with the students (f). (F represents femininity.)

e. The doctors are going to the house with the nurses.

f. The women are sitting in the cars.

g. The car belongs to the doctor.

h. The two engineers (f) are going to the office.

i. The knives from the kitchen are in the room above the desk.

j. The apples are in the basket.

4. Break down the following sentences in to their simplest form of subject, predicate, prepositional phrase, adverbial and acting predicate.

The first one is done for you

1. The students are sitting in the school.

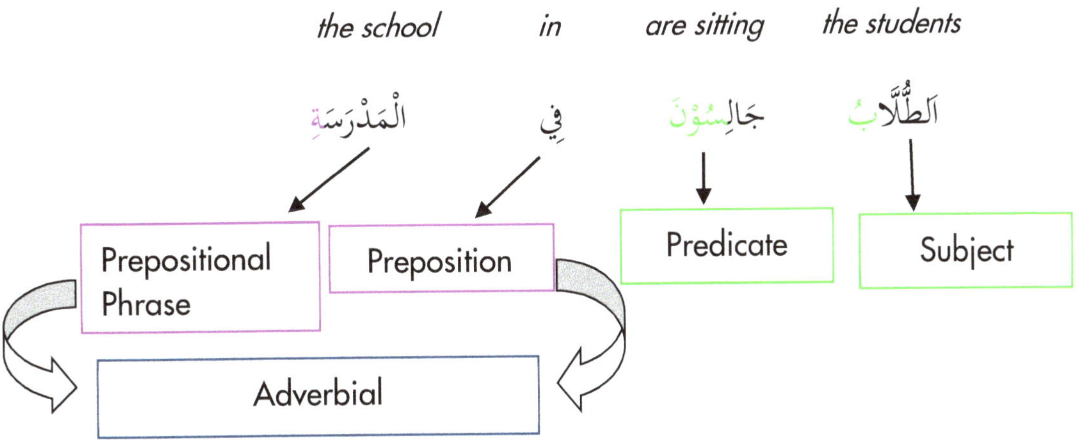


2. The books are in the bag.

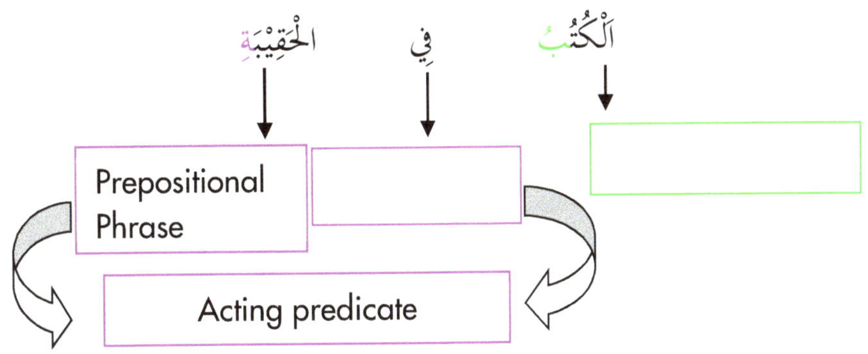

3. The cars are in front of the house.

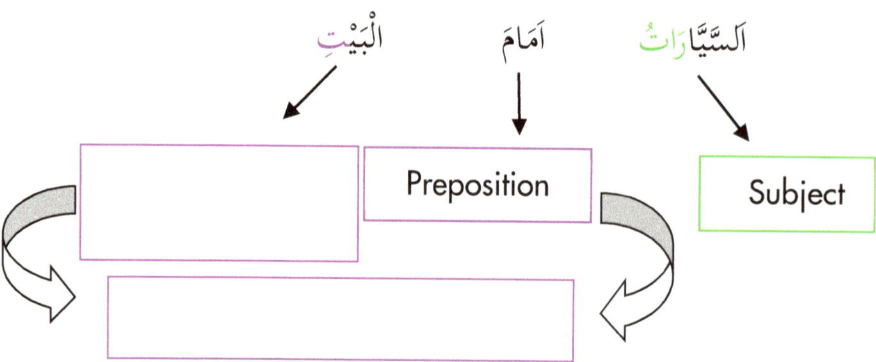


4. The man is sleeping on the bed and the children are in the school.

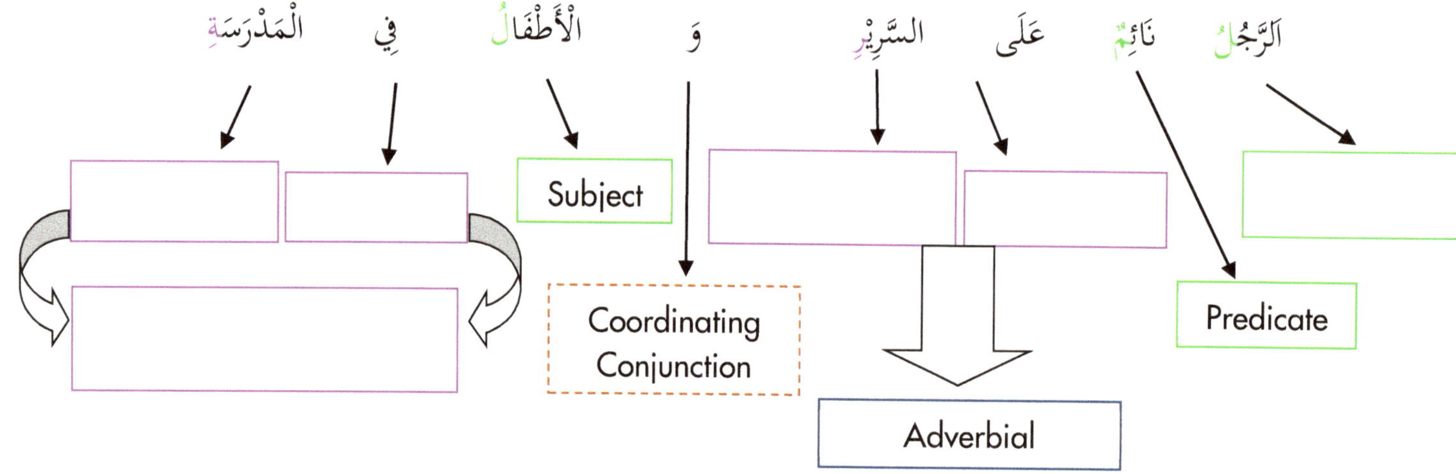

## The advanced prepositional sentence

In English sentences can be varied to make them more effective or interesting. There are many ways of varying sentences, for instance restructuring the order of the sentence. The advanced prepositional sentence is also known as an 'Indefinite subject' sentence.

To create an advanced prepositional sentence, the prepositional phrase will be brought before the subject, for example.

'**The boy** is in the room' can be re-written as;

Prepositional phrase: In the room
Subject: **The boy**

Sentence 1: *'In the room there is **a boy**.'*
Sentence 2: *'There is **a boy** in the room.'*

Both sentences give the same meaning despite being written differently. '**The boy**' in both sentences is given the particle *'There'* due to it being an indefinite subject. This particle merely emphasises the subject, it would not be incorrect to say 'In the room is a **boy**'.

- In Arabic, the prepositional phrase will be brought ahead of its subject and will be in the genitive state. This is known as an advanced predicate.

  E.g. فِي الْغُرْفَةِ (In the room)

- The subject will be in the nominative state. Due to the subject being indefinite the subject will not have the article اَلْ, therefore it will be written with a Tanween.

  E.g. وَلَدٌ (*a boy*)

- The sentence will be grammatically broken down as such;

*'There is a boy in the room.'*

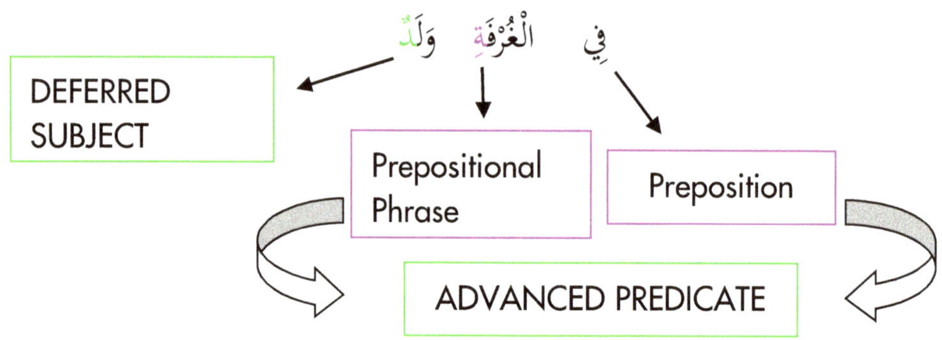


1. Underline the prepositional phrases from the following sentences and circle the subjects within them.

The first one has been done for you.

I. There is a book on that table.

II. In the kitchen there is a plate.

III. Under the table there is a cat.

IV. There is a pen on the desk.

V. In the garden there is a tree.

2. Translate the following sentences in to Arabic using the words from the table below.

The first one has been done for you.

| فِي -In | عَلَى -On | تَحْتَ -Under |
| --- | --- | --- |
| كِتَابٌ -Book | مَكْتَبٌ -Desk | شَجَرَةٌ -Tree |
| تُفَّاحَةٌ -Apple | بِنْتٌ -Girl | بَيْتٌ - House |
| مُعَلِّمٌ -Teacher | مَدْرَسَةٌ -School | سَلَّةٌ -Basket |

a) In the car there is a basket.

فِي السَّيَّارَةِ سَلَّةٌ

b) On the desk there is a book.

c) Under the tree there is an apple.

d) In the house there is a girl.

e) There is a teacher in the school.

## 3. Fill in the missing boxes with the correct grammar.

The first one has been done for you.

1. *'There is a pen on the desk.'*

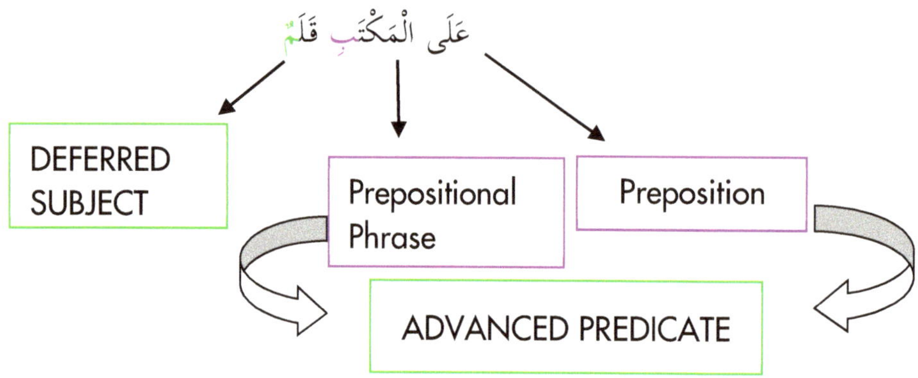


2. *'There is a boy in the school.'*

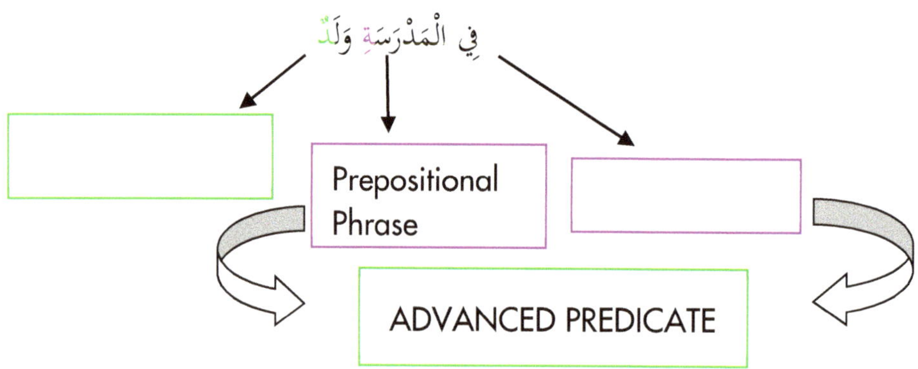


3. *'There is a basket in the room and there is a pen in the office.'*

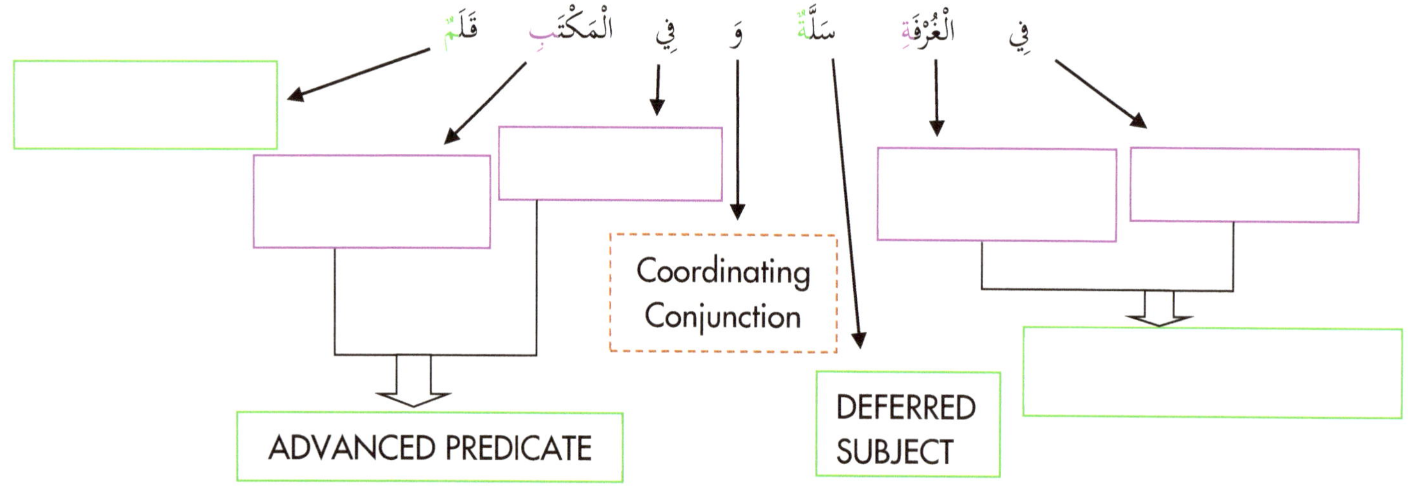

## The advanced prepositional sentence dual/plural agreement

- We have mentioned previously that in Arabic prepositional phrases can act like predicates. Therefore, there will be no agreement between the prepositional phrase and the subject in gender and amount, for instance;

*'The pens are on the desk.'*

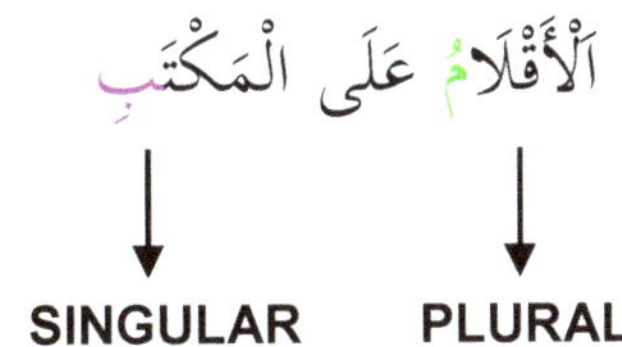


- In the same manner, an advanced prepositional sentence does not need to agree with its subject. For instance;

*'There are pens on the desk.'*

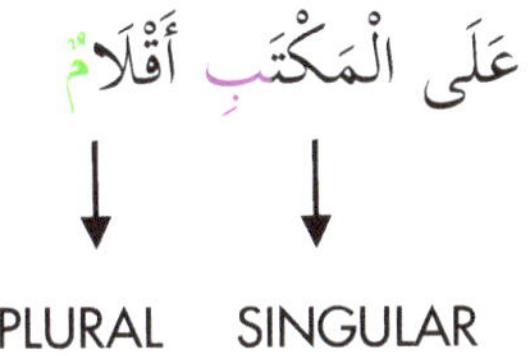


*'There are pens on the two desks.'*

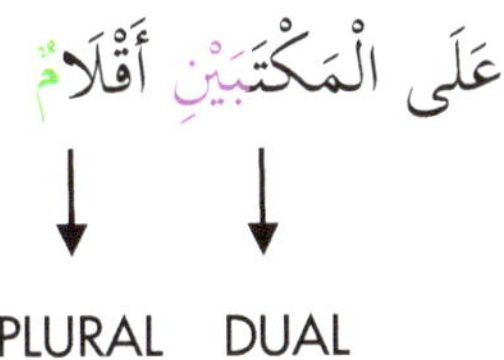


*'There are pens on the desks.'*

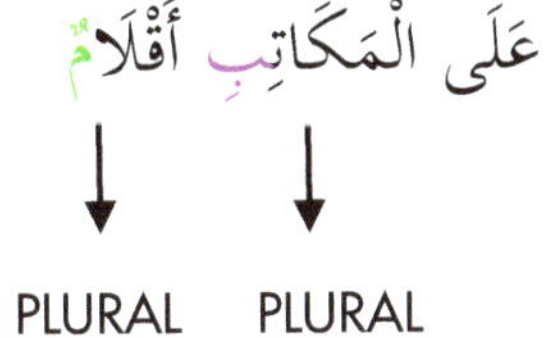

## 1. Using the table of words, translate the following sentences in to Arabic.

The first one has been done for you.

| English | Singular | Plural |
|---|---|---|
| Boy | وَلَدٌ | أَوْلَادٌ |
| Pen | قَلَمٌ | أَقْلَامٌ |
| Office | مَكْتَبٌ | مَكَاتِبُ |
| House | بَيْتٌ | بُيُوتٌ |
| Table | طَاوِلَةٌ | طَاوِلَاتٌ |
| Apple | تُفَّاحَةٌ | تُفَّاحَاتٌ |
| Kitchen | مَطْبَخٌ | مَطَابِخُ |
| Woman | اِمْرَأَةٌ | نِسَاءٌ |
| Room | غُرْفَةٌ | غُرَفٌ |
| Car | سَيَّارَةٌ | سَيَّارَاتٌ |
| Basket | سَلَّةٌ | سِلَالٌ |

The dual form for the:

Nominative state – ◌َانِ

Accusative or Genitive state - ◌َيْنِ

I. There are two baskets in the two cars.

فِي السَّيَّارَتَيْنِ سَلَّتَانِ

II. There are two boys in the two rooms.

III. On the tables there are apples.

IV. There is a woman in the house.

V. There are women in the kitchen.

VI. There are two baskets in the room and there are apples in the two baskets.

# 07

The Arabic Sentence

# Pronouns

# The Arabic Sentence
## Pronouns

Pronouns are words used in place of a noun when the noun directly does not need to be rewritten. For instance, the noun in the sentence; 'The boy is sitting' can be replaced with a pronoun '**He**'.

The boy is sitting. ⟶ **HE** is sitting.

The girls are playing. ⟶ **THEY** are playing.

In English, pronouns are subdivided in to categories depending on the person involved in the statement.

They are the:

THIRD PERSON – people or things that are being talked about;
(**HE** is standing.) (**SHE** is playing.)
(**THEY** are talking.) (**IT** was broken.)

SECOND PERSON – the person being spoken to;
(**YOU** are going.)

FIRST PERSON – the person speaking or writing;
(**I** am sitting.) (**WE** are watching.)

As well as being subdivided, pronouns can be personal, as seen from the examples above, and *possessive*; where the noun belongs to a person or thing. For instance, ***his*** book, ***your*** car, ***my*** house, ***our*** mother, ***her*** bag and ***their*** father.

In English, pronouns can be either be in the nominative, accusative or genitive case depending on their position within a sentence. The table below will illustrate the pronouns used in their respective cases.

| Person | Amount | Personal | | Possessive |
|---|---|---|---|---|
| | | Nominative | Accusative | Genitive |
| 3rd | Singular | He, She, It | Him, Her, It | His, Hers, Its |
| | Plural | They | Them | Their |
| 2nd | Singular | You | You | Your |
| | Plural | You | You | Your |
| 1st | Singular | I | Me | My |
| | Plural | We | Us | Our |

- Pronouns in Arabic are also divided in to two groups; PERSONAL and POSSESIVE. Pronouns in Arabic can be attached with nouns, verbs (as a direct/ indirect object) and prepositions.

For example:

1. **Pronoun** attached to a NOUN ⟶ *'**His** computer'*
2. **Pronoun** attached to a VERB ⟶ *'The girl helped **him**.'*
3. **Pronoun** attached to a PREPOSITION ⟶ *'From **us**'*

## Personal pronouns

- The personal pronouns in Arabic are as follows:

| Personal pronouns | | |
|---|---|---|
| **Third person Masculine** | هُوَ | **He/It (Singular)** |
| | هُمَا | **They (Dual)** |
| | هُمْ | **They (Plural)** |
| **Third person Feminine** | هِيَ | **She/ It (Singular)** |
| | هُمَا | **They (Dual)** |
| | هُنَّ | **They (Plural)** |
| **Second person Masculine** | أَنْتَ | **You (Singular)** |
| | أَنْتُمَا | **You (Dual)** |
| | أَنْتُمْ | **You (Plural)** |
| **Second person Feminine** | أَنْتِ | **You (Singular)** |
| | أَنْتُمَا | **You (Dual)** |
| | أَنْتُنَّ | **You (Plural)** |
| **First person Masculine/ Feminine** | أَنَا | **I (Singular)** |
| | نَحْنُ | **We (Dual/Plural)** |

- Personal pronouns can come in the place of a subject and will agree with the predicate in **gender** and **amount**.

- Prepositions can also come after a personal pronoun and the rules of an acting predicate will take place. For instance,

*(Plural/Feminine)*
'We are in the garden.'

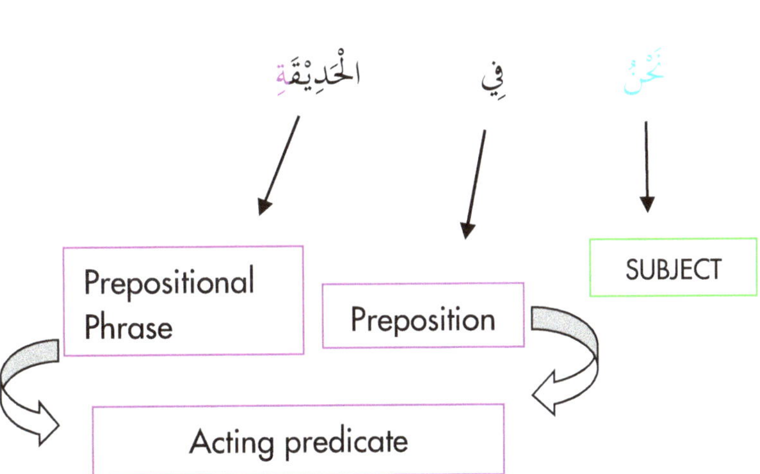


'I am in the house.'

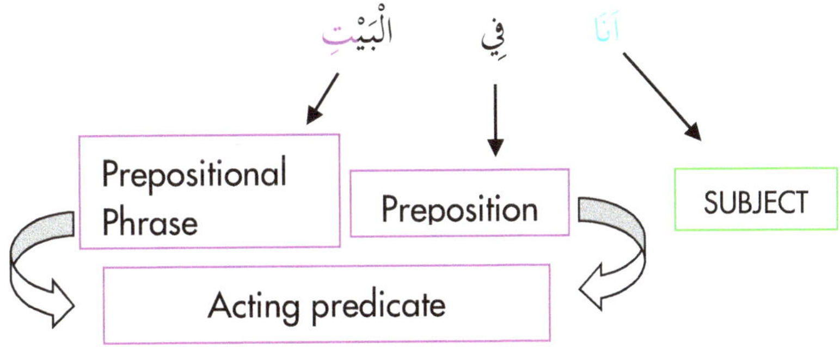

1. The pronouns in the right hand side table have been put in the incorrect order. Using the table on the left write the personal pronouns in their correct order.

| Correct personal pronouns | |
|---|---|
| | He/It (Singular) |
| | They (Dual) |
| | They (Plural) |
| | She/ It (Singular) |
| | They (Dual) |
| | They (Plural) |
| | You (Singular) |
| | You (Dual) |
| | You (Plural) |
| | You (Singular) |
| | You (Dual) |
| | You (Plural) |
| | I (Singular) |
| | We (Dual/Plural) |

| Incorrect personal pronouns | |
|---|---|
| هِيَ | He/It (Singular) |
| اَنْتُنَّ | They (Dual) |
| اَنْتُمَا | They (Plural) |
| اَنَا | She/ It (Singular) |
| هُنَّ | They (Dual) |
| اَنْتِ | They (Plural) |
| هُمَا | You (Singular) |
| نَحْنُ | You (Dual) |
| اَنْتَ | You (Plural) |
| هُمَا | You (Singular) |
| اَنْتُمَا | You (Dual) |
| هُوَ | You (Plural) |
| اَنْتُمْ | I (Singular) |
| هُمْ | We (Dual/Plural) |

## 2. Fill in the missing gaps with the correct pronouns.

i. She is standing. قَائِمَةٌ ----------

ii. I am tall. طَوِيْلٌ ----------

*(Plural/Masculine)*
iii. They are going. ذَاهِبُوْنَ ----------

*(Dual/Feminine)*
iv. You are sitting. جَالِسَتَانِ ----------

*(Singular/Masculine)*
v. It is on the table. عَلَى الطَّاوِلَةِ ----------

## 3. Translate the following English sentences in to Arabic using the words from the box.

| English | Singular | Plural |
|---|---|---|
| Boy | وَلَدٌ | اَوْلَادٌ |
| Pen | قَلَمٌ | اَقْلَامٌ |
| Standing | قَائِمٌ | قَائِمُوْنَ |
| Office | مَكْتَبٌ | مَكَاتِبُ |
| Governors | أَمِيْرٌ | أُمَرَاءُ |
| Going | ذَاهِبٌ | ذَاهِبُوْنَ |
| Sitting | جَالِسٌ | جَالِسُوْنَ |
| Nurse | مُمَرِّضٌ | مُمَرِّضُوْنَ |

| English | Singular | Plural |
|---|---|---|
| Teacher | مُعَلِّمٌ | مُعَلِّمُوْنَ |
| House | بَيْتٌ | بُيُوْتٌ |
| Kitchen | مَطْبَخٌ | مَطَابِخُ |
| Table | طَاوِلَةٌ | طَاوِلَاتٌ |
| Street | شَارِعٌ | شَوَارِعُ |
| Garden | حَدِيْقَةٌ | حَدَائِقُ |
| Room | غُرْفَةٌ | غُرَفٌ |
| Car | سَيَّارَةٌ | سَيَّارَاتٌ |

*NOTE: (M) will represent Masculine*
*(F) will represent Feminine*
*(PL) will represent Plural*

(M. PL)
a. We are standing on the street. نَحْنُ قَائِمُوْنَ عَلَى الشَّارِعِ

(M. Singular)
b. It is on the table.

c. She is sitting in the car behind the teacher.

(F. PL)
d. They are in the house.

(F. Dual)
e. I am sitting in the kitchen and you are standing in the garden.

4. Break down the following sentences in to their simplest form of subject, predicate, prepositional phrase and acting predicate.

The first one is done for you.

(M. PL)
1. You are going to the office.

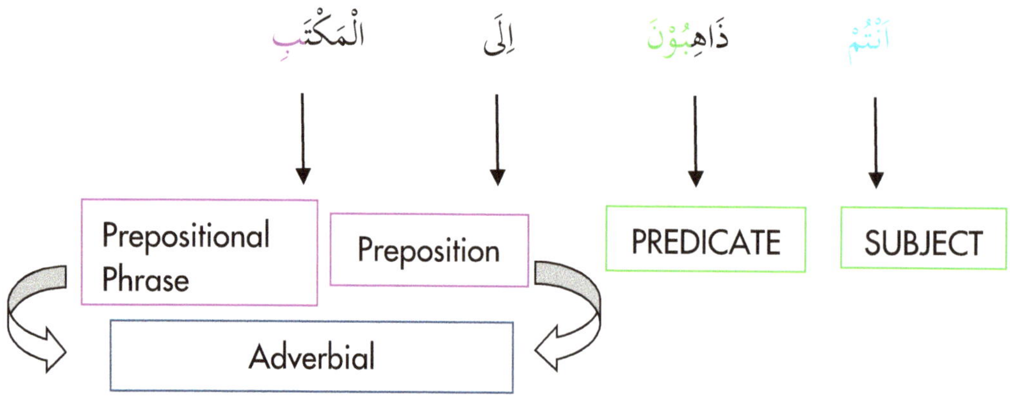

(F. Dual)
2. You are in the garden.

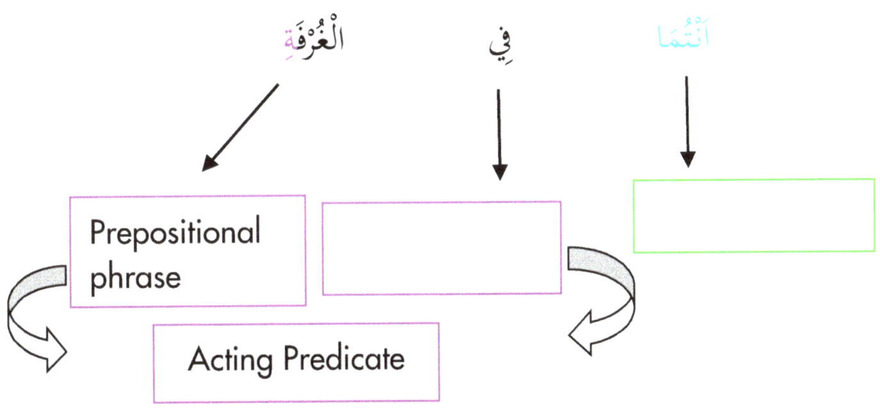


(F. Dual)
3. We are coming to the kitchen.

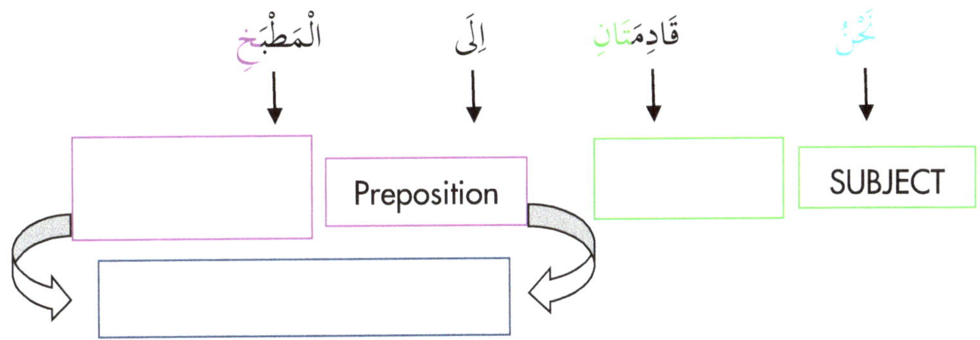

## Possessive pronouns with nouns

Pronouns as mentioned previously can signify possession to a noun, verb and preposition. In English, pronouns that are attributed to a noun are divided in to three categories. They are:

Possessive pronoun ***third person***:

His (**His** book) Hers (**Her** pen)

Theirs (**Their** house) Its (**Its** length)

Possessive pronoun ***second person***:

Yours (singular – **Your** cup)
(Plural – **Your** books)

Possessive pronoun ***first person***:

Mine (**My** car)

Ours (**Our** school)

- In English, the possessive pronoun precedes the noun that follows as cited in the examples above, e.g. **Our** school.
- In Arabic possessive pronouns are attached to the ending of nouns, verbs as a direct/indirect object and prepositions. E.g.

Third person:

كِتَابُهُ – His book
كِتَابُهَا - Her book

Second person:

كِتَابُكَ - Your book (Singular/Masculine)
كِتَابُكِ - Your book (Singular/Feminine)

First person:

كِتَابِيْ - My book
كِتَابُنَا - Our book

## Possessive pronouns

- The possessive pronouns in Arabic are as follows:

| Possessive pronouns | | | Examples |
|---|---|---|---|
| **Third person Masculine** | هُ | His/ Its (Singular) | بَيْتُهُ |
| | هُمَا | Their (Dual) | بَيْتُهُمَا |
| | هُمْ | Their (Plural) | بَيْتُهُمْ |
| **Third person Feminine** | هَا | Her/ Its (Singular) | بَيْتُهَا |
| | هُمَا | Their (Dual) | بَيْتُهُمَا |
| | هُنَّ | Their (Plural) | بَيْتُهُنَّ |
| **Second person Masculine** | ـكَ | Your (Singular) | بَيْتُكَ |
| | ـكُمَا | Your (Dual) | بَيْتُكُمَا |
| | كُمْ | Your (Plural) | بَيْتُكُمْ |
| **Second person Feminine** | ـكِ | Your (Singular) | بَيْتُكِ |
| | ـكُمَا | Your (Dual) | بَيْتُكُمَا |
| | كُنَّ | Your (Plural) | بَيْتُكُنَّ |
| **First person Masculine/ Feminine** | ـِيْ | My (Singular) | بَيْتِيْ |
| | ـنَا | Our (Dual/Plural) | بَيْتُنَا |

## Possessive pronouns with singular nouns

- Possessive pronouns are attached to the ending of nouns in Arabic. When a noun is attached to a possessive pronoun it becomes definite and is not in need of the article اَلْ before the subject. E.g.

قَلَمُهُ - (His pen)

سَيَّارَتِي - (My car)

بَيْتُكِ - (Your house)

- Due to the possessive pronoun's effect on making a noun definite, it therefore cannot take a Tanween and will have a singular vowel as is shown in the examples above.

1. Add the correct possessive pronoun to the following nouns in Arabic.

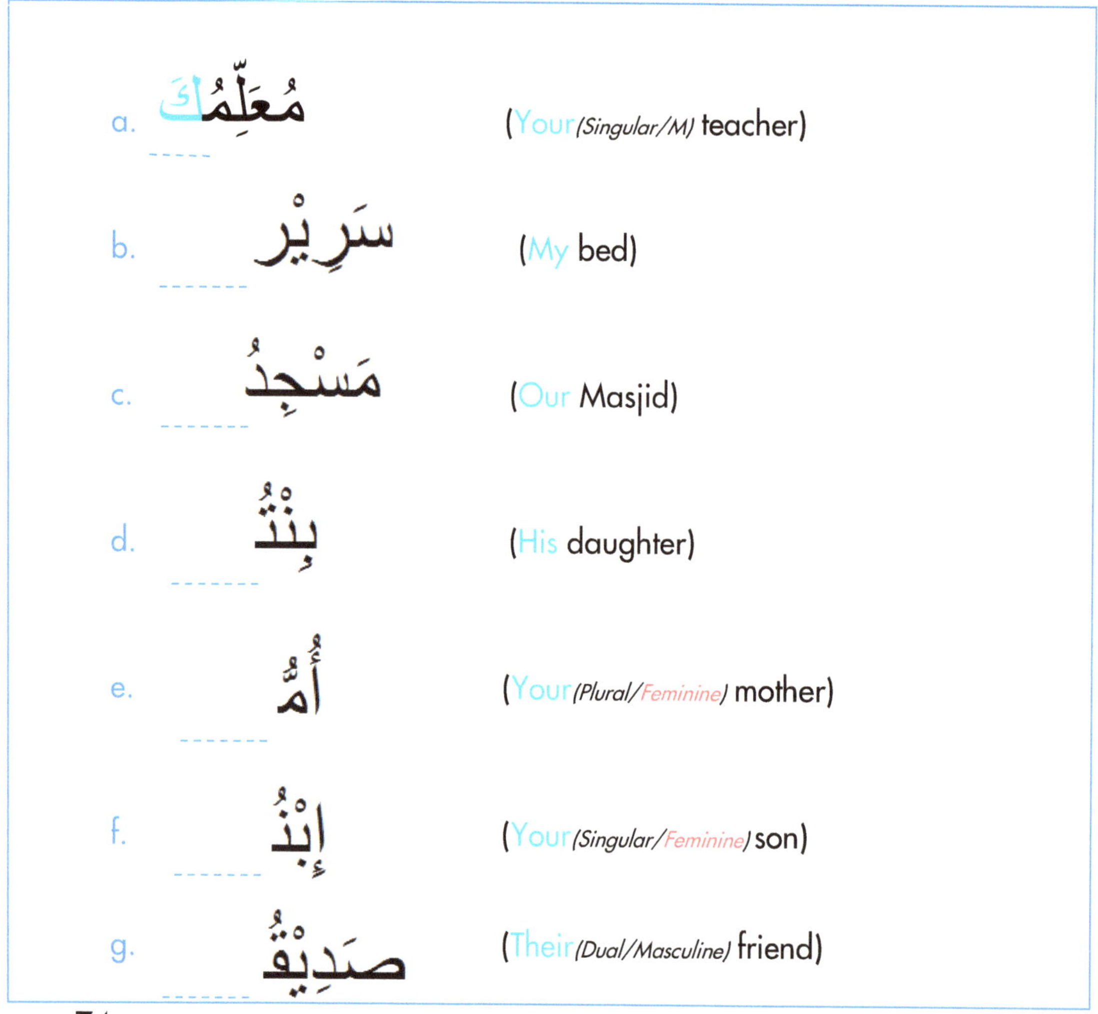

a. مُعَلِّمُكَ (Your (Singular/M) teacher)

b. سَرِيْر (My bed)

c. مَسْجِدُ (Our Masjid)

d. بِنْتُ (His daughter)

e. أُمُّ (Your (Plural/Feminine) mother)

f. إِبْنُ (Your (Singular/Feminine) son)

g. صَدِيْقُ (Their (Dual/Masculine) friend)

## Possessive pronouns (subject and predicate agreement)

- When a possessive pronoun is used as a subject in Arabic, the predicate will agree with the noun being possessed (subject) in **gender** and **amount**. E.g.

*'My car is new.'*

 - In the example above the subject being discussed is the car. The sign of femininity can be found on the Arabic word for car and as a result the predicate will also be in the feminine form. Both subject and predicate are in the singular form and agree in **gender** and **amount**.

- In sentences where a possessive pronoun is attached to a word, the word itself becomes a POSSESSION and the possessive pronoun will become its *POSSESSOR*. Therefore, grammatically in Arabic a sentence which constitutes of a subject and predicate can be split further in to smaller fragments. E.g.

*'Our book is on your table.'*

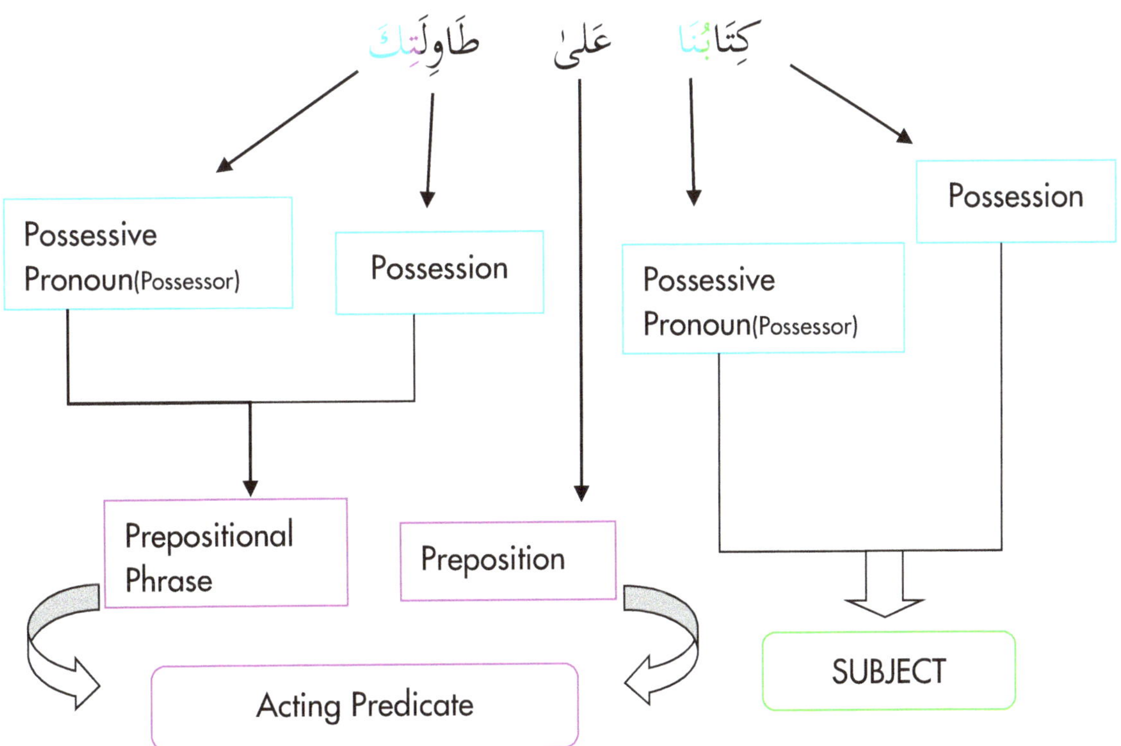

1. Using the words from the table below change the following English sentences in to Arabic.

| English | Singular | English | Singular |
|---|---|---|---|
| Teacher | مُعَلِّمٌ | New | جَدِيْدٌ |
| Pen | قَلَمٌ | Old | قَدِيْمٌ |
| Kitchen | مَطْبَخٌ | Clean | نَظِيْفٌ |
| Room | غُرْفَةٌ | Dirty | وَسِخٌ |
| Table | طَاوِلَةٌ | Small | صَغِيْرٌ |
| Car | سَيَّارَةٌ | Big | كَبِيْرٌ |
| House | بَيْتٌ | Fast | سَرِيْعٌ |

| Plural feminine | Plural masculine | Dual feminine | Dual masculine | Singular feminine | Singular masculine | |
|---|---|---|---|---|---|---|
| هُنَّ | هُمْ | هُمَا | هُمَا | هَا | هُ | 3rd Person |
| كُنَّ | كُمْ | كُمَا | كُمَا | كِ | كَ | 2nd Person |
| نَا | نَا | نَا | نَا | ـِيْ | ـِيْ | 1st Person |

a. His house is small.

b. Our car is fast.

(Singular/M)

c. Your pen is new.

(Plural/M)
d. Their teacher is old.

---

(Plural/F)
e. Your room is dirty.

---

(Dual/M)
f. My house is big and your house is small.

---

g. Her kitchen is clean and his room is dirty.

---

(Dual/F)
h. Their car is old.

---

(Plural/F) (Plural/M)
i. Your table is dirty and their table is clean.

---

(Singular/F)
j. My pen is new and your pen is old.

---

2. Break down the following sentences in to their simplest form of subject, predicate, prepositional phrase, acting predicate, possession and possessive pronoun (possessor).

The first one is done for you.

a. His pen is in the room.

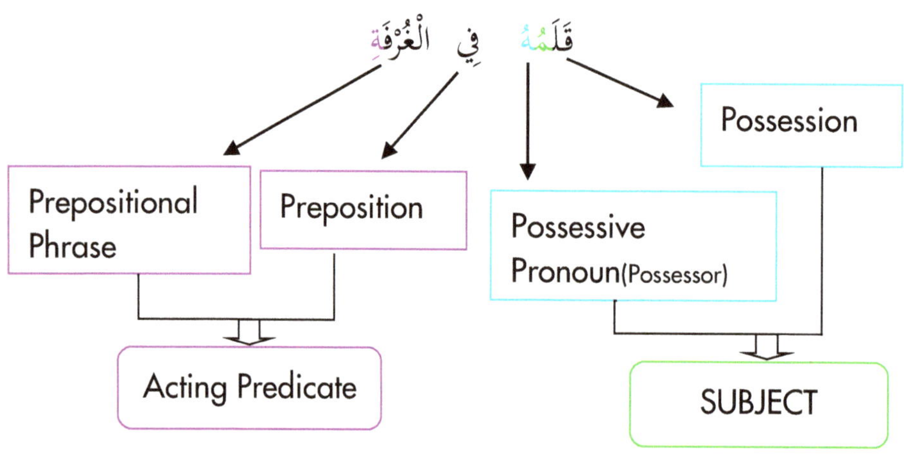


(Plural/Feminine)
b. Their kitchen is new.

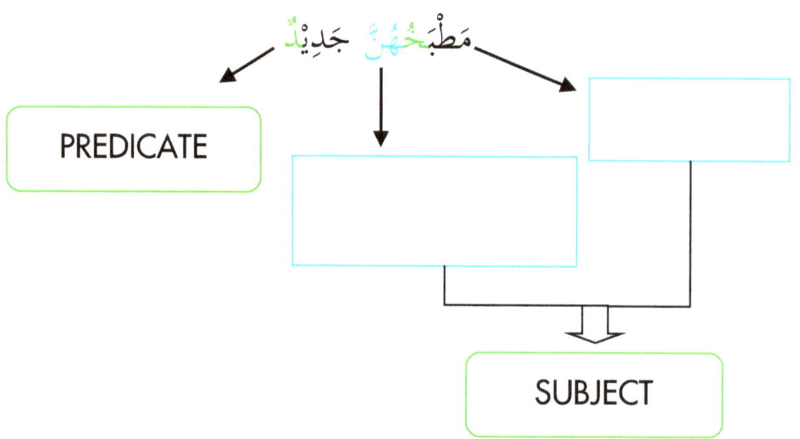

*(Dual/Masculine)*
c. Your car is small.

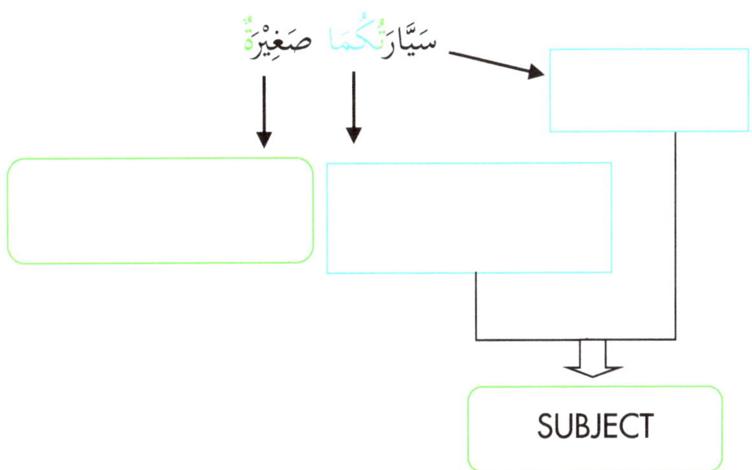


d. My teacher is in the room.

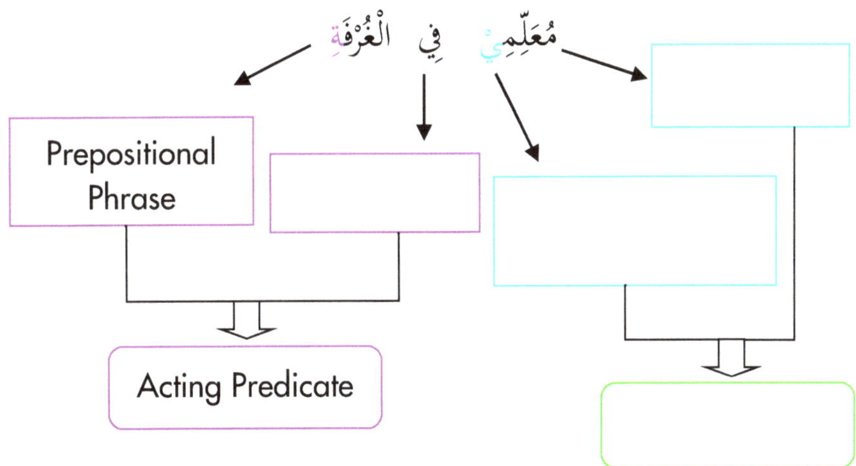

e. Our house is small and our kitchen is big.

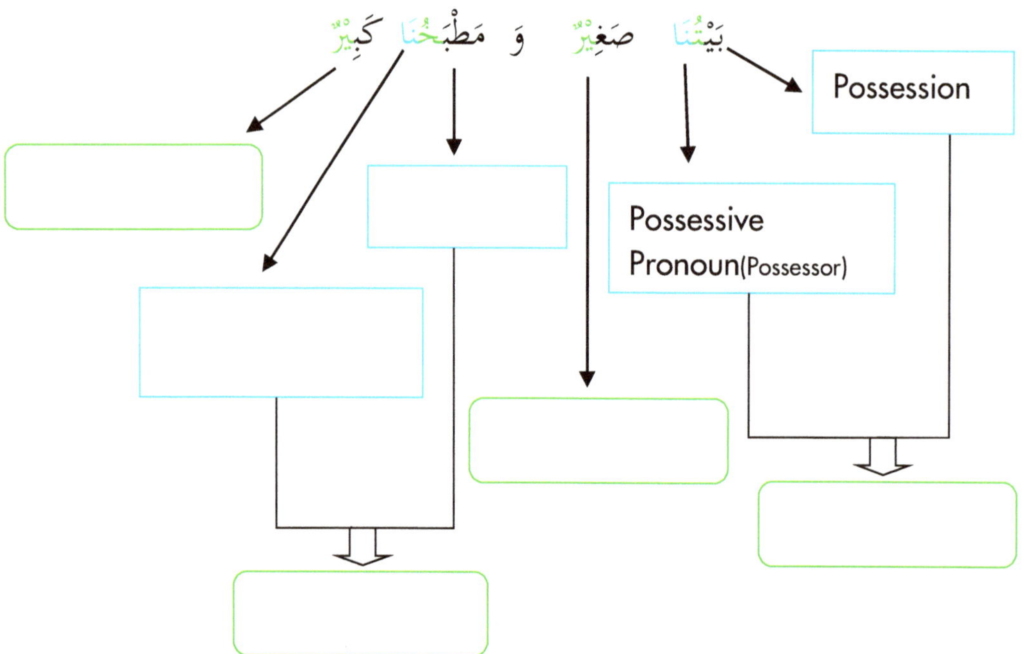

## Possessive pronouns with dual and plural nouns

In English, possessive pronouns can be applied to plural words by affixing the **pronoun** before the noun of possession, e.g.

'**Our** cars'

- Pronouns can be attached to dual and plural words in Arabic as well. However, there are a few rules that need to be discussed.
  We have previously learnt the formation of making a singular word dual and plural;

  For a dual word we add the letters ◌َانِ/ ◌َ يْنِ or تَانِ/ تَيْنِ

  For a plural word masculine form, we add the letters ◌ُ وْنَ or ◌ِيْنَ

  For a plural word in the feminine form we add ◌َاتٌ or ◌َاتٍ

- When we attach a possessive pronoun to a ***dual*** (masculine and feminine form), or to a ***plural masculine*** word, then the ن will be omitted and the pronoun will attach to the end of the word. This will be the case for the third person, second person and only the first person plural possessive pronouns.

| Dual ◌َانِ |
|---|
| كِتَابَاهُ |
| كِتَابَاهُمَا |
| كِتَابَاهُمْ |
| كِتَابَاهَا |
| كِتَابَاهُمَا |
| كِتَابَاهُنَّ |
| كِتَابَاكَ |
| كِتَابَاكُمَا |
| كِتَابَاكُمْ |
| كِتَابَاكِ |
| كِتَابَاكُمَا |
| كِتَابَاكُنَّ |
| كِتَابَانَا |

| Dual ◌َيْنِ |
|---|
| سَيَّارَتَيْهِ |
| سَيَّارَتَيْهِمَا |
| سَيَّارَتَيْهِمْ |
| سَيَّارَتَيْهَا |
| سَيَّارَتَيْهِمَا |
| سَيَّارَتَيْهِنَّ |
| سَيَّارَتَيْكَ |
| سَيَّارَتَيْكُمَا |
| سَيَّارَتَيْكُمْ |
| سَيَّارَتَيْكِ |
| سَيَّارَتَيْكُمَا |
| سَيَّارَتَيْكُنَّ |
| سَيَّارَتَيْنَا |

| Plural ◌ُوْنَ |
|---|
| مُعَلِّمُوْهُ |
| مُعَلِّمُوْهُمَا |
| مُعَلِّمُوْهُمْ |
| مُعَلِّمُوْهَا |
| مُعَلِّمُوْهُمَا |
| مُعَلِّمُوْهُنَّ |
| مُعَلِّمُوْكَ |
| مُعَلِّمُوْكُمَا |
| مُعَلِّمُوْكُمْ |
| مُعَلِّمُوْكِ |
| مُعَلِّمُوْكُمَا |
| مُعَلِّمُوْكُنَّ |
| مُعَلِّمُوْنَا |

| Plural ◌ِيْنَ |
|---|
| مُعَلِّمِيْهِ |
| مُعَلِّمِيْهِمَا |
| مُعَلِّمِيْهِمْ |
| مُعَلِّمِيْهَا |
| مُعَلِّمِيْهِمَا |
| مُعَلِّمِيْهِنَّ |
| مُعَلِّمِيْكَ |
| مُعَلِّمِيْكُمَا |
| مُعَلِّمِيْكُمْ |
| مُعَلِّمِيْكِ |
| مُعَلِّمِيْكُمَا |
| مُعَلِّمِيْكُنَّ |
| مُعَلِّمِيْنَا |

- As we have studied previously, the possessive pronoun for the first person singular form is constructed by attaching ◌ِيْ to the end of a word, e.g.

  سَيَّارَتِيْ 'My car'

- However, when attaching the first person singular pronoun to the ***dual form***, we remove the ن and add a يَ to the end of the word.

- In the ***dual*** ◌َيْنِ ***form***, where the ن is deleted, we are left with two of the same letters. In Arabic, we can join both letters together and use a symbol to denote the merging of two letters; this is known as a Tashdid (◌ّ). Look at the demonstration below;

| Nominative case | Accusative/ Genitive case | |
|---|---|---|
| Dual ◌َانِ | Dual ◌َيْنِ | |
| كِتَابَايَ | كِتَابَيَّ | My books |
| سَيَّارَتَايَ | سَيَّارَتَيَّ | My cars |

- When attaching the first person singular pronoun to the ***plural masculine form***, we also removed the ن and add a يَ to the end of the word. However, there is a process of transformation which occurs to the plural word in the nominative case when adding the first person singular pronoun. Look at the demonstration below;

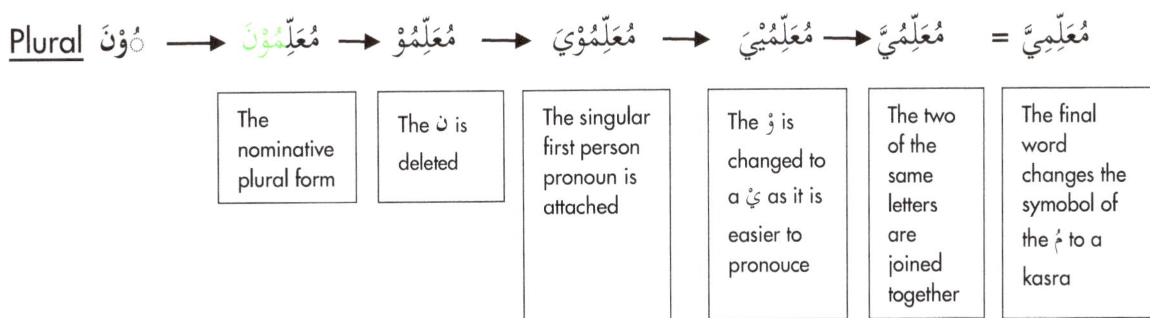


| Nominative case | Accusative/ Genitive case |
|---|---|
| Plural ◌ُوْنَ | Plural ◌ِيْنَ |
| مُعَلِّمِيَّ | مُعَلِّمِيَّ |
| My Teachers | |

- When a possessive pronoun is attached to a ***plural feminine*** word, the pronoun will be joint at the end of the letter and there will be no additional changing to the structure of the word.

| Nominative case | Accusative/ Genitive case |
|---|---|
| مُعَلِّمَاتُهُ | مُعَلِّمَاتِهِ |
| مُعَلِّمَاتُهُمَا | مُعَلِّمَاتِهِمَا |
| مُعَلِّمَاتُهُمْ | مُعَلِّمَاتِهِمْ |
| مُعَلِّمَاتُهَا | مُعَلِّمَاتِهَا |
| مُعَلِّمَاتُهُمَا | مُعَلِّمَاتِهِمَا |
| مُعَلِّمَاتُهُنَّ | مُعَلِّمَاتِهِنَّ |
| مُعَلِّمَاتُكَ | مُعَلِّمَاتِكَ |
| مُعَلِّمَاتُكُمَا | مُعَلِّمَاتِكُمَا |
| مُعَلِّمَاتُكُمْ | مُعَلِّمَاتِكُمْ |
| مُعَلِّمَاتُكِ | مُعَلِّمَاتِكِ |
| مُعَلِّمَاتُكُمَا | مُعَلِّمَاتِكُمَا |
| مُعَلِّمَاتُكُنَّ | مُعَلِّمَاتِكُنَّ |
| مُعَلِّمَاتِي | مُعَلِّمَاتِي |
| مُعَلِّمَاتُنَا | مُعَلِّمَاتِنَا |

- Possessive pronouns can be attached to the end of ***irregular plurals*** as well. The ***irregular plural*** words will keep their shape as can be seen from the table below.

'His books'

كُتُبُهُ

| | 3rd Person | | 2nd Person | | 1st Person |
|---|---|---|---|---|---|
| | Masculine | Feminine | Masculine | Feminine | Masculine & Feminine |
| Singular | كُتُبُهُ | كُتُبُهَا | كُتُبُكَ | كُتُبُكِ | كُتُبِي |
| Dual | كُتُبُهُمَا | كُتُبُهُمَا | كُتُبُكُمَا | كُتُبُكُمَا | كُتُبُنَا |
| Plural | كُتُبُهُمْ | كُتُبُهُنَّ | كُتُبُكُمْ | كُتُبُكُنَّ | كُتُبُنَا |

### 1. Attach the nouns to their pronouns from the words below to make the correct phrase.

The first one has been done for you.

| | | | | | | |
|---|---|---|---|---|---|---|
| e.g. a. | بَيْتَانِ | + | نَا | = | بَيْتَانَا | (Our two houses) |
| b. | سَيَّارَاتُ | + | هُمْ | = | ............ | (Their cars) |
| c. | مُدَرِّسُوْنَ | + | يْ | = | ............ | (My teachers) |
| d. | بُيُوْتُ | + | هُنَّ | = | ............ | (Their houses) |
| e. | مَدْرَسَتَيْنِ | + | كُمَا | = | ............ | (Your two schools) |

### 2. Attach the correct pronouns to the end the following words.

The first one has been done for you.

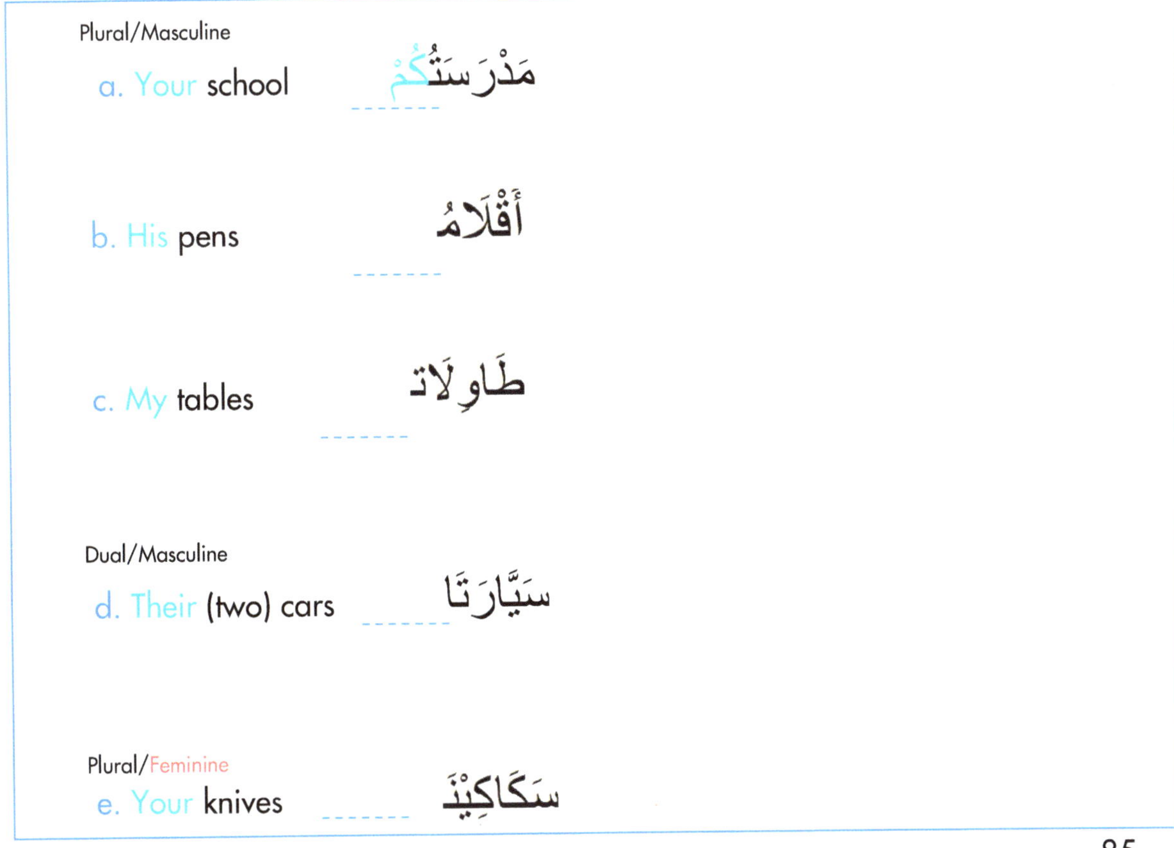

Plural/Masculine

a. Your school ....... مَدْرَسَتُكُمْ

b. His pens ....... أَقْلَامُ

c. My tables ....... طَاوِلَاتُ

Dual/Masculine

d. Their (two) cars ....... سَيَّارَتَا

Plural/Feminine

e. Your knives ....... سَكَاكِيْنُ

## Possessive pronouns with dual and plural nouns (subject and predicate agreement)

- As we have established earlier, a subject will agree with its predicate in **gender** and **amount**. E.g.

| Pronoun | Sentence | Arabic |
|---|---|---|
| Singular/Masculine - | His book is new. | كِتَابُهُ جَدِيْدٌ |
| Dual/Masculine - | Their book is new. | كِتَابُهُمَا جَدِيْدٌ |
| Plural/Masculine - | Their book is new. | كِتَابُهُمْ جَدِيْدٌ |

From the above examples, the predicates are in their **singular** form as the subject for all three sentences are **singular**. Only the pronouns to whom the item belongs to changes.

❖ The predicate will **not** agree with the possessive pronoun.

- If the subject is in the **dual** or **plural** form, then the predicate will be in the **dual** or **plural** form depending on the subject.

| Pronoun | Sentence | Arabic |
|---|---|---|
| Singular/Masculine - | His book is new. | كِتَابُهُ جَدِيْدٌ |
| Dual/Masculine - | Their (two) *books* are new. | كِتَابَاهُمَا جَدِيْدَانِ |
| Plural/Masculine - | Their *books* are new. | كُتُبُهُمْ جَدِيْدَةٌ |

The predicates from the above examples agree with their subject in **gender** and **amount**. The final example is ***SINGULAR FEMININE*** due to the subject being a non-intellectual plural.

## 1. Place the appropriate predicates for the following subjects, use the words from the table provided.

The first one has been done for you.

*** Remember the predicate must agree with the subject in gender and amount. ***

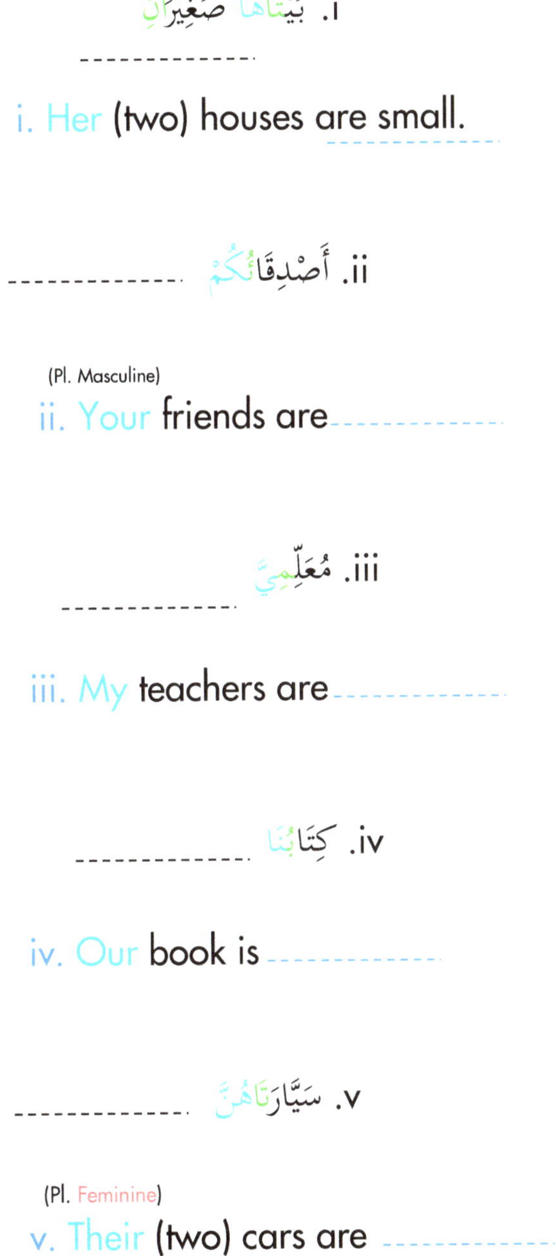

i. بَيْتَاهَا صَغِيْرَانِ

i. Her (two) houses are small.

ii. أَصْدِقَاؤُكُمْ -------------

(Pl. Masculine)

ii. Your friends are -------------

iii. مُعَلِّمِيَّ -------------

iii. My teachers are -------------

iv. كِتَابُنَا -------------

iv. Our book is -------------

v. سَيَّارَتَاهُنَّ -------------

(Pl. Feminine)

v. Their (two) cars are -------------

| English | Singular | Plural |
|---|---|---|
| New | جَدِيْدٌ | جُدُدٌ |
| Truthful | صَادِقٌ | صَادِقُوْنَ |
| Old | قَدِيْمٌ | قُدَمَاءُ |
| Pious | صَالِحٌ | صَالِحُوْنَ |

2. Break down the following sentences in to their simplest form of subject, predicate, prepositional phrase, acting predicate, possession and possessor.

The first one is done for you:

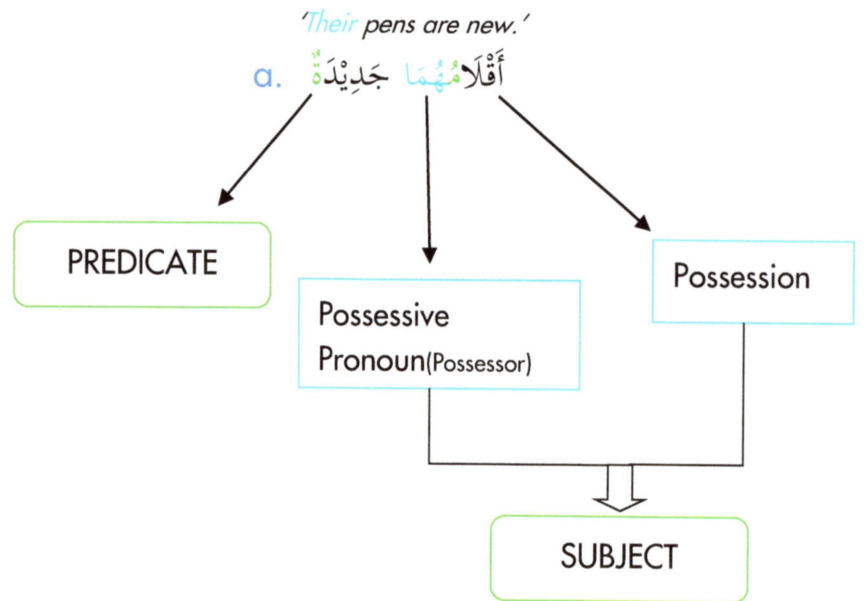

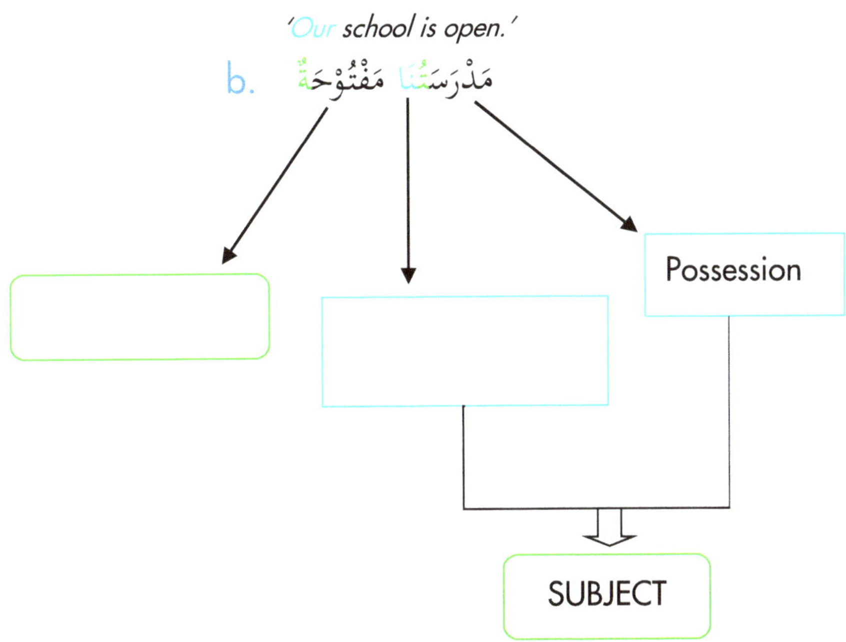
'Our school is open.'
b. مَدْرَسَتُنَا مَفْتُوْحَةٌ
Possession
SUBJECT

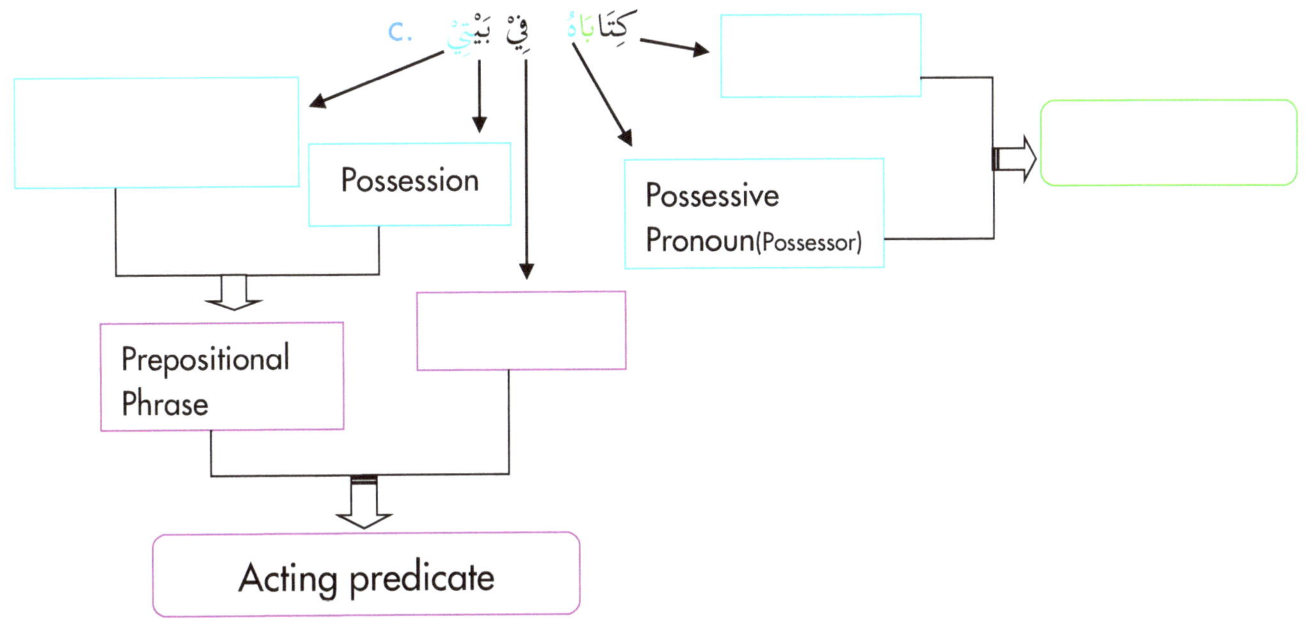
'His (two)books are in my house.'
c. كِتَابَاهُ فِيْ بَيْتِيْ
Possession
Possessive Pronoun(Possessor)
Prepositional Phrase
Acting predicate

*'Your (female)teachers are sitting in front of our school.'*

d. مُعَلِّمَاتُكِ جَالِسَاتٌ أَمَامَ مَدْرَسَتِنَا

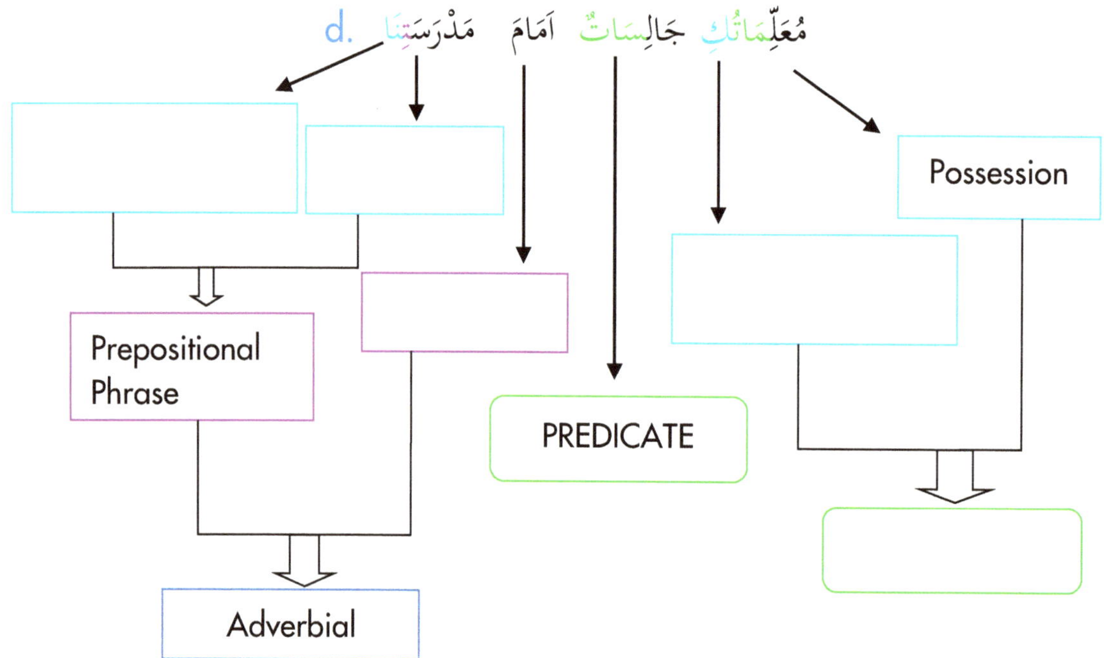

3.Translate the following sentences in to **Arabic** using the words from the table below.

The first one has been done for you.

(Plural/Masculine)
i) Her books*(dual)* are on your tables.

كِتَابَاهَا عَلَىٰ طَاوِلَاتِكُمْ

---

ii) My pens are new.

---

(Dual/Feminine)
iii) Their houses are old.

---

(Plural/Masculine) (Plural/Feminine)
iv) Your cars are in front of their houses*(dual)*.

---

(Singular/Feminine)
v) My teachers are sitting with your teachers.

---

vi) Our schools*(dual)* are open.

---

| English | Arabic |
|---|---|
| Houses (Dual) | بَيْتَانِ |
| Houses | بُيُوْتٌ |
| New | جَدِيْدٌ |
| Pens | اَقْلَامٌ |
| Old | قَدِيْمٌ |
| Cars | سَيَّارَاتٌ |
| Teachers | مُعَلِّمُوْنَ |
| Open | مَفْتُوْحٌ |
| Schools (Dual) | مَدْرَسَتَانِ |
| In front of | اَمَامَ |

4. Add the correct predicate to the following sentences in **Arabic**.

(Plural/Feminine)

a. My house is old and their houses are new.

وَ بُيُوْتُهُنَّ ------------- بَيْتِيْ -------------

(Dual/Feminine)

b. His pens*(dual)* are new and your books are old.

وَ كُتُبُكَ ------------- قَلَمَاهُ -------------

(Plural/Masculine)

c. Our schools are open and your school is closed.

وَ مَدْرَسَتُكُمْ ------------- مَدَارِسُنَا -------------

| English | Arabic |
|---|---|
| Old (Feminine) | قَدِيْمَةٌ |
| Old | قَدِيْمٌ |
| New | جَدِيْدَةٌ |
| New (Dual) | جَدِيْدَانِ |
| Open | مَفْتُوْحَةٌ |
| Closed | مُغْلَقَةٌ |

## Possessive pronouns attached to prepositions

As we have discussed previously, prepositions cannot be understood by themselves and only give meaning when connected structurally to a noun or verb. Prepositions can also be understood when attached to possessive pronouns, however, context would be needed in understanding their intended meaning. For instance;
The response "*From us.*" where the question is "**Who is the gift from?**"

- In Arabic, possessive pronouns will be attached to the end of the preposition. E.g.

| مِنْ | + | هُمْ | = | مِنْهُمْ |
|---|---|---|---|---|
| From | + | Them | = | From them |

- Possessive pronouns when attached to a preposition will be in the genitive state. However, pronouns are **indeclinable**; meaning that they will not change in their structural form, except for some prepositions which will be listed below.

- The structure of some prepositions in Arabic slightly change in pronunciation when attached to a possessive pronoun. E.g.

| عَلى | + | هُمْ | = | عَلَيْهِمْ |
|---|---|---|---|---|
| On | + | Them | = | On them |

- There are five prepositions in which the format of the word slightly changes when connected to a pronoun, they are;

  فِيْ (from)

  عَلى (on/upon)

  إِلى (to/towards)

  بِ (with)

  لِ (for)

| | فِيْ | عَلَى | اِلَى | بِ | لِ |
|---|---|---|---|---|---|
| ـهُ | فِيْهِ | عَلَيْهِ | اِلَيْهِ | بِهِ | لَهُ |
| ـهُمَا | فِيْهِمَا | عَلَيْهِمَا | اِلَيْهِمَا | بِهِمَا | لَهُمَا |
| ـهُمْ | فِيْهِمْ | عَلَيْهِمْ | اِلَيْهِمْ | بِهِمْ | لَهُمْ |
| ـهَا | فِيْهَا | عَلَيْهَا | اِلَيْهَا | بِهَا | لَهَا |
| ـهُمَا | فِيْهِمَا | عَلَيْهِمَا | اِلَيْهِمَا | بِهِمَا | لَهُمَا |
| ـهُنَّ | فِيْهِنَّ | عَلَيْهِنَّ | اِلَيْهِنَّ | بِهِنَّ | لَهُنَّ |
| ـكَ | فِيْكَ | عَلَيْكَ | اِلَيْكَ | بِكَ | لَكَ |
| ـكُمَا | فِيْكُمَا | عَلَيْكُمَا | اِلَيْكُمَا | بِكُمَا | لَكُمَا |
| ـكُمْ | فِيْكُمْ | عَلَيْكُمْ | اِلَيْكُمْ | بِكُمْ | لَكُمْ |
| ـكِ | فِيْكِ | عَلَيْكِ | اِلَيْكِ | بِكِ | لَكِ |
| ـكُمَا | فِيْكُمَا | عَلَيْكُمَا | اِلَيْكُمَا | بِكُمَا | لَكُمَا |
| ـكُنَّ | فِيْكُنَّ | عَلَيْكُنَّ | اِلَيْكُنَّ | بِكُنَّ | لَكُنَّ |
| ـيْ | فِيَّ | عَلَيَّ | اِلَيَّ | بِيْ | لِيْ |
| ـنَا | فِيْنَا | عَلَيْنَا | اِلَيْنَا | بِنَا | لَنَا |

- The remaining prepositions will have no further alterations to the structure of the word. e.g.

| مِنْهُ | عَنْهُ | اَمَامَهُ | عِنْدَهُ | مَعَهُ |
|---|---|---|---|---|

1. Complete the table below by putting in the correct forms of the word.

| | خَلْفَ | عَلىٰ | مِنْ | بِ | فَوْقَ |
|---|---|---|---|---|---|
| ـهُ | | عَلَيْهِ | مِنْهُ | | |
| ـهُمَا | | | | | فَوْقَهُمَا |
| ـهُمْ | خَلْفَهُمْ | | | بِهِمْ | |
| ـهَا | | عَلَيْهَا | | | فَوْقَهَا |
| ـهُمَا | | | مِنْهُمَا | بِهِمَا | |
| ـهُنَّ | خَلْفَهُنَّ | | | بِهِنَّ | |
| ـكَ | | عَلَيْكَ | مِنْكَ | | |
| ـكُمَا | | | | بِكُمَا | |
| ـكُمْ | | عَلَيْكُمْ | | | |
| ـكِ | | | | بِكِ | فَوْقَكِ |
| ـكُمَا | | | مِنْكُمَا | | |
| ـكُنَّ | خَلْفَكُنَّ | | | بِكُنَّ | |
| ـيْ | | عَلَيَّ | مِنِّي | | فَوْقِي |
| ـنَا | | | مِنَّا | بِنَا | |

2. Write the correct form in Arabic by joining up the words.

a. عَلىٰ + هُمَا =

b. لِ + كُنَّ =

c. فِيْ + نَا =

d. اِلىٰ + كُمْ =

## Possessive pronouns in a prepositional phrase

A prepositional phrase constitutes of two parts; the *preposition* and a **noun**. For instance;

"*in* the **car**."

فِي السَّيَّارَةِ

Possessive pronouns can be attached to a prepositional phrase by affixing a pronoun to the noun. E.g.

"*in* HIS **car**."

The noun (car) is made definite by the third person singular masculine pronoun - HIS.

- In Arabic, the possessive pronouns will be attached to the end of the **noun**. The particle اَلْ is removed as the word becomes definite by the pronoun. The **noun** will be in the genitive state due to the preposition.

"*in* HIS **car**."

فِيْ سَيَّارَتِهِ

- The possessive pronouns for the third person category will be written with a Kasra due to the phonetics of the word structure.

| | 3rd person pronoun | |
|---|---|---|
| | Masculine | Feminine |
| Singular | فِيْ سَيَّارَتِهِ | فِيْ سَيَّارَتِهَا |
| Dual | فِيْ سَيَّارَتِهِمَا | فِيْ سَيَّارَتِهِمَا |
| Plural | فِيْ سَيَّارَتِهِمْ | فِيْ سَيَّارَتِهِنَّ |

The rest of the possessive pronouns will remain the same.

1. Using the table of words below, translate the following phrases in to Arabic.

The first one has been done for you.

| English | Arabic |
|---|---|
| A. In our house. | فِيْ بَيْتِنَا |
| (Plural/Masculine) B. To their school. | |
| C. On my table. | |
| (Dual/Feminine) D. From your office. | |
| E. Behind her room | |

| بَيْتٌ House | غُرْفَةٌ Room | مَكْتَبٌ Office | طَاوِلَةٌ Table | مَدْرَسَةٌ School |
|---|---|---|---|---|
| عَلَى On | إِلَى To | مِنْ From | فِيْ In | خَلْفَ Behind |

| Plural | | Dual | | Singular | | |
|---|---|---|---|---|---|---|
| Feminine | Masculine | Feminine | Masculine | Feminine | Masculine | |
| هِنَّ | هِمْ | هِمَا | هِمَا | هَا | هِ | 3rd Person |
| كُنَّ | كُمْ | كُمَا | كُمَا | كِ | كَ | 2nd Person |
| نَا | نَا | نَا | نَا | ـيْ | ـيْ | 1st Person |

2. Break down the following sentences grammatically in to its smallest unit of ion, possession, possessive pronoun and prepositional phrase.

The first one has been done for you.

a. 'With our teacher.'

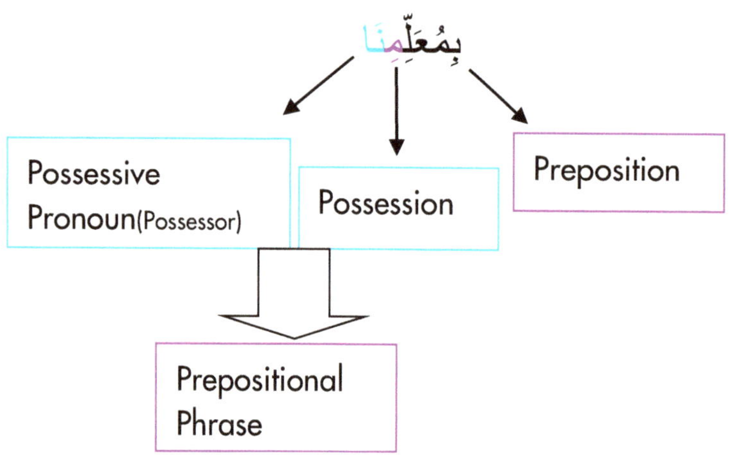


b. 'In their car.'

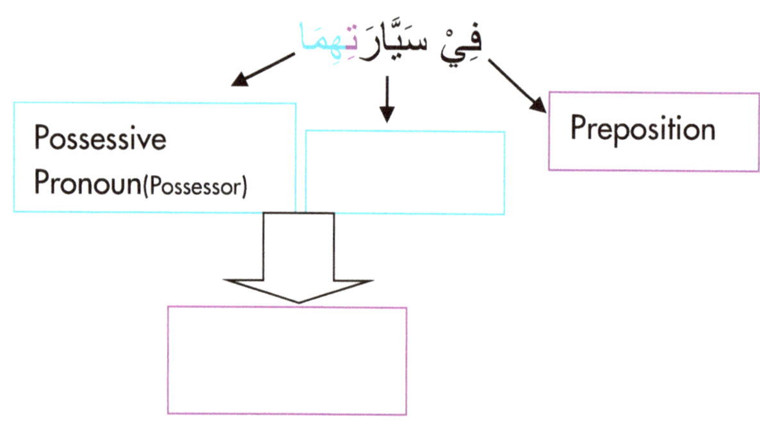


c. 'From my school.'

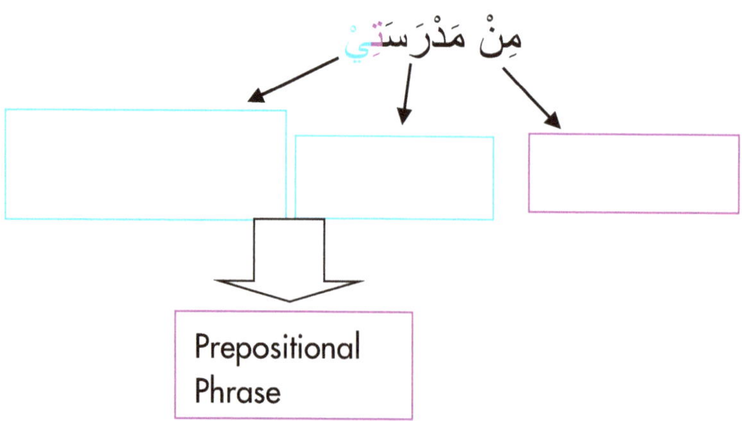

## Possessive pronouns in a prepositional phrase (dual/plural)

In English, possessive pronouns can be applied to plural words by affixing the pronoun before the **noun of possession** in a prepositional phrase. E.g.

'*In* HIS **cars**.'

- In Arabic, the dual and plural forms of the word will be in the genitive state due to the preposition. The forms of the dual and plural structure are listed in the table below.

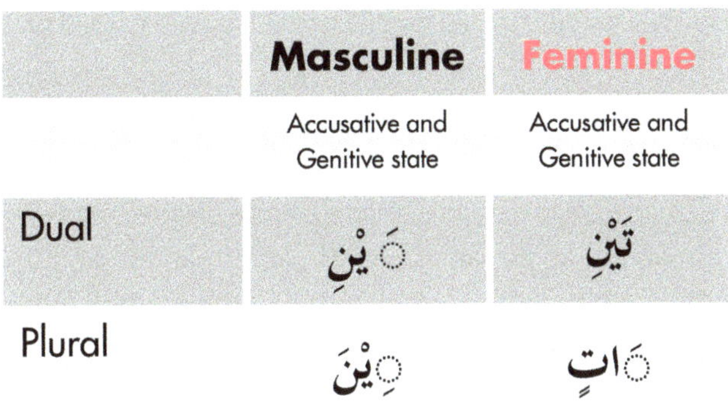

| | **Masculine**<br>Accusative and Genitive state | **Feminine**<br>Accusative and Genitive state |
|---|---|---|
| Dual | ◌َيْنِ | تَيْنِ |
| Plural | ◌ِيْنَ | ◌َاتٍ |

- Possessive pronouns can be attached to dual and plural words in Arabic as well. However, as mentioned previously, for the dual (masculine and feminine) and plural masculine form, the ن will be omitted and the pronoun will be attached to the end of the word. For example;

'With their teachers.'

- When attaching the **first person singular pronoun** to the <u>dual</u> and **<u>regular plural</u>** masculine form, we remove the ن and add a يَّ to the end of the word, as we have seen before.

- When a possessive pronoun is attached to a **<u>regular plural</u>** **<u>feminine</u>** noun in a prepositional phrase, the pronoun will be joined at the end of the noun and there will be no additional changes to the structure of the word.

'*In* HER **cars**.'

فِيْ سَيَّارَاتِهَا

Possessive Pronoun(Possessor) | Possession | Preposition

Prepositional Phrase

- Possessive pronouns can be attached to the end of irregular plurals in a prepositional phrase. The irregular plural word will keep its shape and will be in the genitive state.

'*On* HIS **books**.'

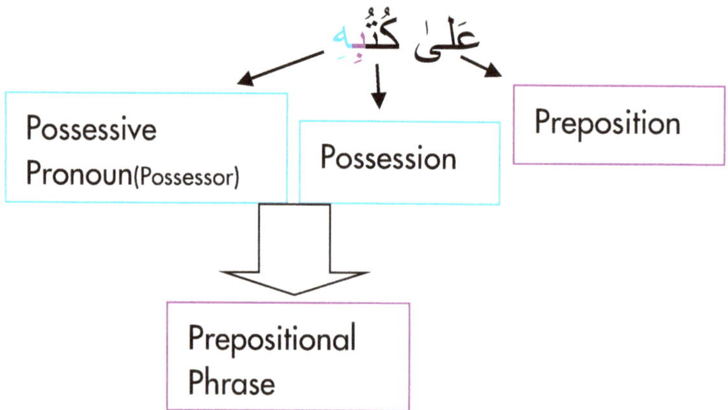

## Possessive pronouns in a prepositional phrase sentence

From the previous section, possessive pronouns can attach themselves to their respected nouns in the form of a prepositional phrase. E.g.

'In his car.'

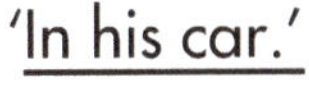

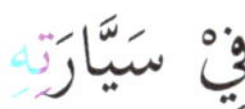

- The above phrase makes part of a sentence, by adding a suitable subject we can make a simple sentence in Arabic, as has been discussed previously.

By adding the subject **'The boy'** before the prepositional phrase a simple sentence is created;

'**The boy** is in his car.'

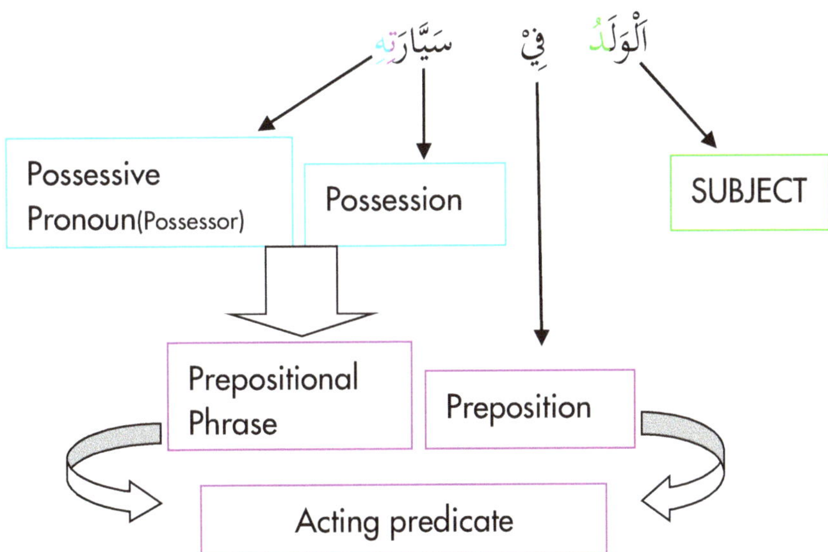

- As discussed previously, the subject can also be deferred until after the prepositional phrase which will come as an advanced predicate. The grammatical formation will be different as is illustrated below.

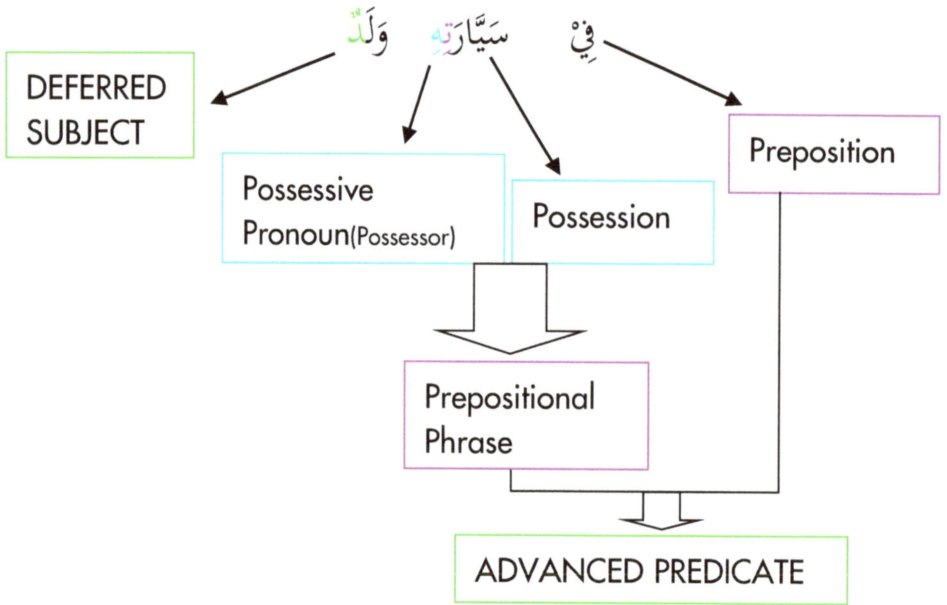


1. Rearrange the following sentences in Arabic by putting the prepositional phrase ahead of the subject. The first one has been done for you.

a. The man is in my room. اَلرَّجُلُ فِيْ غُرْفَتِيْ

فِيْ غُرْفَتِيْ رَجُلٌ

b. The book is on his bed. اَلْكِتَابُ عَلَى سَرِيْرِهِ

---

c. The girl is in your school. اَلْبِنْتُ فِيْ مَدْرَسَتِكُنَّ

---

## Possessive pronouns in an advanced prepositional phrase

It has been discussed, earlier in the book, the concept of the advanced prepositional phrase. This section will clarify the changes to the meaning of a sentence in Arabic and the grammar when the possessive pronoun is attached to the **preposition** and not the noun.

In the previous section we looked at how the possessive pronoun attaches to the noun in a prepositional phrase sentence, for example;

*'With* HER **teacher**.'

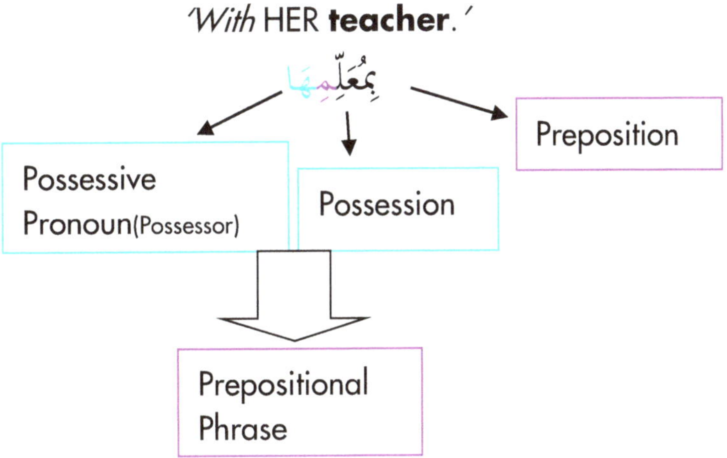


- When the possessive pronoun is attached to the **preposition** instead of the noun, both the meaning and the grammatical structure change. For instance; in the above example, by changing the position of the possessive pronoun it will alter the meaning of the sentence.

*'There is a teacher with her.'*

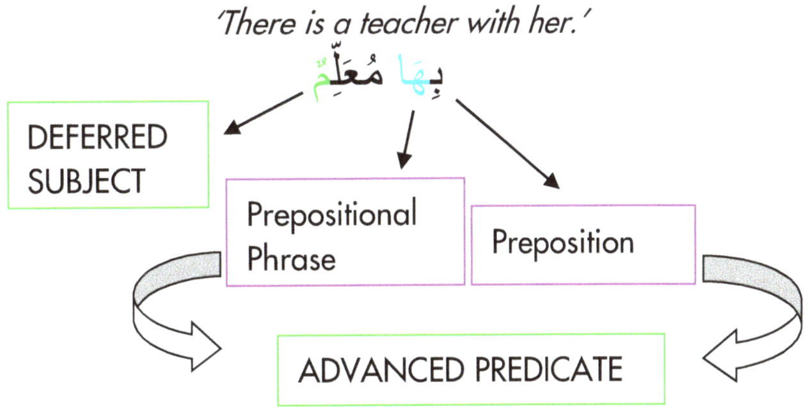


- A word to word translation of the above example will be 'with her is a teacher'. This is a complete sentence, whereas the above example 'with her teacher' is a phrase; a fragment of a sentence.

- Below is another example to clarify the difference of meaning and structure between the two sentence variation.

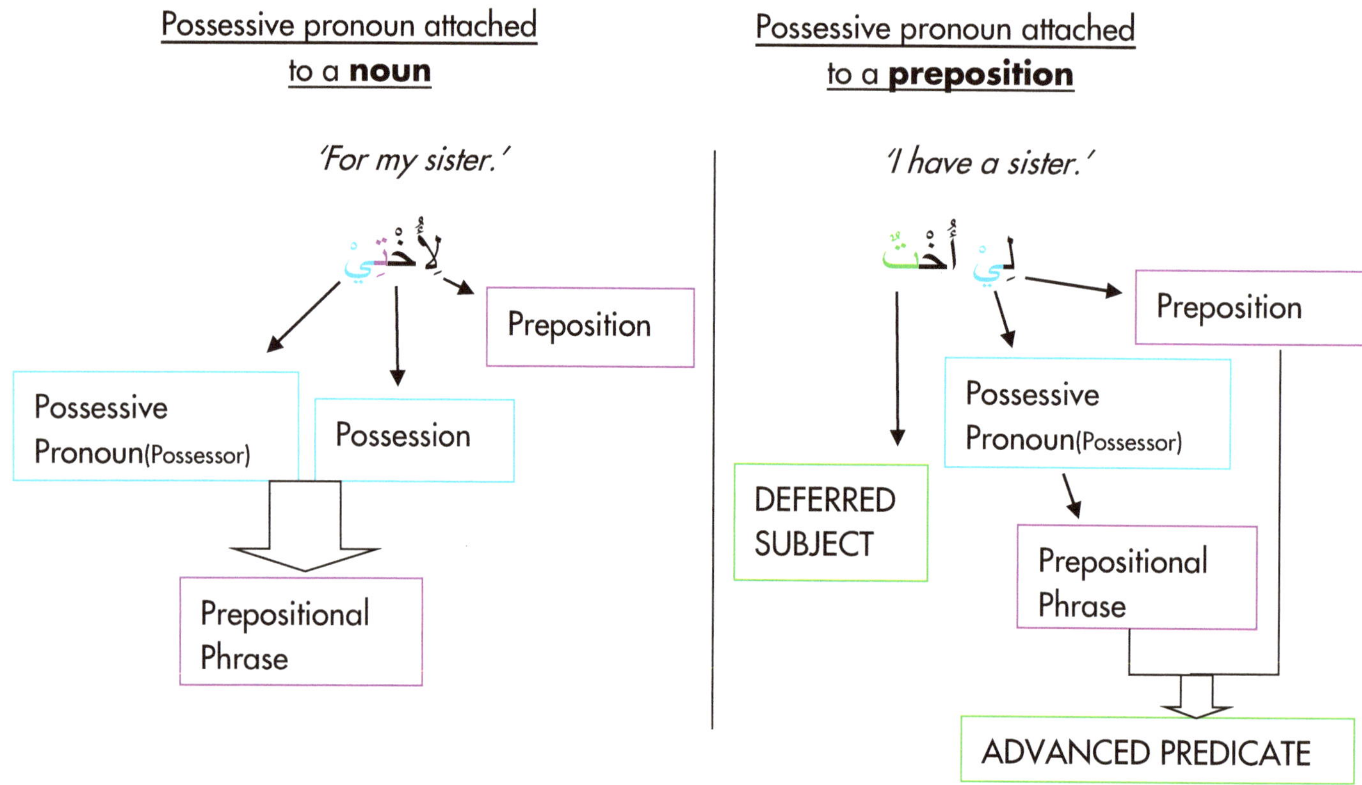

1. State whether the possessive pronouns for the following sentences are connected to the NOUN or the PREPOSITION.

The first one has been done for you.

| Sentence | Possessive pronoun connected to… |
|---|---|
| There is a house in front of us. | PREPOSITION |
| From their house. | |
| In my car. | |
| There is a pen under him. | |
| From my letter. | |
| There is a letter from me. | |

*****Hint- pronouns when attached to a preposition in English come after the preposition, and when attached to nouns come before the noun. *****

2. Place the correct preposition and personal pronoun for each sentence. The first one has been done for you.

*(Singular/Feminine)*

a. In it there is a book. فِيْهَا كِتَابٌ

b. With us there is a child. طِفْلٌ ------

*(Plural/Masculine)*

c. In front of you there is a doctor. طَبِيْبٌ ---------

*(Plural/Masculine)*

d. There is a letter from them. رِسَالَةٌ ---------

e. There is a pen for me. قَلَمٌ ---------

## 3. Translate the following sentences in to Arabic using the words from the box.

a. The pen is in his book. ................................................

b. There is a cat in my room. ................................................

*(Dual/Feminine)*

c. Our bag is in your car. ................................................

d. There are men in the room. ................................................

*(Plural/Feminine)*

e. Our sons are in their garden. ................................................

f. Her teacher is with us. ................................................

| مُعَلِّمٌ | حَقِيْبَةٌ | رِجَالٌ | غُرْفَةٌ | قِطَّةٌ |
|---|---|---|---|---|
| Teacher | Bag | Men | Room | Cat |
| كِتَابٌ | أَقْلَامٌ | أَبْنَاءٌ | سَيَّارَةٌ | حَدِيْقَةٌ |
| Book | Pens | Sons | Car | Garden |

4. Break down the following sentences grammatically in to its smallest unit of preposition, possession, possessive pronoun, prepositional phrase, subject and predicate.

Write the English translation for the following sentences.

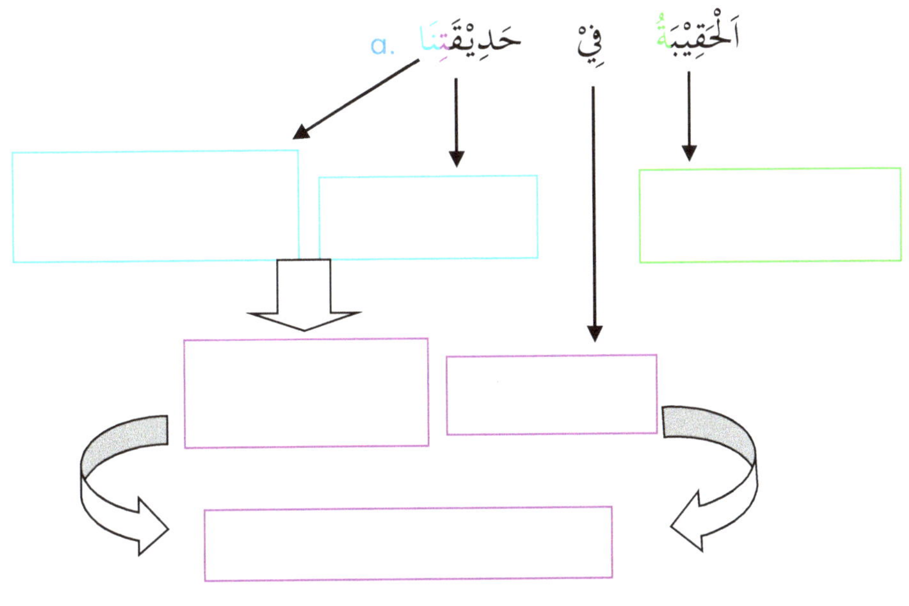


-----------------------------------------------

b. اَلْكِتَابُ فِيْ حَقِيْبَتِيْ

-----------------------------------------------

c. اَلْأَقْلَامُ لِمُعَلِّمِكَ

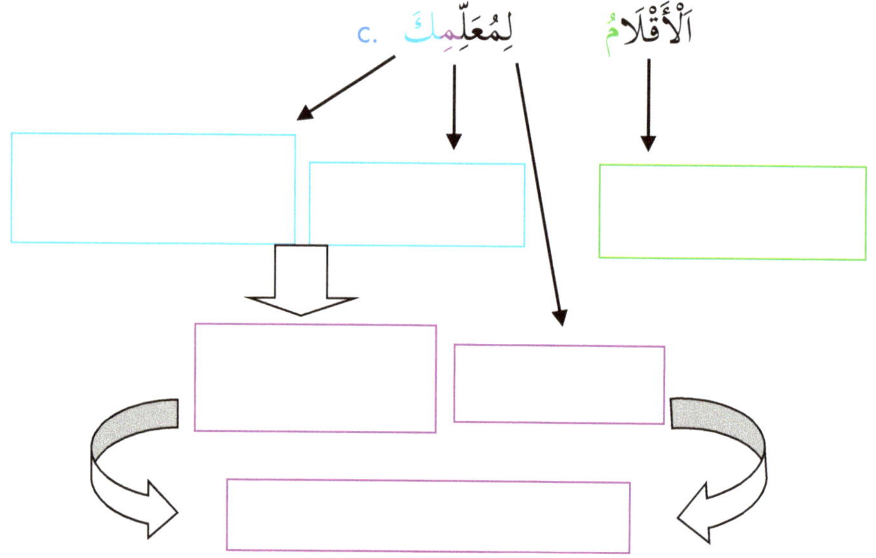

d. فِيْ حَدِيْقَتِهِنَّ قِطَّةٌ

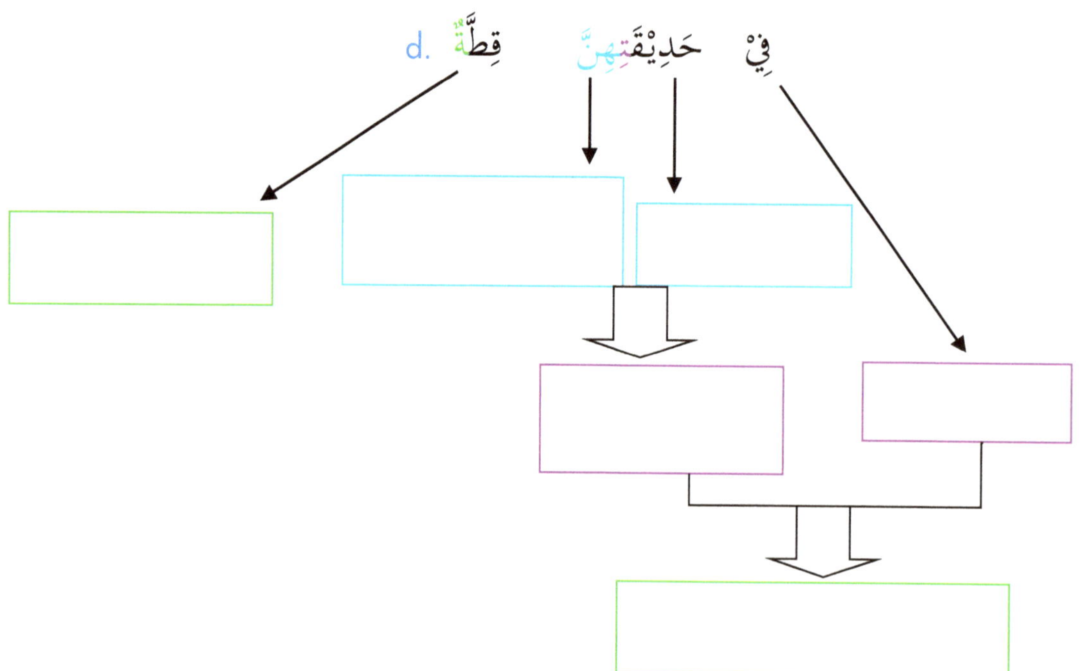

5. Complete the Arabic sentences by placing the correct diacritical marks (Dhamma, Fatha, Kasra) on those letters that have none.

a. *'The boy is sitting in our garden.'*

اَلْوَلَد جَالِس فِيْ حَدِيْقَتنا

b. *'The girl is going with her two sisters.'*

اَلْبِنْت ذَاهِبَة مَعَ أُخْتيها

c. *'His pens are on my table.'*

اَقْلَامه عَلٰى طَاوِلَتي

d. *'There is a man in your car.'*

فِيْ سَيَّارَتكم رَجُل

e. *'Their teachers are in our school.'*

مُعَلِّموهم فِيْ مَدْرَسَتنا

f. *'The school is in front of the house.'*

اَلْمَدْرَسَة اَمَامَ الْبَيْت

## Identifying personal and possessive pronouns in compound sentences

Pronouns, as stated earlier, replace the noun within the sentence and are classed in to two types; Personal and Possessive.

Personal pronouns can form either the subject or predicate of a sentence. For example; *'He is standing.'*, the personal pronoun forms the subject.

Possessive pronouns, however, cannot be a subject or predicate in of themselves. Rather, they are fragments attached to a word that in turn becomes the subject or predicate, for instance; *'His brother is standing.'*, the possessive pronoun is attached to the word 'brother' which in turn becomes the subject.

- Compound sentences can be created in Arabic using the coordinating conjunction وَ (And).

- In Arabic, just as in English, we can replace nouns with pronouns in compound sentences. When creating longer sentences, we must ensure the correct pronoun is being used.

For instance;

Possessive Pronoun | Possessive Pronoun | Possessive Pronoun

**My** name is Muhammad. **I** have a brother and **his** name is Bilal. **He** is a teacher in a school.

Personal Pronoun

Possessive Pronoun | Possessive Pronoun | Possessive Pronoun

اِسْمِي مُحَمَّدٌ ، لِيْ اَخٌ وَ اِسْمُهُ بِلَالٌ ،

Personal Pronoun

هُوَ مُعَلِّمٌ فِيْ مَدْرَسَةٍ

اِسْمٌ - Name
اَخٌ - Brother

## 1. Read the following extract and answer the following questions.

a. Highlight all the personal pronouns in yellow and all the possessive pronouns in blue. Some have been done for you.

*My name is Khadija. My family is small. I have a dad, his name is Muhammad and he is a doctor. I have a mum she is a teacher. Our house is big, in it there are rooms. My room is small; in it there is a bed, table and chair. Our kitchen is small and our garden is big. In our garden there are trees and they are big. My two sisters are students and they are clever. Their room is big. In their room there are two beds and two windows.*

### b. Using the table below list all of the nouns that are attached to the possessive pronouns.

| Pronoun | Possession | Pronoun | Possession |
|---|---|---|---|
| *e.g. My* | *Name* | | |
| | | | |
| | | | |
| | | | |
| | | | |
| | | | |
| | | | |
| | | | |

### c. Write the correct possessive pronoun for the following sentences.

i. He is a doctor. طَبِيْبٌ ------

ii. She is a teacher. مُعَلِّمَةٌ ------

iii. They *(Dual/Feminine)* are clever. ذَكِيَّتَانِ ------

2. Place the correct pronouns in the missing gaps in Arabic. Some of them have been done for you.

اِسْمِي خَدِيْجَة، عَائِلَتِ ___ صَغِيْرَة. لِيْ اَب، اِسْمُ ___ مُحَمَّد

*My name is Khadija. My family is small. I have a dad, his name is Muhammad*

وَ ___ طَبِيْب. لِيْ اُمٌّ وَ ___ مُعَلِّمَة. بَيْتُ ___ كَبِيْر، فِيْهِ غُرَف.

*and he is a doctor. I have a mum and she is a teacher. Our house is big, in it there are rooms.*

غُرْفَتِ ___ صَغِيْرَة، فِيْ ___ سَرِيْر وَ طَاوِلَة وَ كُرْسِي.

*My room is small, in it there is a bed, table and chair.*

مَطْبَخُنَا صَغِيْر وَحَدِيْقَتُ ___ كَبِيْرَة. فِيْ حَدِيْقَتِ ___ اَشْجَار

*Our kitchen is small and our garden is big. In our garden there are trees*

وَ هِيَ كَبِيْرَة. اُخْتَا ___ طَالِبَتَانِ وَ ___ ذَكِيَّتَانِ.

*and they are big. My two sisters are students and they are clever.*

غُرْفَتُ ___ كَبِيْرَة، فِيْهَا سَرِيْرَانِ وَ شُبَّاكَانِ.

*Their room is big. In it there are two beds and two windows.*

3. Break down the following sentences grammatically in to its smallest unit of preposition, possession, possessive pronoun, prepositional phrase, subject and predicate.

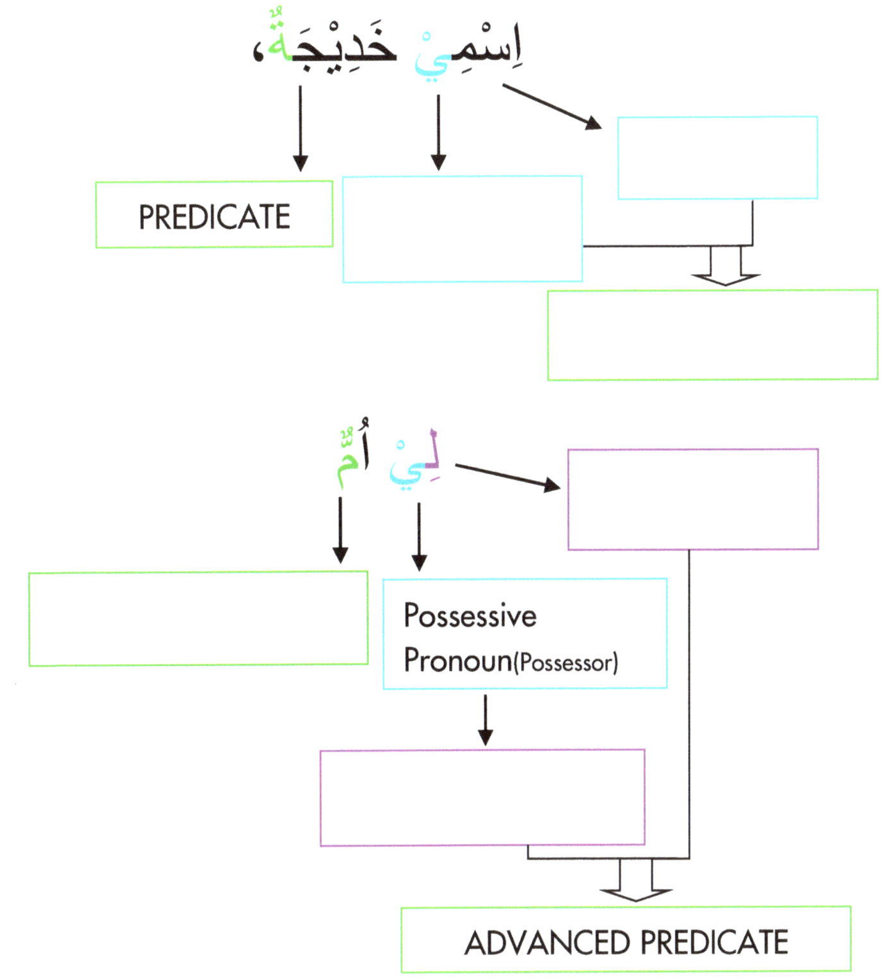


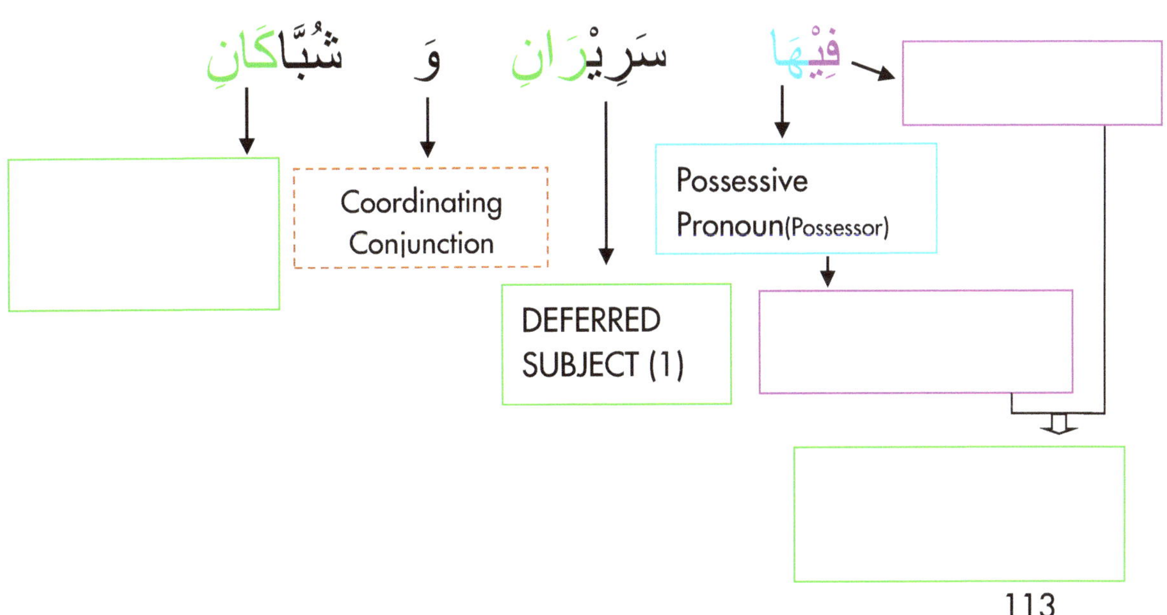

# 08

## The Arabic Sentence

Review

# The Arabic Sentence Review

## Points to remember

- ✓ In Arabic, prepositions will render the noun that follows it in to the genitive state.

- ✓ The preposition and the noun together make a prepositional phrase which in turn can be used as an **acting predicate** or as an **Adverbial** in a sentence.

- ✓ The genitive state for the dual and plural forms are:

| | Accusative and Genitive state | Accusative and Genitive state |
|---|---|---|
| Dual | ◌َ يْنِ | تَيْنِ |
| Plural | ◌ِيْنَ | ◌َاتٍ |

- ✓ An ADVANCED PREDICATE sentence is formed when the prepositional phrase is brought ahead of the subject. There is no agreement of **gender** and **amount**.

- ✓ Pronouns replace nouns and can either be personal or possessive.

| نَحْنُ | اَنَا | اَنْتُنَّ | اَنْتُمَا | اَنْتِ | اَنْتُمْ | اَنْتُمَا | اَنْتَ | هُنَّ | هُمَا | هِيَ | هُمْ | هُمَا | هُوَ |
|---|---|---|---|---|---|---|---|---|---|---|---|---|---|
| ـنَا | ـِيْ | كُنَّ | ـكُمَا | ـكِ | كُمْ | ـكُمَا | ـكَ | هُنَّ | هُمَا | هَا | هُمْ | هُمَا | هُ |

✓ Personal pronouns will agree with its predicate in **gender** and **amount**.

✓ Possessive pronouns can be attached to the end of nouns, verbs and prepositions.

✓ When a possessive pronoun is attached to nouns in the dual or plural forms, then the نْ of the dual and plural form will be omitted.

✓ Possessive pronouns can be attached to prepositions in which they alter the structure of the word.

✓ Possessive pronouns can be attached to a prepositional phrase by which the meaning and grammar changes.

* * *

# The Arabic Sentence
# Demonstrative Pronouns

Demonstrative pronouns (also known as determiners) are pronouns that specify a noun in relation to its proximity of distance; i.e. being close or far, as well as in time and place.

E.g. **THIS** is a book and **THAT** is a pen.

In the above sentence, the words this and that are demonstrative pronouns; which indicate the position as well as the place of the nouns they are referring to.

Demonstrative pronouns, as seen from the example above, can be regarded as a subject or a predicate by themselves. They can also be used to modify nouns in which they form a phrase.

E.g. **THIS** book is new.

The demonstrative pronoun modifies the noun and is now not a subject by itself, rather a phrase. The rulings for a demonstrative phrase will be clarified in detail in its relevant chapter.

The demonstrative pronouns are:

| Demonstrative pronouns | |
|---|---|
| Singular | Plural |
| This | These |
| *e.g. This is a car.* | *e.g. These are flowers* |
| That | Those |
| *e.g. That is a school.* | *e.g. Those boys are playing.* |

- As Arabic is more varied in its ability to differentiate between **gender** and **amount**, the demonstrative pronouns in Arabic will be classified according to their **gender** and **amount**.

| | Demonstrative pronoun "This/These" | |
|---|---|---|
| | Masculine | Feminine |
| Singular | هٰذَا | هٰذِهِ |
| Dual (Nominative state) | هٰذَانِ | هَاتَانِ |
| (Accusative & Genitive state) | هٰذَيْنِ* | هَاتَيْنِ* |
| Plural | هٰؤُلَاءِ | هٰؤُلَاءِ |

| | Demonstrative pronoun "That/Those" | |
|---|---|---|
| | Masculine | Feminine |
| Singular | ذَالِكَ | تِلْكَ |
| Dual (Nominative state) | ذَانِكَ | تَانِكَ |
| (Accusative & Genitive state) | ذَيْنِكَ* | تَيْنِكَ* |
| Plural | أُولٰئِكَ | أُولٰئِكَ |

- All demonstrative pronouns are **indeclinable**; they cannot change their structure except for the *dual form* in the accusative and genitive state. They are indicated in the tables above with an asterisk (*).

## Sentences using demonstrative pronouns

Sentences are constructed via two components namely a subject and a predicate and are by default in the nominative state. Demonstrative pronouns can take the position as a subject as they are definite within a sentence and the article اَلْ will not be needed.

E.g. This is a car.
These are houses.

The above sentence 'This is a car' is singular. Whereas, the sentence 'These are houses' is plural as the predicate is in the plural form (s). In both sentences the subject is a demonstrative pronoun.

- Nominal sentences in Arabic, as we have learnt, have to agree in **amount** as well as in **gender**. Therefore, the correct demonstrative pronoun will be used depending on the noun that it is referring to. For instance;

'A car' in Arabic is feminine and singular – سَيَّارَةٌ

The demonstrative pronoun in Arabic will also be feminine and singular – هٰذِهِ(This)

'This is a car.'

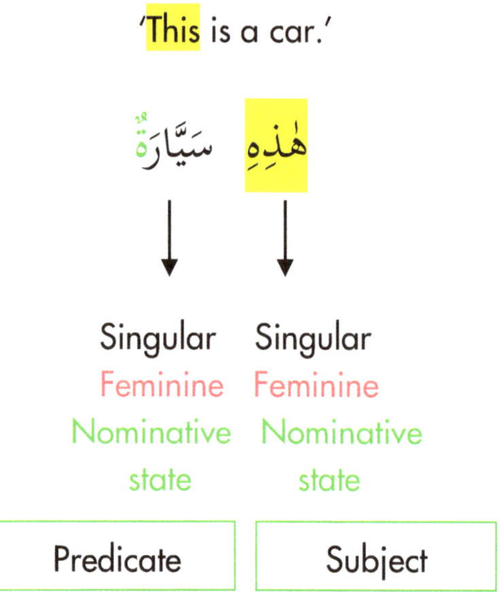

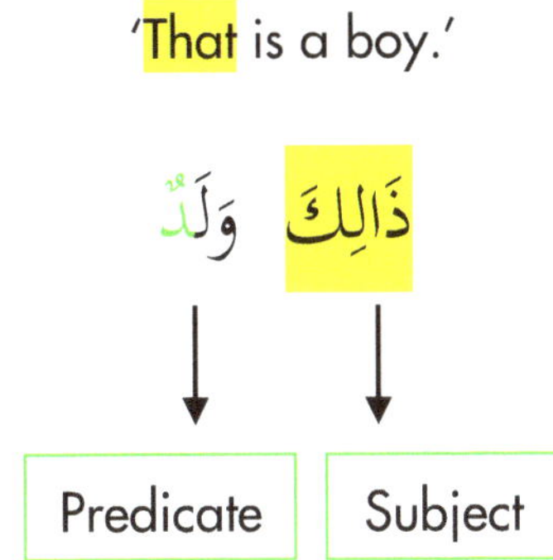


- The same rule will be applied to the dual and the plural form (for words that are **not** classified as non-intellectual beings).

Dual form:

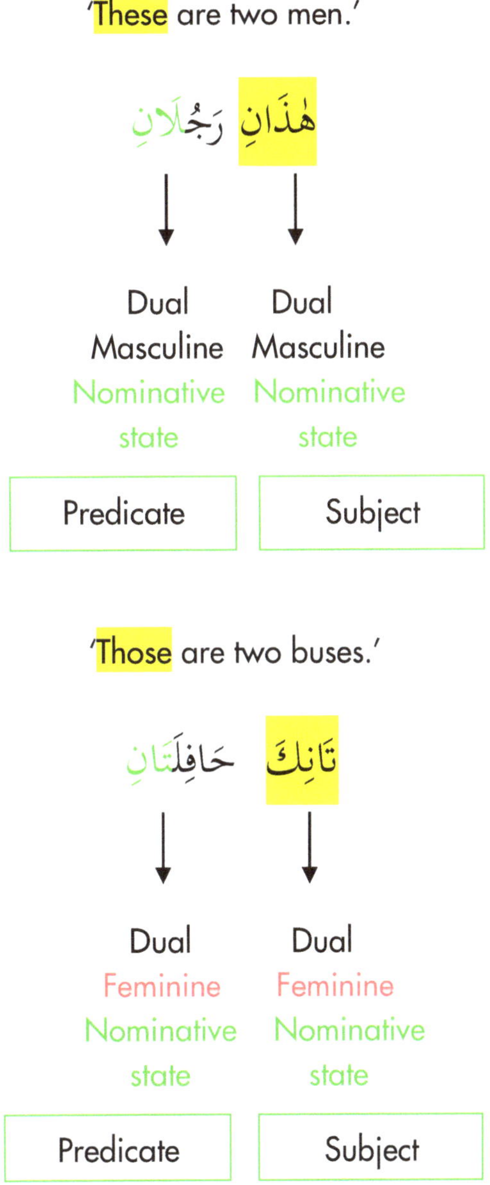

Plural form:

'These are teachers.'

Plural form (non-intellectual beings)

- The ruling of a Plural non-intellectual being has been discussed previously. The same ruling will apply here as well, by which the demonstrative pronoun will come in the ***SINGULAR FEMININE*** form.

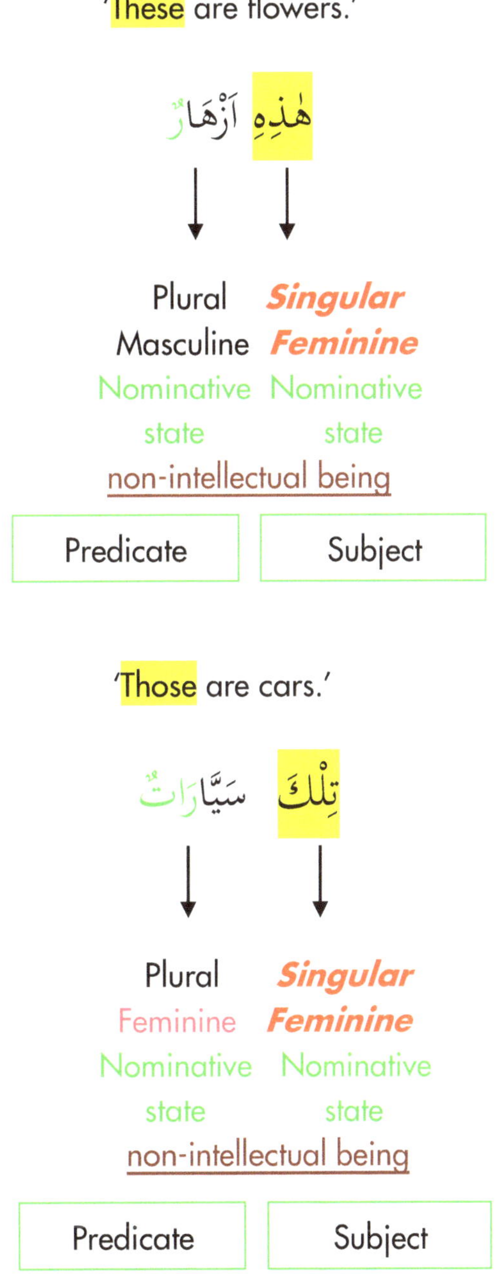

1. Circle the demonstrative pronouns from each of the sentences below.

The first one has been done for you.

I. That is a school.

II. Those are pens and these are pencils.

III. These are my books.

IV. This is for my sister and that is for my dad.

V. These are two students.

2. Complete the table by putting the correct demonstrative pronouns in Arabic.

Some have been done for you.

| Demonstrative Pronouns | | | |
|---|---|---|---|
| Masculine | Feminine | Masculine | Feminine |
| | هٰذِهِ | ذَالِكَ | |
| هٰذَانِ<br>هٰذَيْنِ | | | |
| | | | أُولٰئِكَ |

3. Add the correct demonstrative pronoun to the following sentences.

The first one has been done for you.

a. These are two boys.

b. That is a house.

c. Those are teachers.

d. Those are cars.

e. This is a school and that is a teacher.

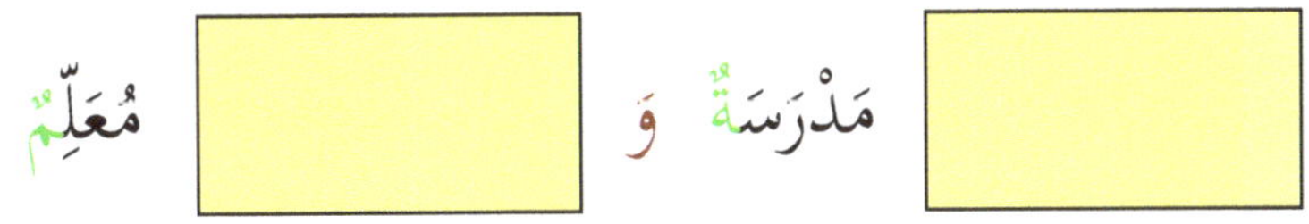

4. Translate the following sentences in to Arabic using the words provided below.

The first one has been done for you.

| جَدِيْدٌ | قَدِيْمٌ | كَبِيْرٌ |
|---|---|---|
| New | Old | Big |
| صَغِيْرٌ | نَظِيْفٌ | وَسِخٌ |
| Small | Clean | Dirty |

(Feminine) (Feminine)
I. This is old and that is new.

هٰذِهِ قَدِيْمَةٌ وَ تِلْكَ جَدِيْدَةٌ

(Masculine) (Feminine)
II. That is clean and this is dirty.

----------------------------------------

(Masculine/Dual) (Masculine/Dual)
III. These are small and those are big.

----------------------------------------

(Feminine)
IV. This is new.

----------------------------------------

(Masculine)
V. That is dirty.

----------------------------------------

## Prepositions attached to demonstrative pronouns

Prepositions, as we have learnt previously, can be attached to nouns as well as pronouns. In the same manner, prepositions can attach themselves to demonstrative pronouns, by which new connectives and adverbial phrases can be created.

For instance, the phrase *'Due to this'* or *'after that'* can be formed in Arabic by the combination of a preposition and a demonstrative pronoun.

- In Arabic, the preposition will be attached to the **FRONT** of the demonstrative pronoun as is done for nouns and pronouns.

E.g.

Preposition + demonstrative pronoun

كَ + ذَالِكَ = كَذَالِكَ

Like + That = Like that (In that way)

- Prepositions render the following word in to the genitive state. However, demonstrative pronouns are **indeclinable**, by which they will **NOT** alter the ending of a demonstrative pronoun but will be presumed as though it is in the genitive state.

E.g.

Preposition + Demonstrative Pronoun

مِنْ + هٰذَا = مِنْ هٰذَا

From + This = From this

1. Join the prepositions to the demonstrative pronouns below using the rules that have been explained.

The first one has been done for you.

| | Preposition | + | Demonstrative Pronoun | | |
|---|---|---|---|---|---|
| 1. | On | | That | | Upon that |
| | عَلَى | + | ذَالِكَ | = | عَلَى ذَالِكَ |
| 2. | After | | That | | ______ |
| | بَعْدَ | + | ذَالِكَ | = | |
| 3. | Before | | This | | ______ |
| | قَبْلَ | + | هٰذَا | = | |
| 4. | For | | That | | ______ |
| | لِ | + | ذَالِكَ | = | |
| 5. | With | | This | | ______ |
| | بِ | + | هٰذَا | = | |

## Demonstrative pronouns in a prepositional phrase sentence (acting predicate)

A prepositional phrase can be placed, instead of a predicate, to complete a sentence; by which it acts like a predicate. However, the rulings of **gender** and **amount** are not as stringent when forming these style of sentences.

Prepositional phrases are created by the usage of a preposition and a noun or even an attached pronoun.

For instance, *'From a boy'* and *'From him'*.

Both sentences have a preposition (*From*) and are proceeded by a noun (*boy*) and a pronoun (*him*).

Adding a demonstrative pronoun to the prepositional phrases above will enable the sentences to be complete.

e.g. 'This is *from a boy*.'

'Those are *from him*.'

- In Arabic, the demonstrative pronoun will be placed first in sequence then the prepositional phrase. For instance,

'This is *from a boy*.'

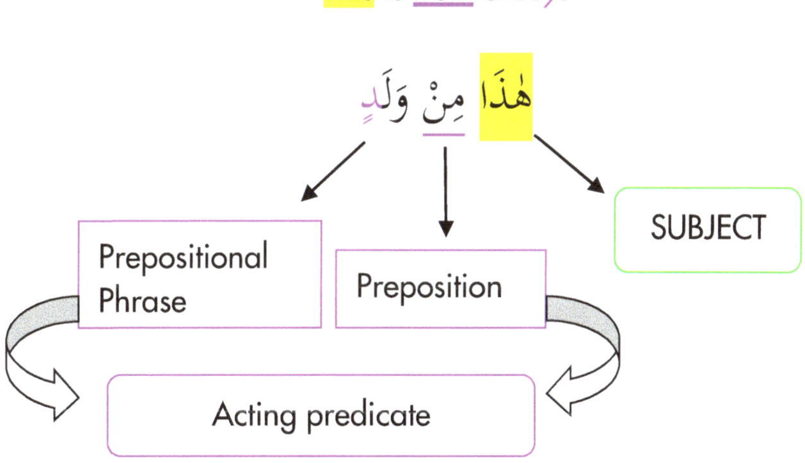

- The demonstrative pronoun will not need to agree to the prepositional phrase in gender and amount. For instance,

(Plural/Feminine)
'Those are *from* *him*.'

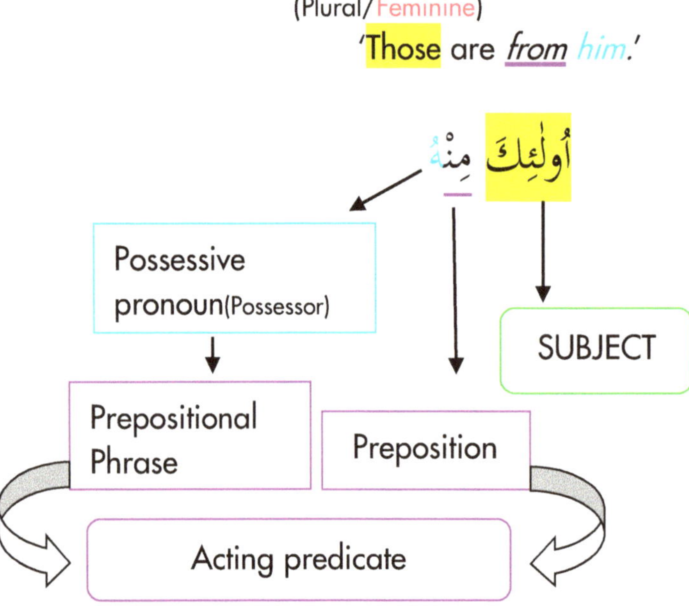


- The prepositional phrase can be made more complicated by affixing an attached pronoun to the noun. Again, agreement of **gender** and **amount** will not be in effect. For instance,

(Plural/Masculine)
'These are from her teacher.'

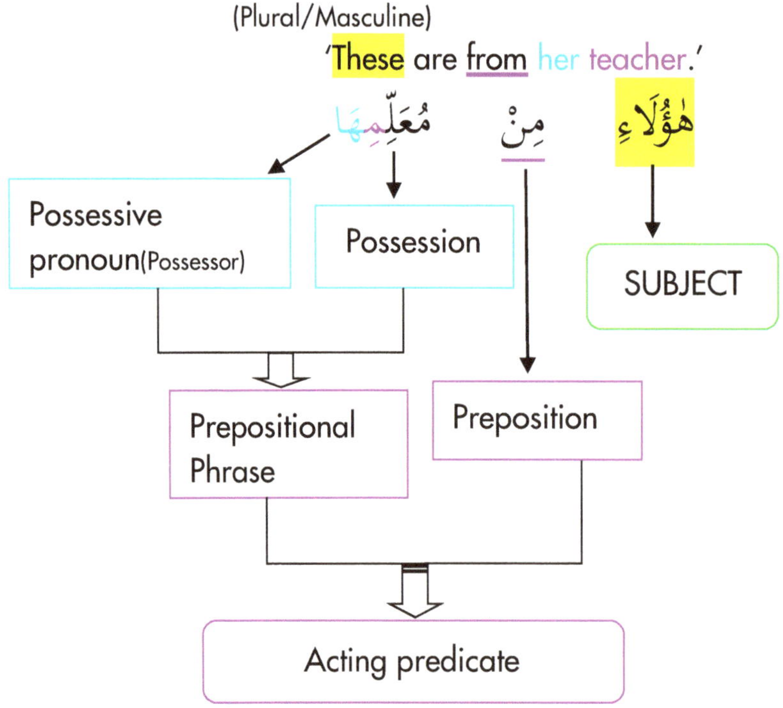

**1. Translate the following sentences in to Arabic using the words below.**

The first one has been done for you.

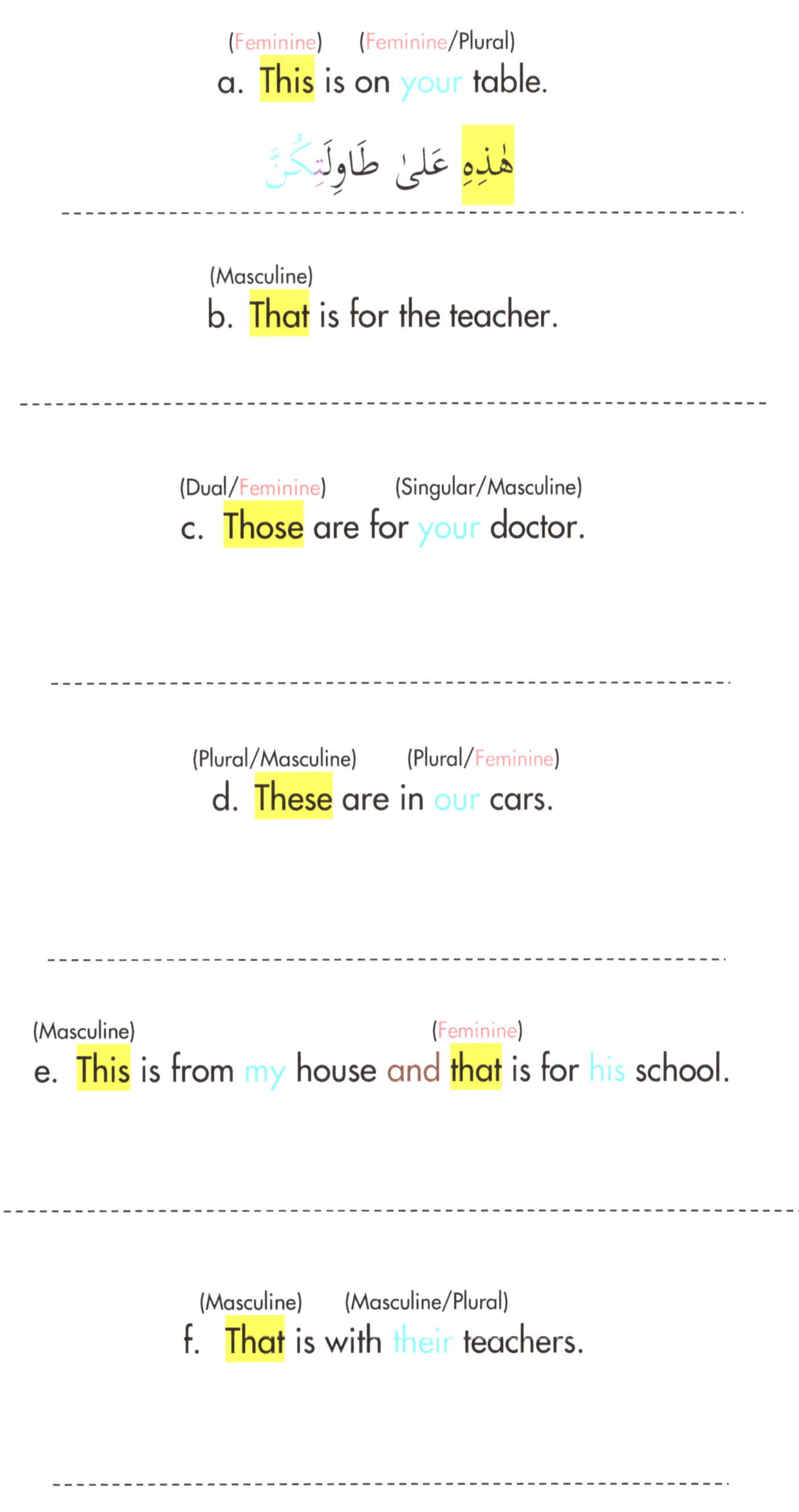

(Feminine) (Feminine/Plural)

a. This is on your table.

هٰذِهِ عَلىٰ طَاوِلَتِكُنَّ

---

(Masculine)

b. That is for the teacher.

---

(Dual/Feminine) (Singular/Masculine)

c. Those are for your doctor.

---

(Plural/Masculine) (Plural/Feminine)

d. These are in our cars.

---

(Masculine) (Feminine)

e. This is from my house and that is for his school.

---

(Masculine) (Masculine/Plural)

f. That is with their teachers.

---

| Nouns | | |
|---|---|---|
| English | Singular | Plural |
| Table | طَاوِلَةٌ | طَاوِلَاتٌ |
| Teacher | مُعَلِّمٌ | مُعَلِّمُوْنَ |
| School | مَدْرَسَةٌ | مَدَارِسُ |
| House | بَيْتٌ | بُيُوْتٌ |
| Car | سَيَّارَةٌ | سَيَّارَاتٌ |
| Doctor | طَبِيْبٌ | اَطِبَّاءُ |

| Prepositions | |
|---|---|
| English | Arabic |
| From | مِنْ |
| With | بِ |
| For | لِ |
| In | فِيْ |
| On | عَلٰى |

2. Translate the following sentences in to ENGLISH using the words above.

The first one has been done for you.

١. هٰذَا مِنْ بَيْتِهِمْ

This is from their house.

---

٢. ذَانِكَ فِيْ مَدْرَسَتِهَا

---

٣. أُولٰئِكَ بِنَا

---

٤. هٰذَا فِيْ سَيَّارَتِيْ وَ ذَالِكَ عَلَى الطَّاوِلَةِ

---

3. Break down the following sentences grammatically in to its smallest unit of preposition, possession, possessive pronoun, prepositional phrase, subject and predicate.

Some boxes have been done for you.

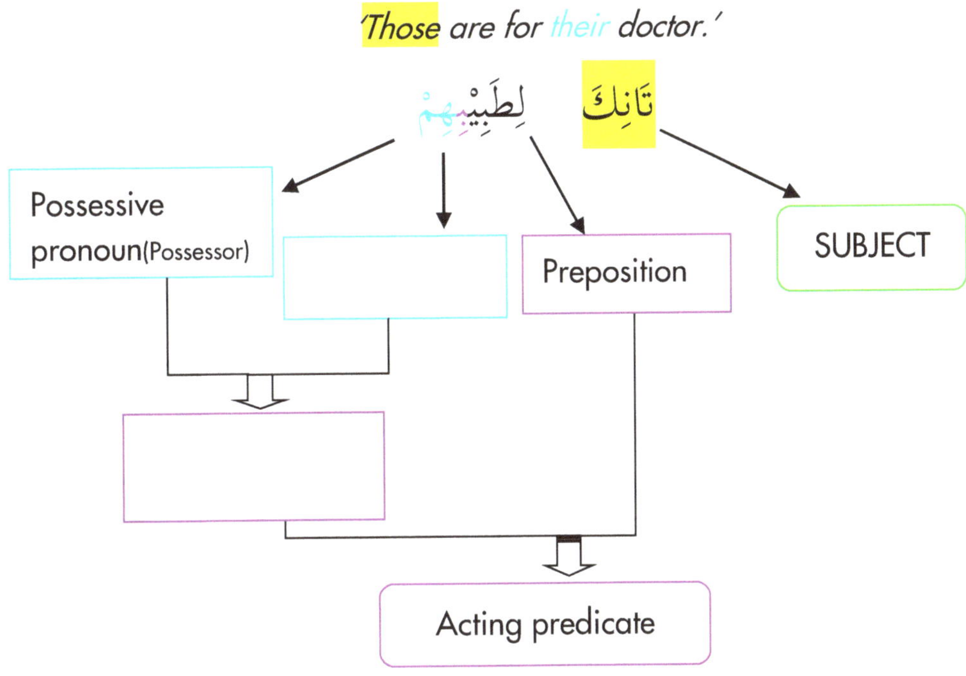


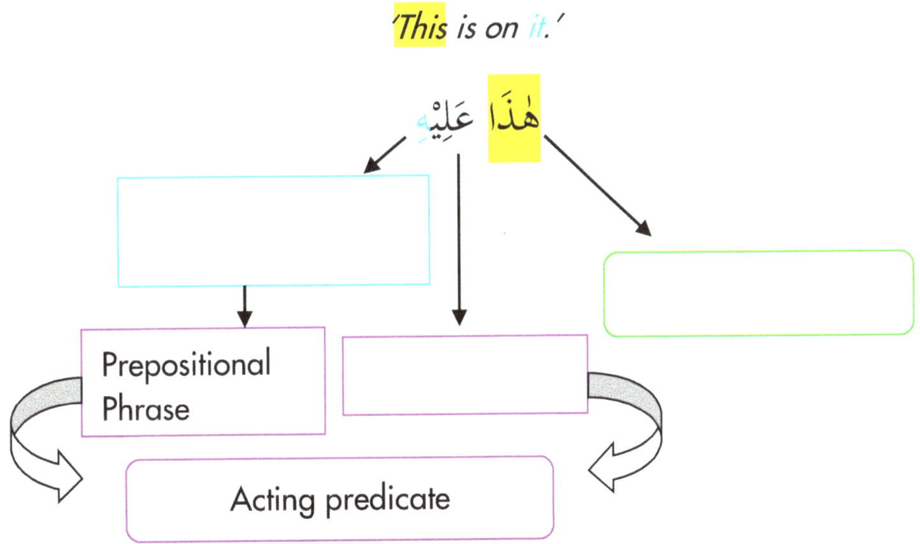

## Definitive demonstrative pronouns

The previous section has discussed the usage of demonstrative pronouns in a general aspect, in which the demonstrative pronoun does not clearly specify the person, place, thing, state or quality and therefore they are not absolutely definitive.

For instance, the statement '*This is small.*', does not specify the true nature of the subject, which is described as small.

Demonstrative pronoun can be made definitive by adding a noun which limits/restricts the demonstrative pronoun. This is classed as a **demonstrative phrase**.

For example, the statement above can be made absolutely definitive by restricting the demonstrative pronoun to a specific noun, e.g. '**CAR**'

'*This* **CAR** *is small.*' The subject in this sentence is now known.

- In Arabic, a demonstrative pronoun can be made definitive by adding a definite noun. The particle اَلْ will be affixed to the noun.

e.g. 'This boy'

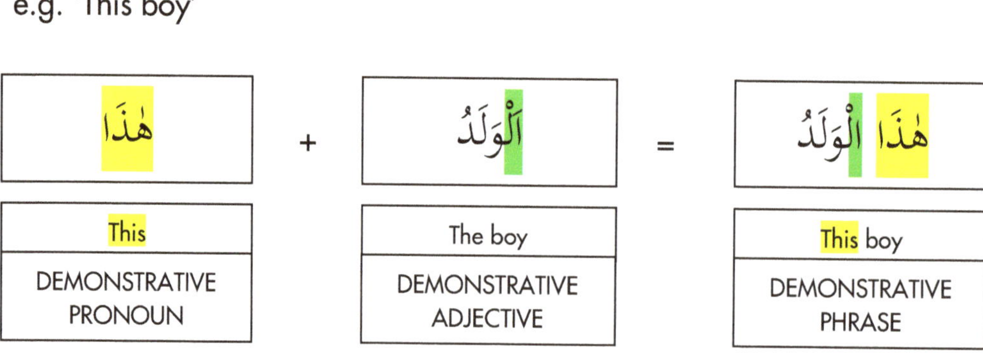

- The demonstrative pronoun will agree to the definite noun in **gender** and **amount**.

| | Masculine | Feminine |
|---|---|---|
| Singular – | (This man)<br>هٰذَا الرَّجُلُ | (This woman)<br>هٰذِهِ الْمَرْأَةُ |
| Dual – | (These men)<br>هٰذَانِ الرَّجُلَانِ | (These women)<br>هَاتَانِ الْمَرْأَتَانِ |
| Plural – | (These men)<br>هٰؤُلَاءِ الرِّجَالُ | (These women)<br>هٰؤُلَاءِ النِّسَاءُ |

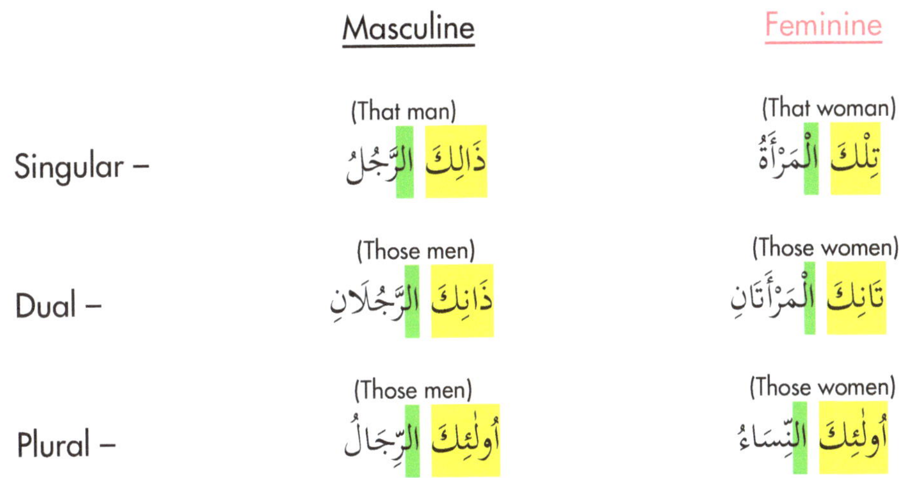

| | Masculine | Feminine |
|---|---|---|
| Singular – | (That man)<br>ذَالِكَ الرَّجُلُ | (That woman)<br>تِلْكَ الْمَرْأَةُ |
| Dual – | (Those men)<br>ذَانِكَ الرَّجُلَانِ | (Those women)<br>تَانِكَ الْمَرْأَتَانِ |
| Plural – | (Those men)<br>أُولٰئِكَ الرِّجَالُ | (Those women)<br>أُولٰئِكَ النِّسَاءُ |

- A predicate can be attached to complete these demonstrative phrases. The subsequent rulings of subject and predicate will also be applicable. I.e. The predicate will agree with the subject in **gender** and **amount**.

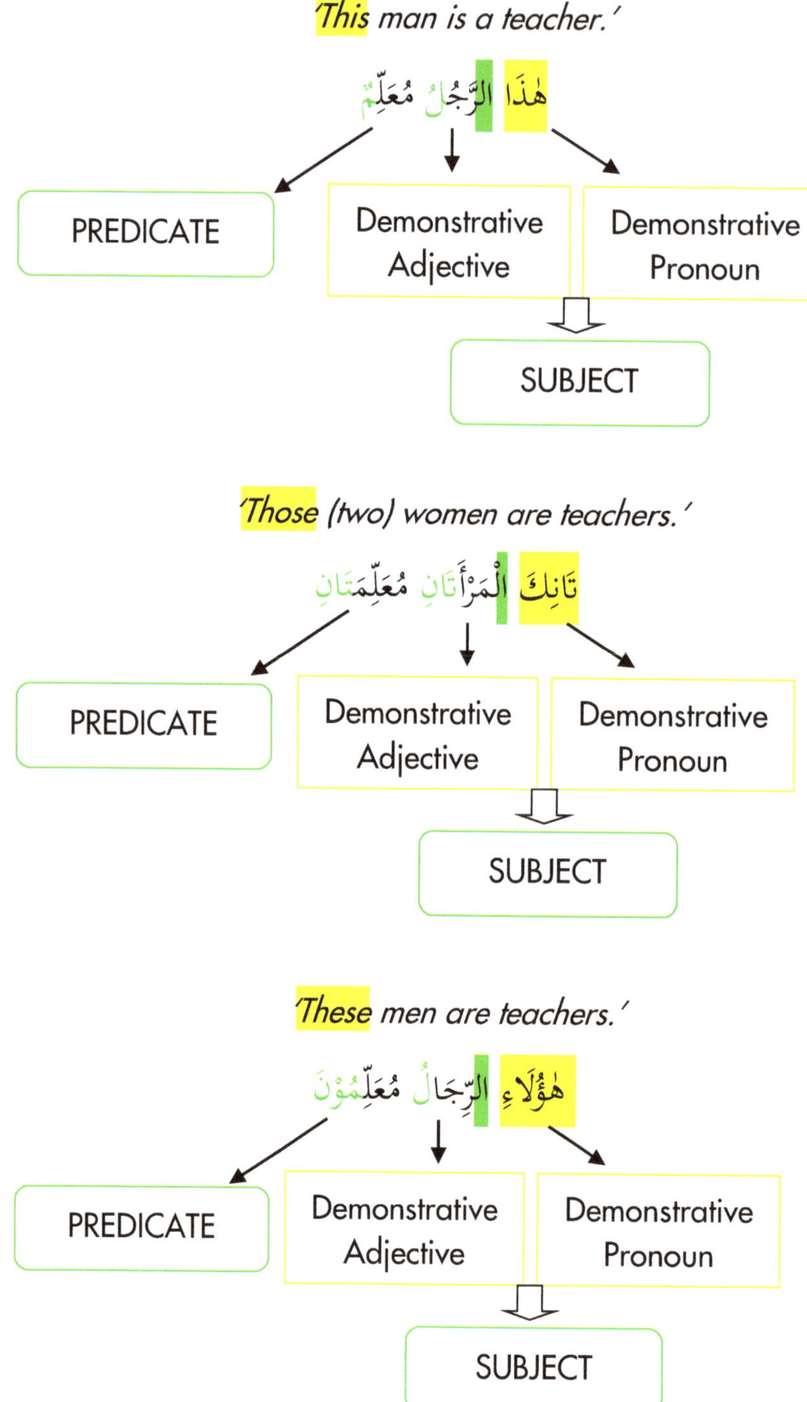

1. State whether the demonstrative pronouns in the following sentences are **general** or *definitive.*

The first one has been done for you.

| | | |
|---|---|---|
| I. | That is broken. | **General** |
| II. | Those pens are new. | ______ |
| III. | These books belong to the school. | ______ |
| IV. | This is large. | ______ |
| V. | These two houses are old. | ______ |

2. Join the correct demonstrative pronouns to the nouns given below.

*** Remember they must agree in **gender** and **amount**. ***

The first one has been done for you.

| | | |
|---|---|---|
| a. This car | اَلسَّيَّارَةُ | هٰذِهِ |
| b. These teachers (Plural/Masculine) | اَلْمُعَلِّمُوْنَ | |
| c. That school | اَلْمَدْرَسَةُ | |
| d. These children (Dual/Masculine) | اَلطِّفْلَانِ | |
| e. Those girls (Plural/Feminine) | اَلْبَنَاتُ | |

3. Using the words below, translate the following sentences in to Arabic.

*** Remember the predicate must agree to its subject in **gender** and **amount**. ***

The first one has been done for you.

| English | Singular | Plural |
|---|---|---|
| Boy | وَلَدٌ | أَوْلَادٌ |
| Pen | قَلَمٌ | أَقْلَامٌ |
| Standing | قَائِمٌ | قَائِمُوْنَ |
| New | جَدِيْدٌ | جُدُدٌ |
| Governors | أَمِيْرٌ | أُمَرَاءُ |
| Going | ذَاهِبٌ | ذَاهِبُوْنَ |
| Sitting | جَالِسٌ | جَالِسُوْنَ |
| Nurse | مُمَرِّضٌ | مُمَرِّضُوْنَ |

1. Those governors are going.

هٰؤُلَاءِ الْأُمَرَاءُ ذَاهِبُوْنَ

---------------------------------

2. That boy is sitting.

---------------------------------

(Dual/Masculine)
3. These pens are new.

---------------------------------

4. This nurse is standing.

---------------------------------

(Plural/Feminine)
5. Those governors are new.

---------------------------------

(Plural/Feminine)
6. Those nurses are sitting and these boys *(dual)* are standing.

---------------------------------

7. That governor is going and this boy is new.

---------------------------------

(Plural)
8. These boys are going and that nurse is going.

---------------------------------

**4. Break down the following sentences to its smallest units of subject and predicate.**

The first one has been done for you.

*'These cars are new.'*

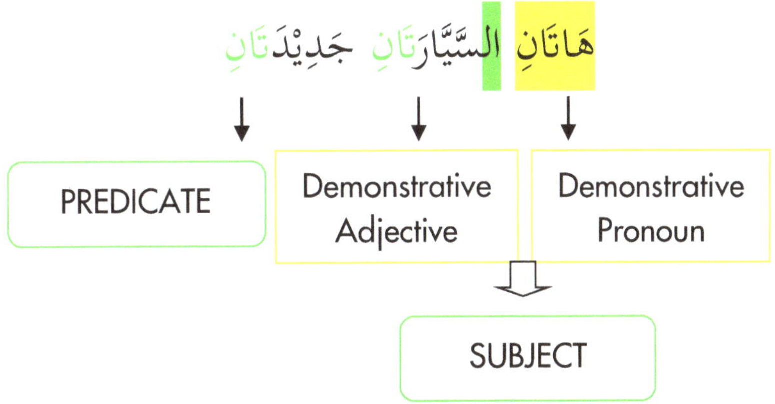


*'That girl is sitting.'*

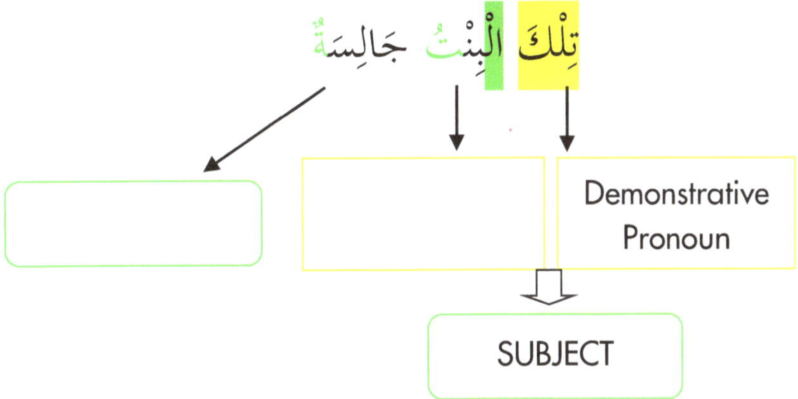


*'Those men are standing.'*

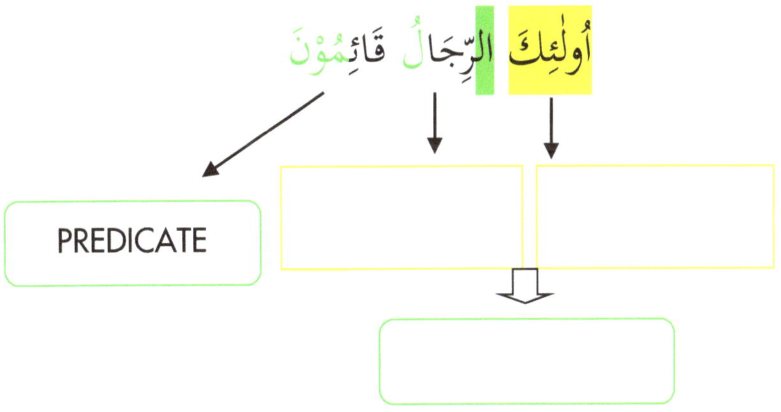

## Definitive demonstrative pronouns for the plural non-intellectual being form

The demonstrative pronoun will have to agree with the noun it is specifying in its gender and amount. This is the case for both Arabic and English; for the plural of 'This house' would be '**These** house**s**'. However, in Arabic as we have learnt preiviously there is an exception for plural non-intellectual being forms.

- In Arabic, when the noun is a plural non-intellectual being, then any words associated with that given noun will be ***SINGULAR FEMININE***. Therefore, the predicate and demonstrative pronoun will be ***SINGULAR FEMININE***.

E.g. *'These houses are new.'*

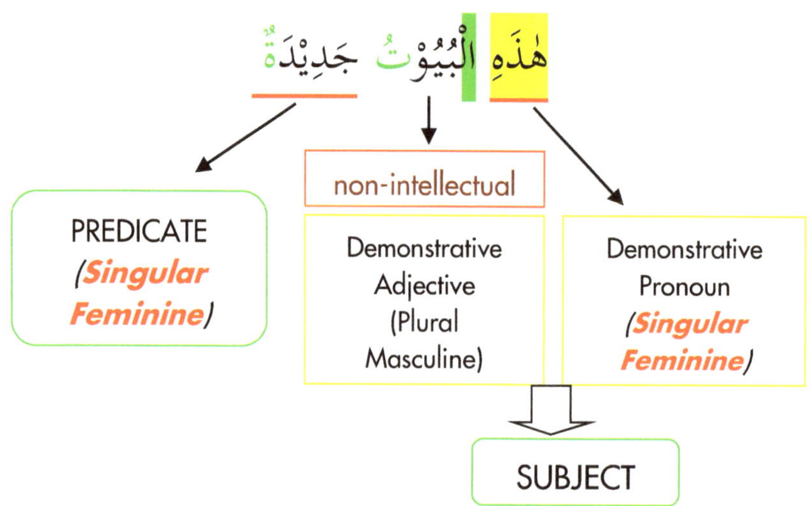


E.g. *'These pens are old.'*

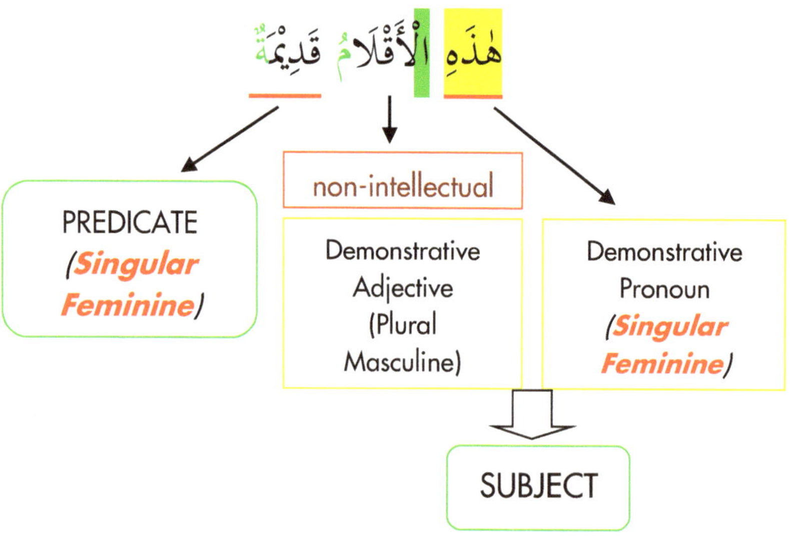

1. Using the words below, translate the following sentences in to Arabic.

*** Remember the ruling for the plural non-intellectual beings ***

The first one has been done for you.

| | | | |
|---|---|---|---|
| بُيُوْتٌ<br>Houses | سَيَّارَاتٌ<br>Cars | نَظِيْفٌ<br>Clean | مَفْتُوْحٌ<br>Open |
| كُتُبٌ<br>Books | غُرَفٌ<br>Rooms | قَدِيْمٌ<br>Old | مَكْسُوْرٌ<br>Broken |
| قُمُصٌ<br>Shirts | سُرُرٌ<br>Beds | كَبِيْرٌ<br>Big | صَغِيْرٌ<br>Small |

I. Those shirts are small.

---------------------------------------------------

II. Those houses are open.

---------------------------------------------------

III. These books are old.

---------------------------------------------------

IV. Those rooms are clean and these houses are big.

---------------------------------------------------

V. These beds are broken.

---------------------------------------------------

VI. Those cars are clean and those books are small.

---------------------------------------------------

2. Add the correct diacritical marks (Dhamma, Fatha, Kasra and Tanween) on the following sentences.

The first one has been done for you.

These houses are small.

١. هٰذِهِ الْبُيُوْتُ صَغِيْرَةٌ

That boy is sitting.

٢. ذَالِكَ الْوَلَد جَالِس

These men are from the school.

٣. هٰؤُلَاءِ الرِّجَال مِنَ الْمَدْرَسَة

These pens are broken.

٤. هٰذِهِ الْأَقْلَام مَكْسُوْرَة

That is a book.

٥. ذَالِكَ كِتَاب

Those (two) cars are new.

٦. تَانِكَ السَّيَّارَتَان جَدِيْدَتَان

This is his shirt.

٧. هٰذَا قَمِيْصه

## Definitive demonstrative pronouns in a prepositional phrase sentence (acting predicate)

A prepositional phrase can be included into to a definitive demonstrative pronoun sentence. The prepositional phrase will not need to agree in **gender** and **amount** to the definitive noun. For instance- '*These books are from the school.*'

The above sentence refers to a plural noun (*These books*) which is the definitive demonstrative phrase. The prepositional phrase (*from the school)* comes as an acting predicate and is in the singular form.

- In Arabic, the demonstrative phrase will be placed first in sequence then the prepositional phrase will follow after. For instance,

  *These books* - هٰذِهِ الْكُتُبُ

  *from the school*- مِنَ الْمَدْرَسَةِ

  'These books are from the school.'
  هٰذِهِ الْكُتُبُ مِنَ الْمَدْرَسَةِ

- Possessive pronouns can also be attached to a preposition in a demonstrative phrasal sentence.

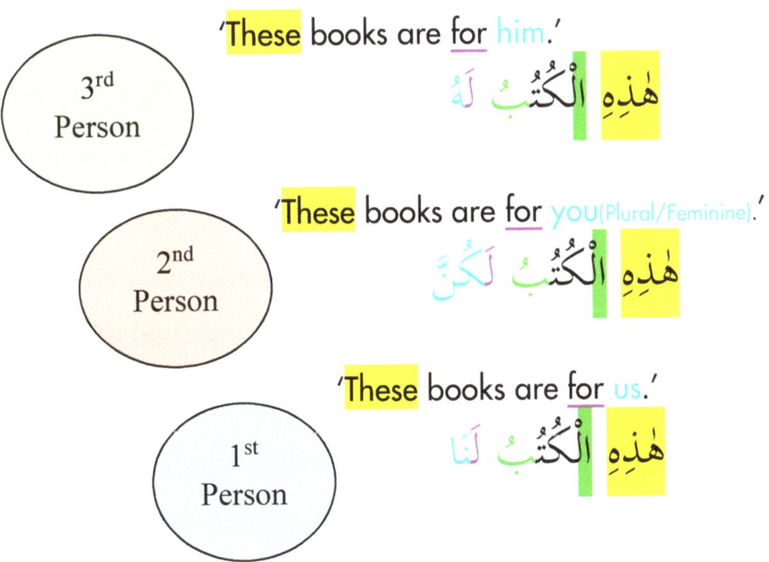

- The prepositional phrase can be made more complicated by affixing an attached pronoun to the noun. Again, agreement of **gender** and **amount** will not be needed. For instance,

'These books are from your school.'

(The noun within the phrase 'from your school' is made definite by the second person pronoun. Therefore, the definite particle اَلْ will not be attached to the noun.)

- The sentence will be broken down to its smallest grammatical unit in the following manner.

'These books are from your school.'

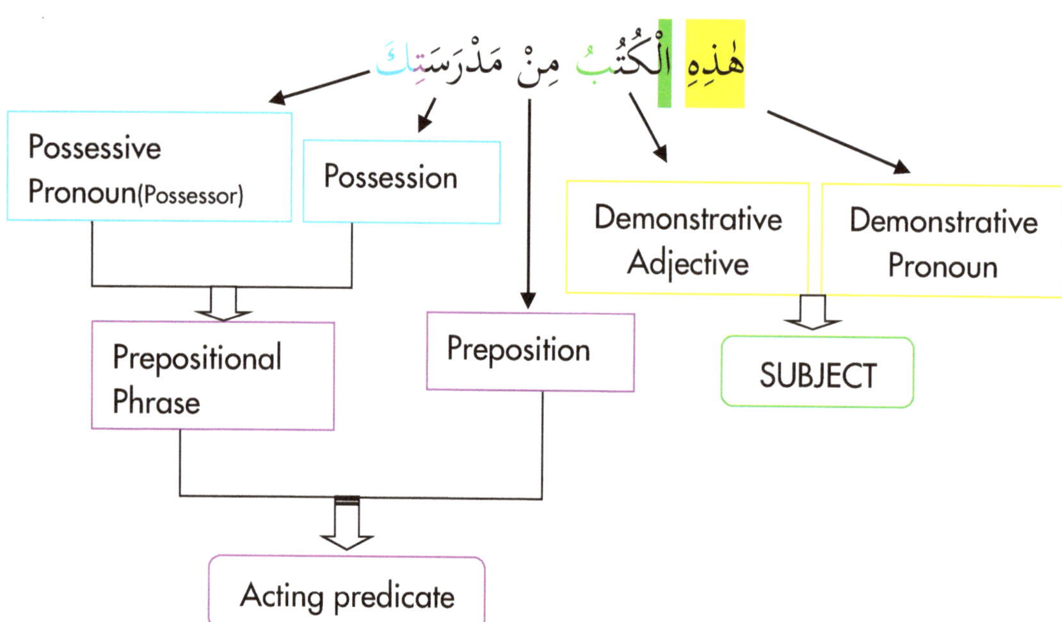

- If a predicate is used within the sentence, then as we have seen previously the predicate will agree with the subject and the prepositional phrase will be regarded as an **Adverbial** (extra information).

'These books from your school are old.'

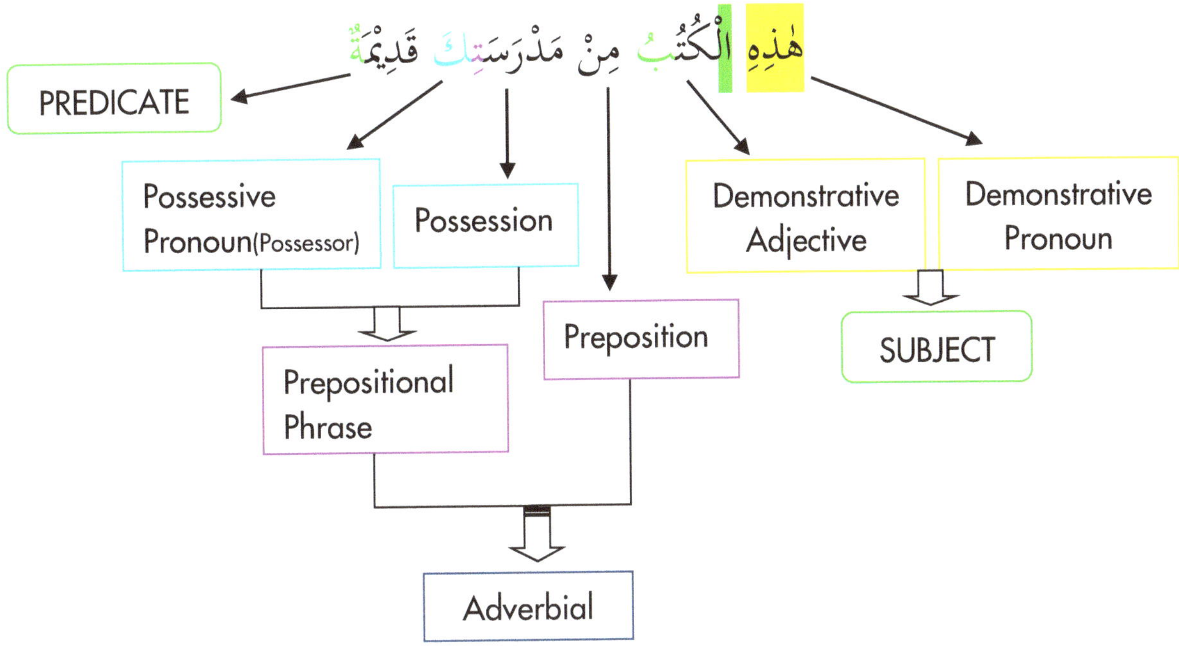


- The noun within the phrase 'from your school' is made definite by the second person pronoun. Therefore, the particle اَلْ will not be attached to the noun.

- Due to the predicate being present in this sentence the prepositional phrase will give more information regarding the subject. Without the **Adverbial**, the sentence is grammatically correct – 'These books are old'.

- The predicate (old) and the demonstrative pronoun (These) in this sentence are ***SINGULAR FEMININE*** as the subject (books) is a plural non-intellectual being.

1. Using the words below, translate the following sentences in to Arabic.

The first one has been done for you.

| بَيْتٌ | وَلَدٌ | قَلَمٌ | سَرِيْرٌ | مَدْرَسَةٌ |
|---|---|---|---|---|
| House | Boy | Pen | Bed | School |
| كِتَابٌ | كُتُبٌ | غُرْفَةٌ | قُمُصٌ | مُعَلِّمٌ |
| Book | Books | Room | Shirts | Teacher |
| نَظِيْفٌ | قَدِيْمٌ | مَكْسُوْرٌ | جُدَدٌ | اَمَامَ |
| Clean | Old | Broken | New (Plural) | In front of (Preposition) |

I. Those shirts from his house are clean.

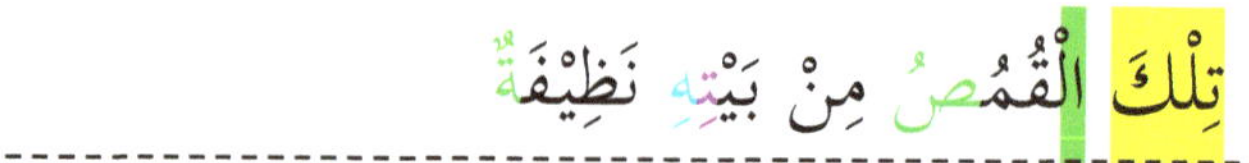

II. This boy is from the school.

III. That book is for my teacher.

IV. These two beds are old and that bed in our room is broken.

V. That pen is for you and these books are for your teacher.

VI. Those teachers in front of our school are new and these boys are from my school.

2. Break down the following sentences to its smallest units of subject and predicate.

The first one has been done for you.

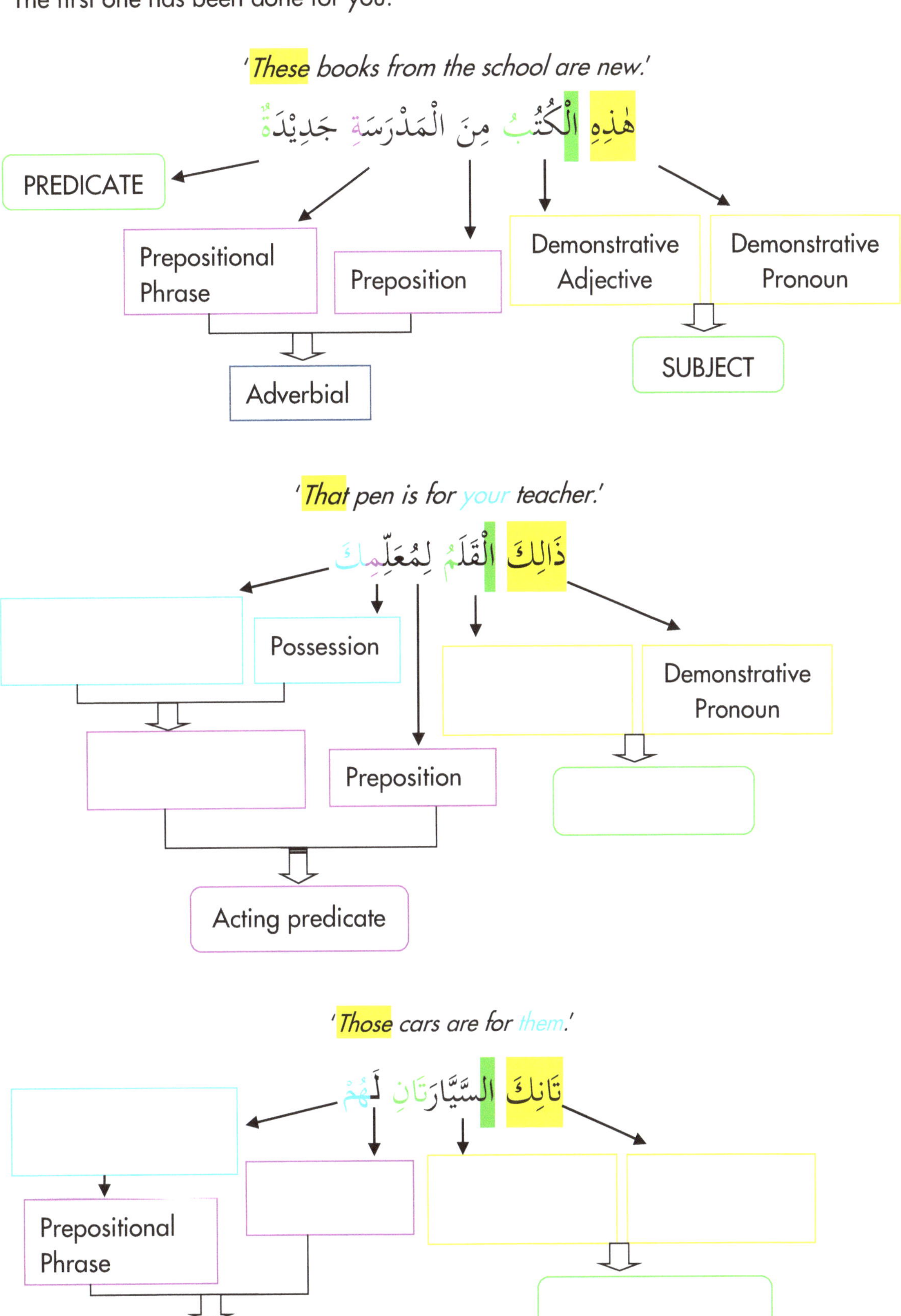

## Using demonstrative pronouns with personal pronouns

In English, a variety of sentences can be formed due to the unrestricted ability of definitiveness, which allows a scope of ease when constructing sentences. Arabic, as we have seen, follows a systematic method which restricts sentences to cases and definitiveness which makes grammar seem more complicated.

As a result of the unrestricted concept of definitiveness within English, we can produce the statement – '*This is the boy.*'

The above statement is a complete sentence by which a general demonstrative pronoun (*This*) is used as a SUBJECT and a definite noun (*the boy*) as a PREDICATE.

- In Arabic, when adding the definite particle اَلْ to the noun the sentence becomes an incomplete phrase. For instance,

'*This boy*'

- To prevent the definite article اَلْ from having an effect within the phrase, a ***personal pronoun*** can be placed between the demonstrative pronoun and the definite noun. This ***personal pronoun*** will have to agree with the definite noun in its **gender** and **amount**.

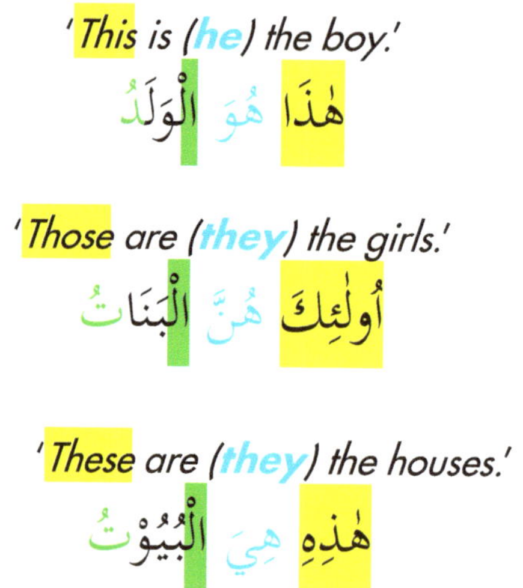


❖ In this last sentence the word '*houses*' is a plural non-intellectual being. Therefore, the demonstrative pronoun and personal pronoun are ***SINGULAR FEMINIE***.

1. Using the words below, translate the following sentences in to Arabic.

The first one has been done for you.

I. Those are the shirts.

تِلْكَ هِيَ الْقُمُصُ

II. That is the school.

---

III. These are the men and those are the women.

---

IV. This is the book.

---

V. These are the (two) boys and these are the (two) girls.

---

VI. Those are the pens and that is the book.

---

| بَيْتٌ | وَلَدٌ | أَقْلَامٌ | مَدْرَسَةٌ |
|---|---|---|---|
| House | Boy | Pens | School |
| | رِجَالٌ | | |
| | Men | | |
| كِتَابٌ | بِنْتٌ | قُمُصٌ | اَلنِّسَاءُ |
| Book | Girl | Shirts | Women |

## Using demonstrative pronouns with possessive pronouns

Possessive pronouns as we have seen previously are attached to its noun to indicate possession, e.g. '*his house*'. These set of pronouns are known as dependent – as they are dependent on a **noun** or **preposition** for their grammatical application.

There is another set of possessive pronouns in English that are known as independent, by which, their meaning establishes possession and their grammatical usage is independent.
The independent possessive pronouns are: *mine, yours, his, hers, its, ours, yours and theirs*. For instance, 'This book of yours' or 'That is mine'.

- In Arabic, there is only one set of possessive pronouns and their application will alter in its meaning depending on the formation of the phrase and the state(case) they are regulated under.

- To form the sentence 'This book of yours' in Arabic, the structure of the phrase will have to be rearranged.

If we were to say - هٰذَا كِتَابُكَ (This is your book.)

This will not give our intended meaning as this sentence is a complete sentence. Therefore, we need to rearrange the structure of the sentence by putting the definite noun ahead of the **demonstrative Pronoun**. E.g.

هٰذَا كِتَابُكَ (This is your book.) → كِتَابُكَ هٰذَا (This book of yours)

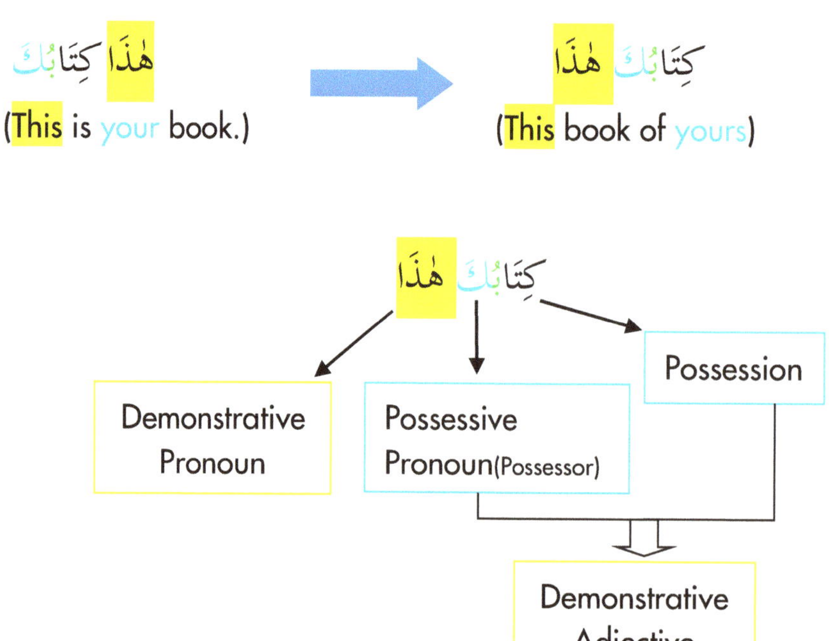

- The sentence '*This book of yours*' can be furthered by adding a predicate or an acting predicate to complete its meaning.

Adding a predicate – '*This book of yours is new.*'

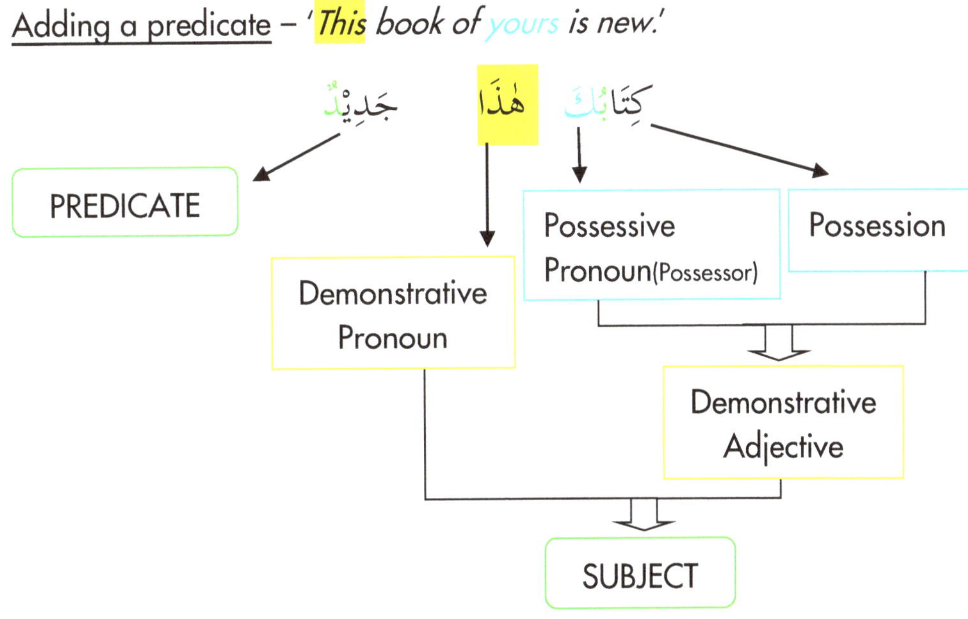


Adding an acting predicate – '*This book of yours is from the school.*'

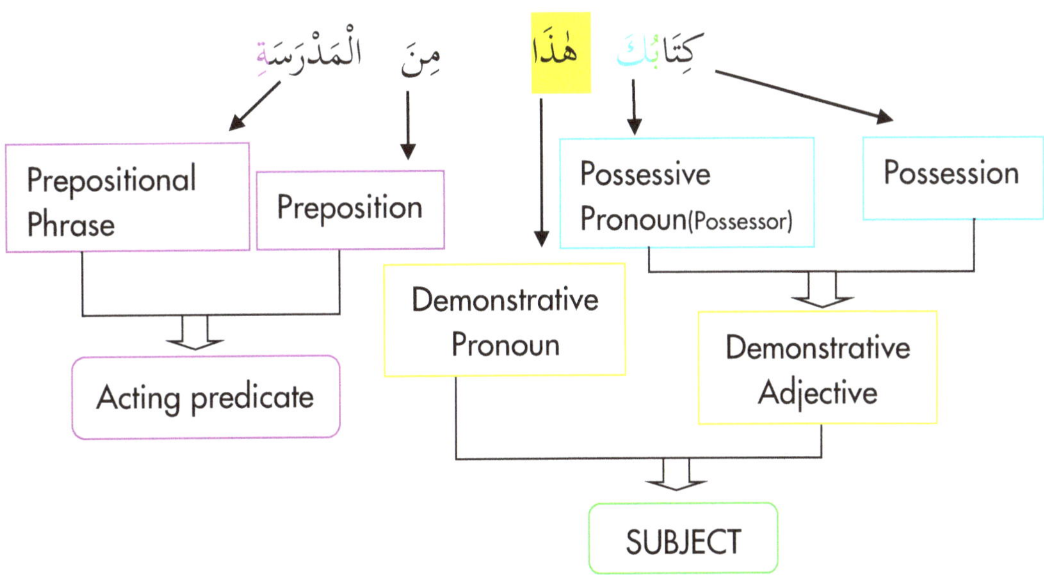

- The sentence '*This is mine*' or '*That is theirs*' in Arabic is created using the Preposition لِ (for/belongs) with the possessive pronoun. For example,

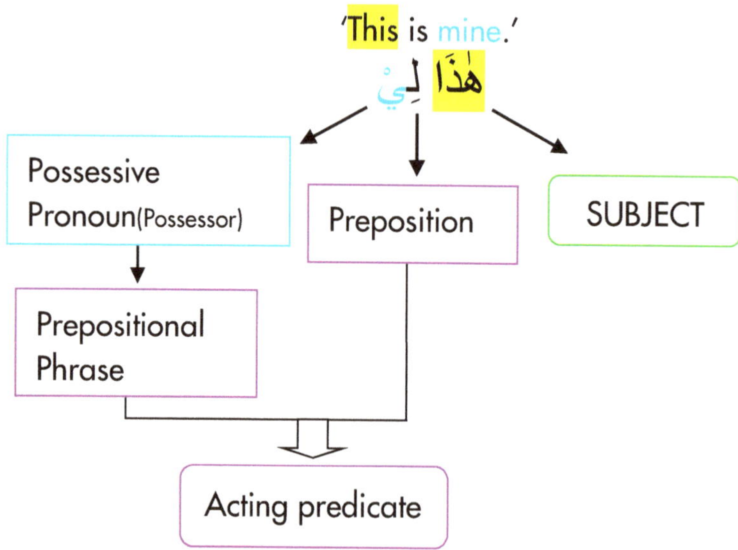


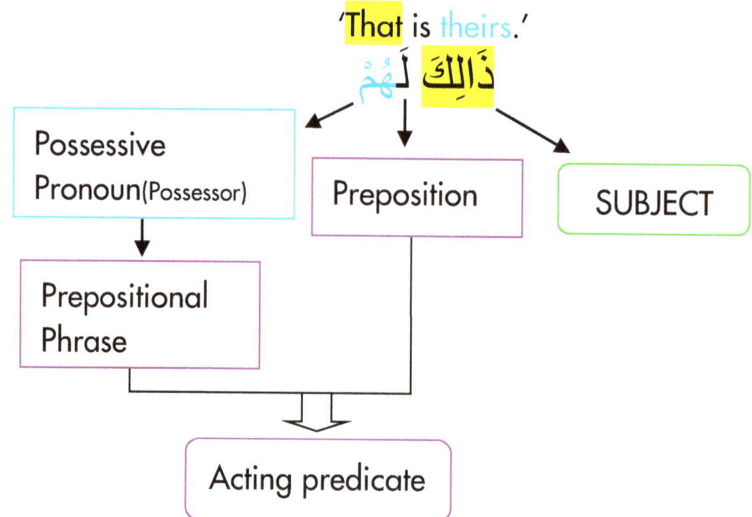

## 1. Using the words below, translate the following sentences in to Arabic.

The first one has been done for you.

I. This house of mine is new.

بَيْتِيْ هٰذَا جَدِيْدٌ

---

II. That car of hers is clean.

---

III. This is yours.

---

IV. Those pens of ours are from his school.

---

V. That book of hers from our school is old.

---

(Plural/Masculine)
VI. These are mine.

---

(Plural/Feminine)
VII. That is theirs.

---

VIII. This school of yours is clean and that house of his is new.

---

| بَيْتٌ | مَدْرَسَةٌ | اَقْلَامٌ | كِتَابٌ | سَيَّارَةٌ | جَدِيْدٌ | قَدِيْمٌ | نَظِيْفٌ |
|---|---|---|---|---|---|---|---|
| House | School | Pens | Book | Car | New | Old | Clean |

## 2. Break down the following sentences in to their smallest grammatical units

Some boxes have been done for you.

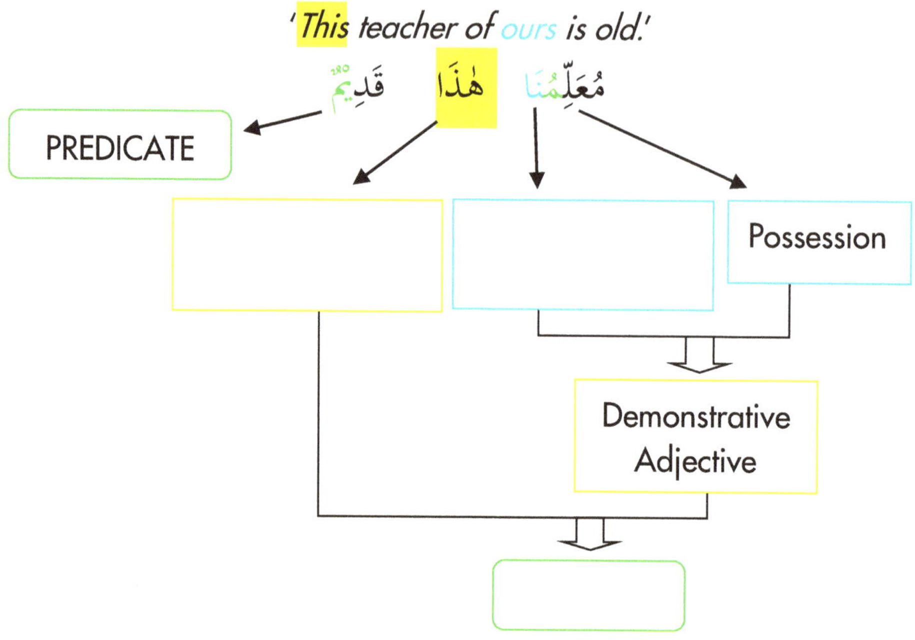


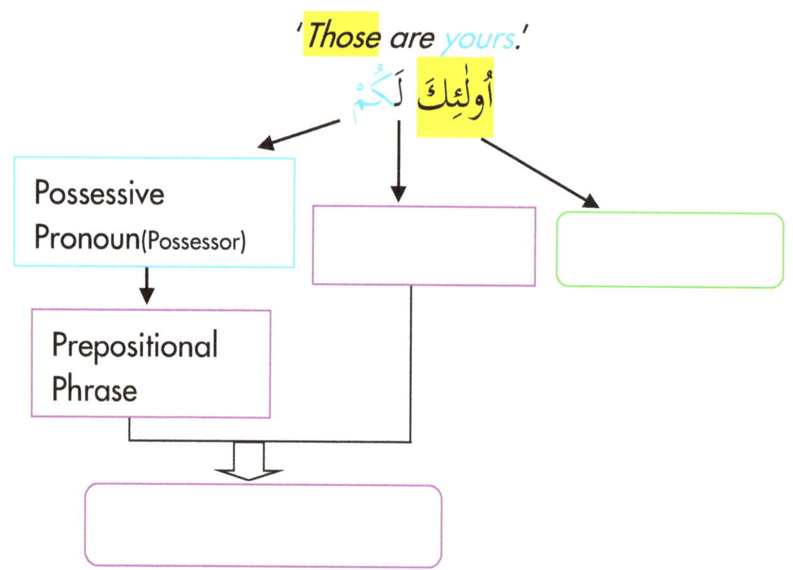

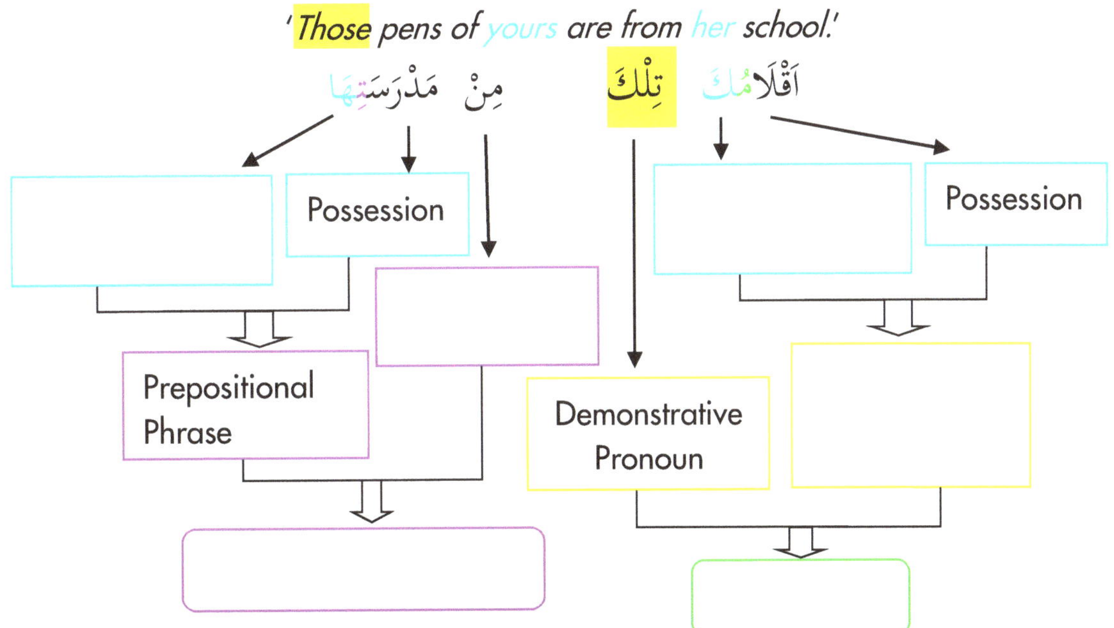
'Those pens of yours are from her school.'
مِنْ مَدْرَسَتِهَا تِلْكَ أَقْلَامُكَ
Possession
Possession
Prepositional Phrase
Demonstrative Pronoun

## Using more than one demonstrative pronoun in a sentence

By now we have established the grammatical rules pertaining to a demonstrative phrase; the relationship of the noun with the demonstrative pronoun and their agreement in gender and amount. As a result, we can now place more than one demonstrative phrase, not only to lengthen our sentence but also make the meaning more specific.

- More than one demonstrative pronoun can be used in a sentence by the coordinating conjunction وَ (And) as seen in previous examples.

*'This house is new and that car is old.'*

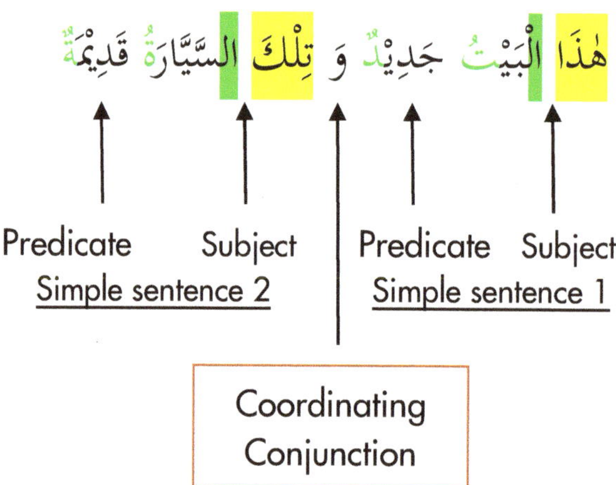


- Demonstrative pronouns are **indeclinable**. Therefore, prepositions will **NOT** alter the ending of a demonstrative pronoun, but the demonstrative adjective will be effected and rendered in to the genitive state.

*'That student is from this house.'*

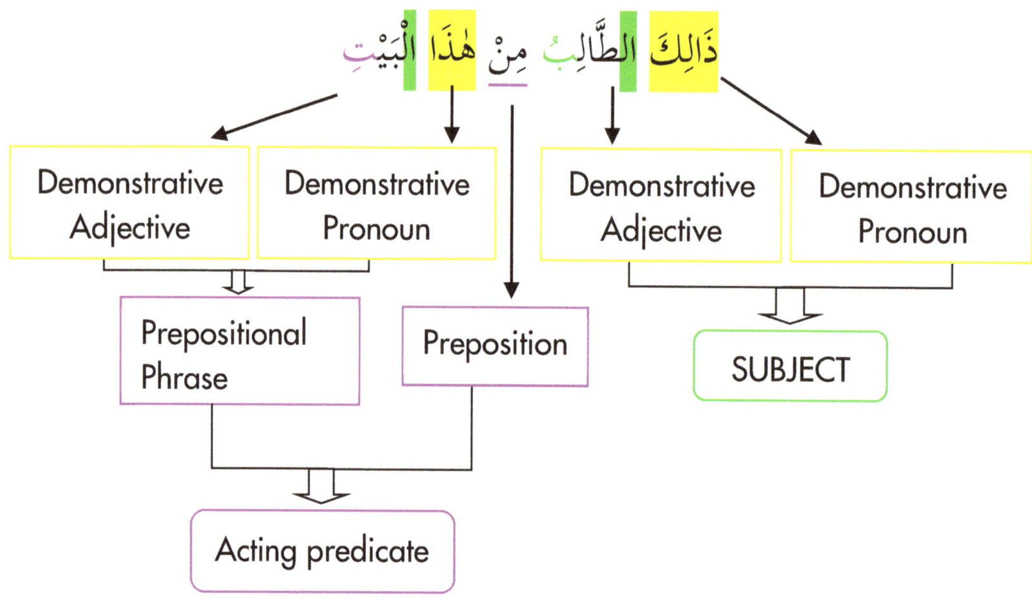

- Demonstrative pronouns in the dual form that come after prepositions will change in their structure.

| | Demonstrative pronoun in the dual form for the accusative and genitive state | |
|---|---|---|
| | These | Those |
| Masculine | هٰذَيْنِ* | ذَيْنِكَ* |
| Feminine | هَاتَيْنِ* | تَيْنِكَ* |

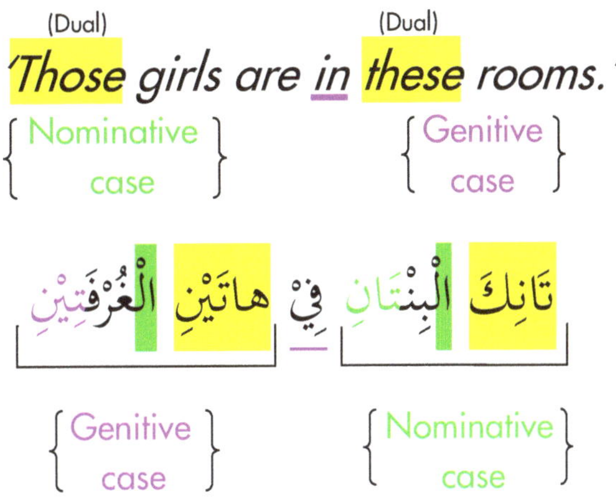


- Predicates can also be added in to sentences that have more than one demonstrative pronoun. As we have learnt before, predicates must agree with their subjects in **gender** and **amount**.

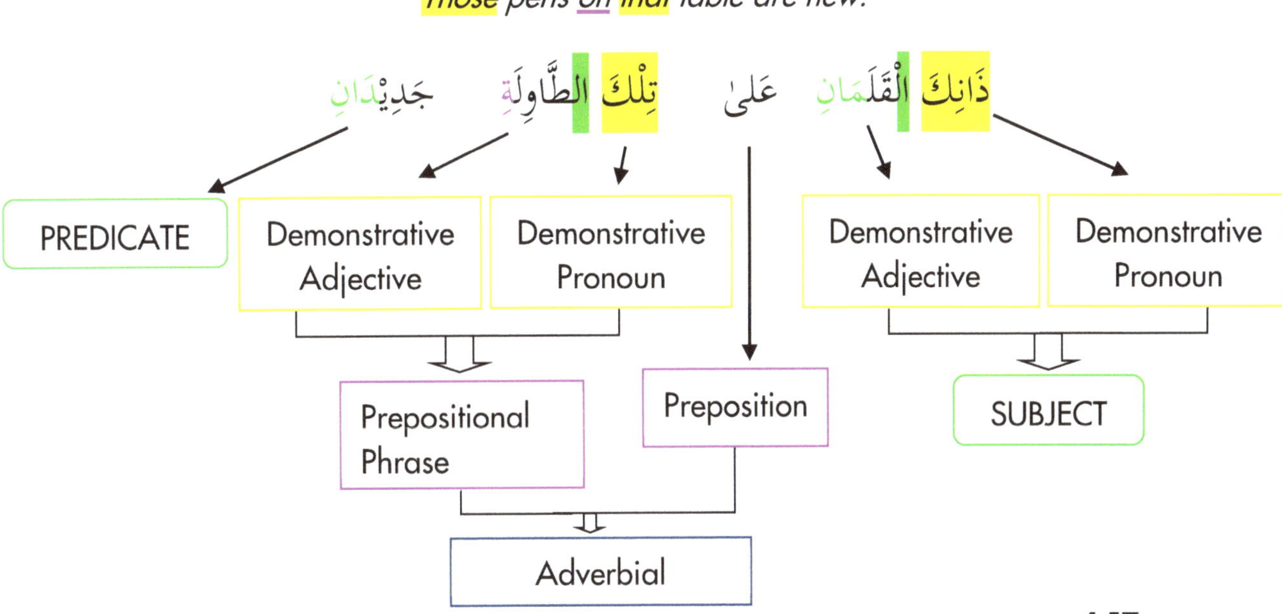

- Demonstrative pronouns can be used in an advanced prepositional phrase. Sentences of this type will be loosely translated and a word-to-word translation may not always be appropriate.

*'In this house there is a boy.'*

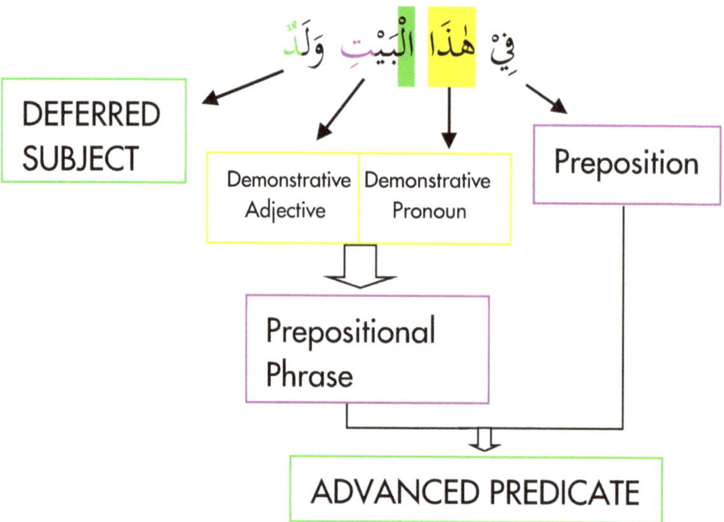


- In an advanced prepositional phrase, we can include a demonstrative pronoun to the deferred subject, as can be seen from the example below.

*'On this table there is that pen.'*

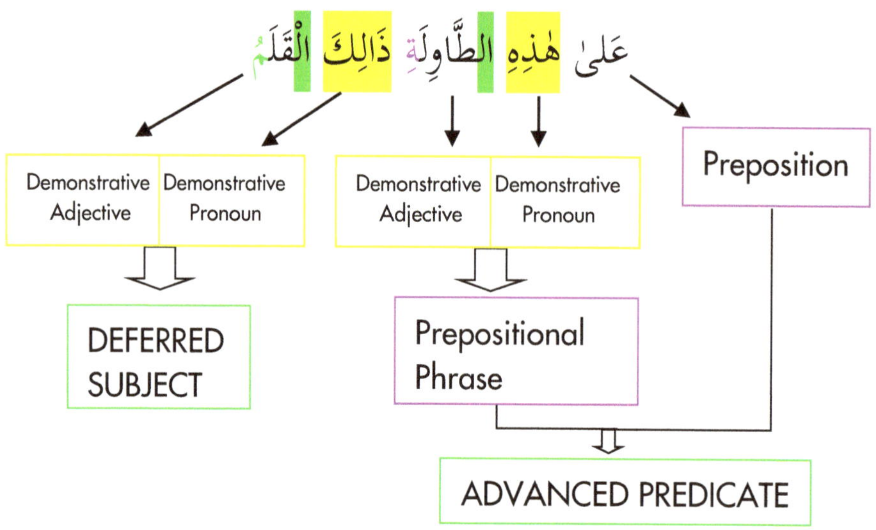

## 1. For the following English sentences...

a. Highlight in yellow all the demonstrative pronouns
b. Underline the prepositions in purple
c. Circle the attached and detached pronouns in blue

The first one has been done for you.

I. Those books of yours are in the school.

II. Those are new and these are in that car.

III. In my house there is that table.

IV. These children are playing in that garden.

V. These students from that school and those boys are going with their fathers to that museum.

## 2. Using the words below, translate the following sentences in to Arabic.

The first one has been done for you.

I. In that school there is this teacher.

فِيْ تِلْكَ الْمَدْرَسَةِ هٰذَا الْمُعَلِّمُ

II. That book of hers is new.

--------------------------------------------------

III. This is my car and that is our house.

--------------------------------------------------

IV. These boys from that school are going with their teachers.

---------------------------------------------------------------

V. That man is sitting in his car.

---------------------------------------------------------------

VI. These girls are going to that school.

---------------------------------------------------------------

(Plural/Feminine)

VII. This teacher of yours from that school is going to those museums.

---------------------------------------------------------------

(Dual/Masculine)

VIII. We are going to these houses and they are going to your school.

---------------------------------------------------------------

IX. That man is from that museum and this woman is from that school.

---------------------------------------------------------------

X. Our teacher is sitting in that room and that man from that school is sitting with him.

---------------------------------------------------------------

---------------------------------------------------------------

| | | | | | | | |
|---|---|---|---|---|---|---|---|
| مَدْرَسَةٌ | School | رَجُلٌ | Man | مَتْحَفٌ | Museum | جَالِسٌ | Sitting |
| مُعَلِّمٌ | Teacher | بِنْتٌ | Girl | مَتَاحِفُ | Museums | جَدِيْدٌ | New |
| مُعَلِّمُوْنَ | Teachers | بَنَاتٌ | Girls | سَيَّارَةٌ | Car | ذَاهِبٌ | Going |
| بَيْتٌ | House | غُرْفَةٌ | Room | أَوْلَادٌ | Boys | مَعَ | With |
| بُيُوْتٌ | Houses | كِتَابٌ | Book | اِمْرَأَةٌ | Woman | مِنْ | From |

**3. Complete the sentences by pairing the subject on the right side of the page with its predicate from the left side of the page.**

The first one has been done for you.

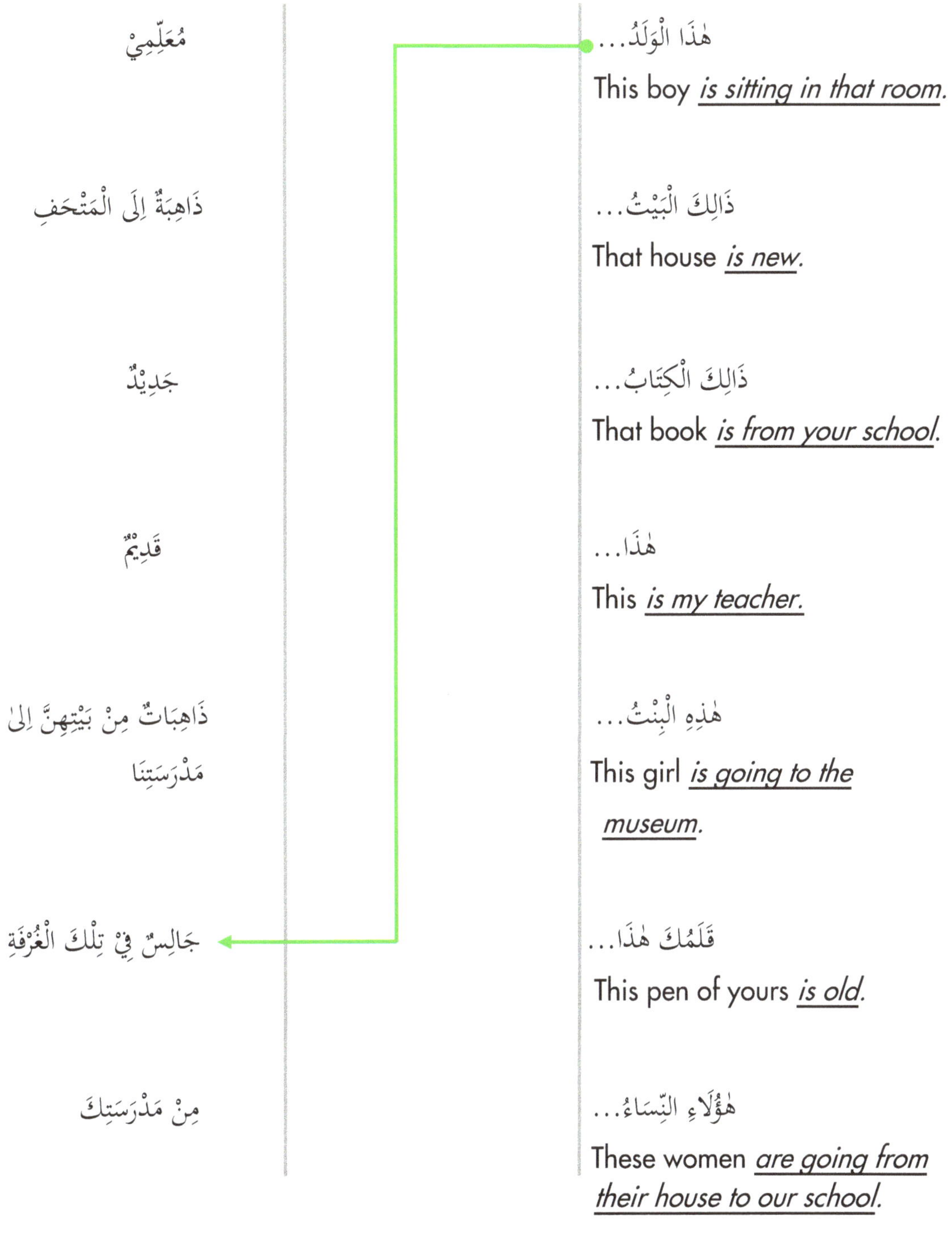

4. Break down the following sentences to its smallest units of subject and predicate.

Some boxes have been done for you.

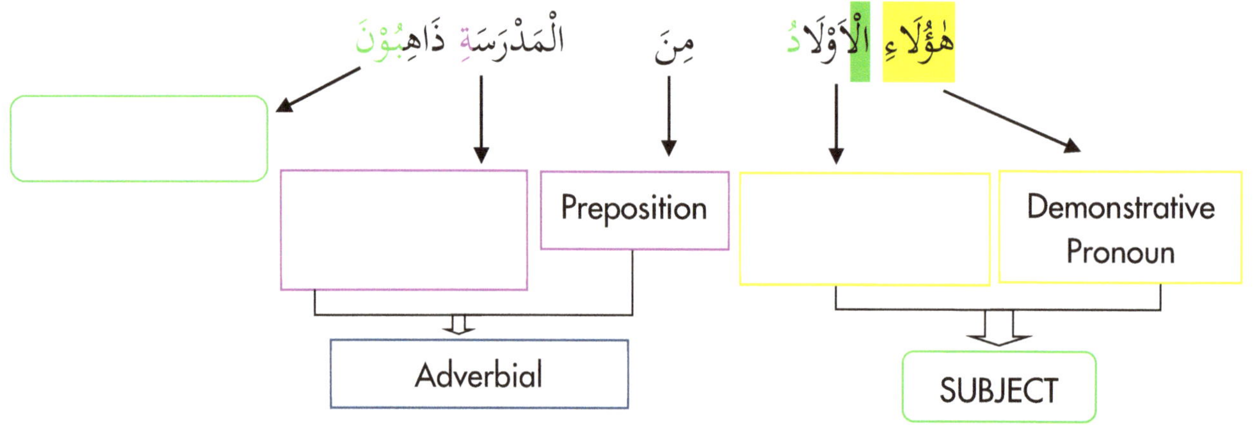


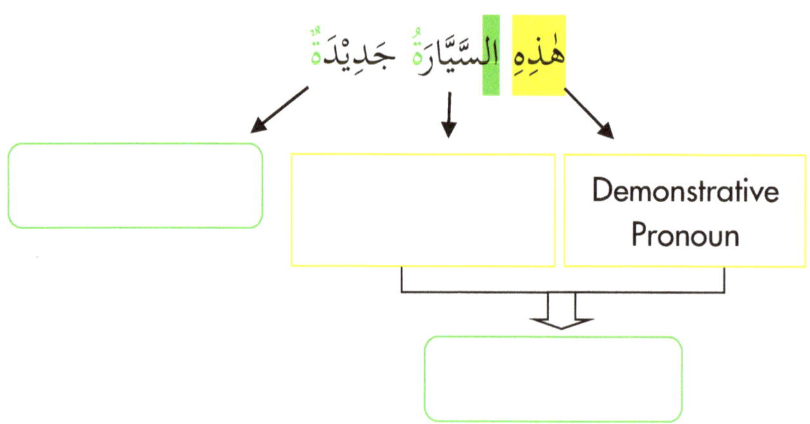


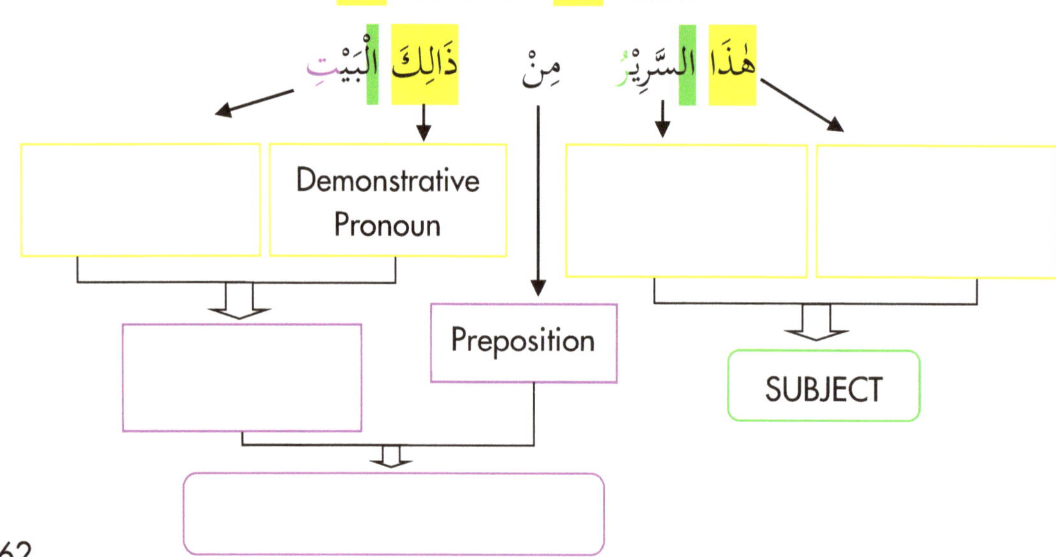

5. Put the correct diacritical marks on the following sentences using the words below **and translate them in to English.**

The first one has been done for you.

1) اَلْمُعَلِّمُ جَالِسٌ فِي الْمَكْتَبِ بِطُلَّابِهِ

1) The teacher is sitting in the office with his students.

2) هذا الْوَلَد ذَاهِب مَعَ أُمِّهِ اِلىٰ ذَالِكَ الْمَتْحَف

---

3) اَلْمُهَنْدِسَتَانِ مِنْ تلك الْمَدْرَسَة قَائِمَتان عِنْدَ اَصْدِقَائهما

---

4) اَلطَّبِيْبات قَادِمَاتٌ مِنْ ذَيْنِكَ الْبَيْتين وَ هُنَّ ذَاهِبات اِلىٰ هذين الْبَيْتين

---

---

| مُهَنْدِسٌ | Engineer | مَدْرَسَةٌ | School | مَتْحَفٌ | Museum | اَصْدِقَاءُ | Friends |
|---|---|---|---|---|---|---|---|
| قَادِمٌ | Coming | أُمٌّ | Mother | طُلَّابٌ | Students | مَكْتَبٌ | Office |
| عِنْدَ | With | طَبِيْبٌ | Doctor | مِنْ | From | ذَاهِبٌ | Going |
| بَيْتَيْنِ | Two Houses | وَلَدٌ | Boy | قَائِمٌ | Standing | مَعَ | With |

6. Using the words from the table above and any additional words write 5 of your own senences in Arabic

(i
---

(ii
---

(iii
---

(iv
---

(v
---

# Negative Sentences

10

The Arabic Sentence

# The Arabic Sentence
# Negative Sentences

Up until now the sentences that have been discussed have all been in the positive form. Negative sentences are quite easy to recognise because their meanings are in the negative form. In English, negative sentences are constructed by adding the particle **NOT** before the predicate.
For instance,

The boy is sitting.

The boy is **NOT** sitting.

Adding the particle 'NOT' before the predicate

The particle **NOT** can also be used as a contraction with the word 'is' and will be written as ***isn't***. The same meaning is implied from both sentences.

is not - The boy is **NOT** sitting.

isn't - The boy is**n't** sitting.

In Arabic, negative sentences can be created by adding a negative particle. There are some grammatical rulings that need to be considered when making a sentence negative.

1. Change the following sentences in to the **negative form** in English.

The first one has been done for you.

i. The man is going to the museum.

The man is **NOT** going to the museum.

ii. That car is clean and this bus is dirty.

-------------------------------------------

iii. Those teachers are from your school.

-------------------------------------------

- The particle مَا **(NOT)** will come before the subject in Arabic to make the sentence negative. The subject will remain in the nominative state which will be marked by a Dhamma (◌ُ). E.g.

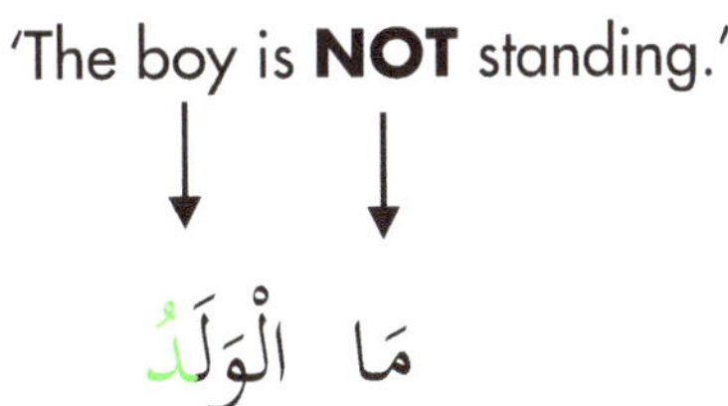


- The particle مَا **(NOT)** will render the predicate in to the accusative state. As the predicate bears a Fathataan (◌ً), an Alif (ا) is usually written at the end of the word. E.g.

'The boy is **NOT** standing.'

مَا الْوَلَدُ قَائِمًا

- As this is a nominal sentence which consists of a subject and a predicate, the agreement of **gender** and **amount** will be applicable.

E.g.

'The girl is **NOT** going.'

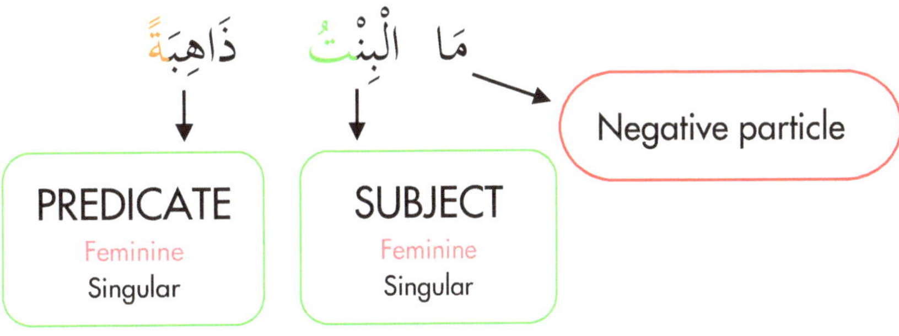


❖ The Alif (ا) will be written on all the letters that have a Fathataan except for the letter ة as can be seen in the example above.

## 1. Add the correct predicates to the following sentences in Arabic.

The first one has been done for you.

a. The man is **NOT** tall. 

b. The car is **NOT** big. 

c. The student is **NOT** present. 

d. The house is **NOT** clean. مَا الْبَيْتُ ______

e. The school is **NOT** open. مَا الْمَدْرَسَةُ ______

f. The teacher is **NOT** coming and the student is **NOT** going.

مَا الْمَعُلِّمُ ______ وَ مَا الطَّالِبَةُ ______

Big
كَبِيْرَةً

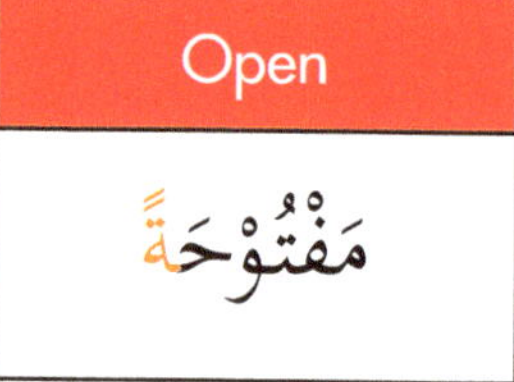


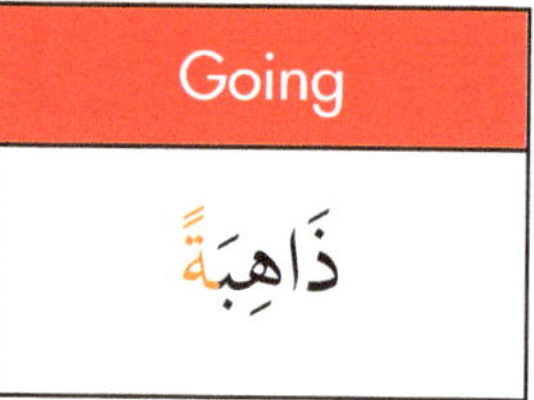


نَظِيْفًا
Clean

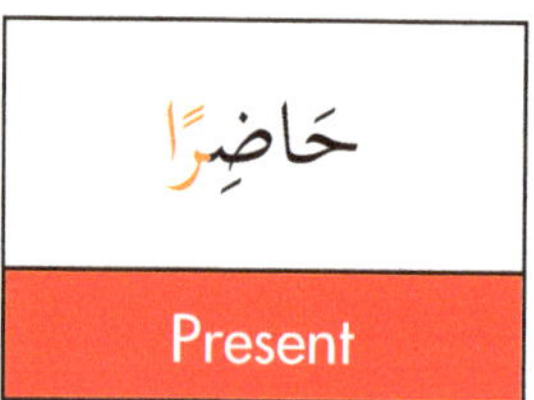

## Negative sentences (dual and plural)

In English, the dual and plural form of a sentence is created by the pluralisation of the subject and the changing of 'is' to 'are'. For instance,

| Singular | Plural |
| --- | --- |
| 'The house is **NOT** new.' | 'The house**s** *are* ***NOT*** new.' |
| or | or |
| 'The house is**n't** new.' | 'The house**s** *aren't* new.' |

- The dual form in Arabic, as we have learnt, is constructed by altering the ending of the singular word.

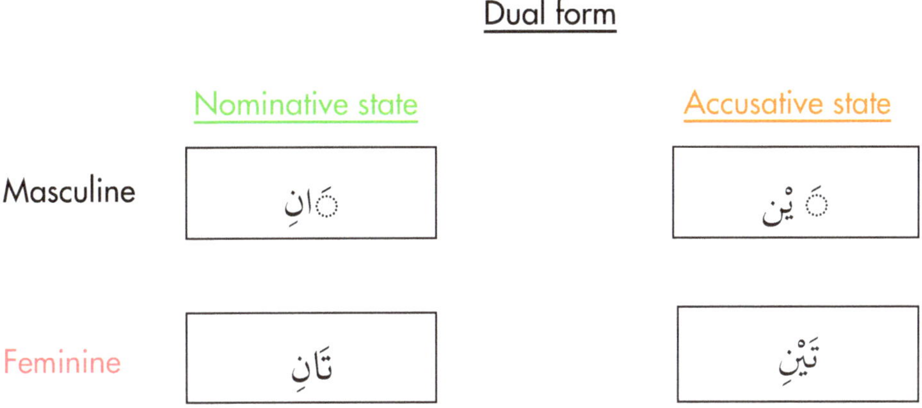

Dual form

| | Nominative state | Accusative state |
| --- | --- | --- |
| Masculine | ◌َانِ | ◌َ يْنِ |
| Feminine | تَانِ | تَيْنِ |

- The subject will be in the nominative state and due to the negative particle, the predicate will be in the accusative state.

'The two men are **NOT** coming.'

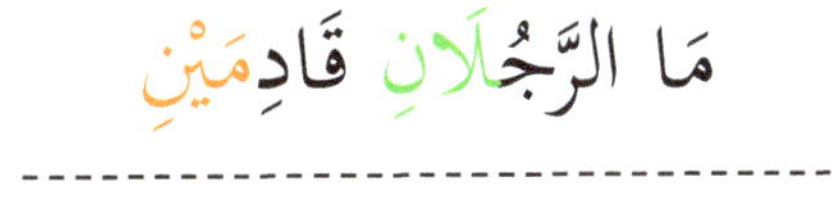

مَا الرَّجُلَانِ قَادِمَيْنِ

'The two nurses(f) are NOT present.'

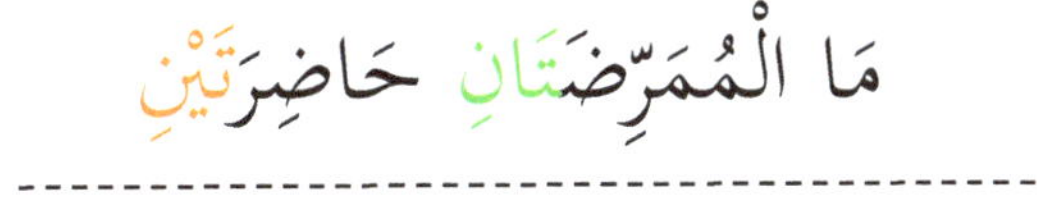

مَا الْمُمَرِّضَتَانِ حَاضِرَتَيْنِ

- The plural regular form in Arabic is constructed by altering the ending of the singular word.

Plural (regular) form

'The teachers are **NOT** going.'

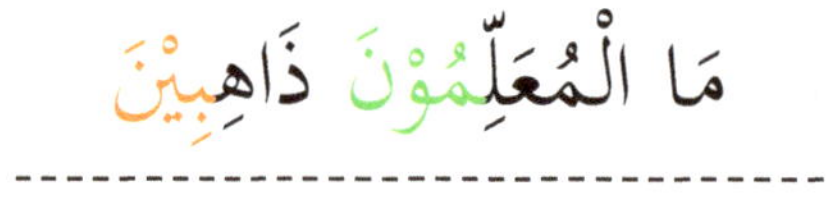

'The female pupils are **NOT** sitting.'

- Irregular plurals that refer to an intellectual being will follow the rules as mentioned above. E.g. 'The boys are **NOT** hardworking.'

- Subsequently, a word that has an irregular plural form can be used as a predicate for an intellectual being. However, the irregular plural word will be in the accusative state.

E.g. 'The boys are **NOT** sitting.'

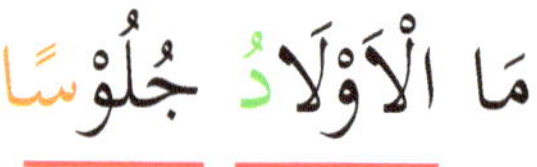

- Sentences that contain a plural non-intellectual being will render the predicate in to the ***SINGULAR FEMININE*** form. The predicate will be in the accusative state.
  For instance;

'The houses are **NOT** new.'

مَا الْبُيُوْتُ جَدِيْدَةً

1. Change the following Arabic sentences in to the **Dual form**.

The first one has been done for you.

a. مَا الْمُعَلِّمُ صَغِيْرًا → مَا الْمُعَلِّمَانِ صَغِيْرَيْنِ

'The teacher is **NOT** small.'

b. مَا الْبِنْتُ قَائِمَةً → ------------------------------

'The girl is **NOT** standing.'

c. مَا الطَّبِيْبُ فَرِحًا → ------------------------------

'The doctor is **NOT** happy.'

d. مَا الْمُهَنْدِسَةُ كَرِيْمَةً → ------------------------------

'The female engineer is **NOT** generous.'

## 2. Translate the following English sentences into Arabic using the words below.

The first one has been done for you.

1) The pens are **NOT** new. مَا الْأَقْلَامُ جَدِيْدَةً

2) The women are **NOT** going.

3) The doors are **NOT** closed.

4) The students are **NOT** skilful.

5) The female nurses are **NOT** truthful.

6) The apples are **NOT** new.

7) The boys are **NOT** thin.

8) The rooms are **NOT** open.

9) The offices are **NOT** long.

10) The teachers are **NOT** hardworking.

11) The nurses are **NOT** sitting and the women are **NOT** standing.

12) The cars are **NOT** going.

| English | Singular | Plural |
|---|---|---|
| Boy | وَلَدٌ | أَوْلَادٌ |
| Pen | قَلَمٌ | أَقْلَامٌ |
| Office | مَكْتَبٌ | مَكَاتِبُ |
| Thin | نَحِيْفٌ | نِحَافٌ |
| Skilful | مَاهِرٌ | مَاهِرُوْنَ |
| Apple | تُفَّاحَةٌ | تُفَّاحَاتٌ |
| Going | ذَاهِبٌ | ذَاهِبُوْنَ |
| Woman | اِمْرَأَةٌ | نِسَاءٌ |
| Closed | مُغْلَقٌ | مُغْلَقُوْنَ |
| Standing | قَائِمٌ | قَائِمُوْنَ |
| Sitting | جَالِسٌ | جَالِسُوْنَ |
| Nurse | مُمَرِّضٌ | مُمَرِّضُوْنَ |

| English | Singular | Plural |
|---|---|---|
| Teacher | مُعَلِّمٌ | مُعَلِّمُوْنَ |
| House | بَيْتٌ | بُيُوْتٌ |
| Open | مَفْتُوْحٌ | مَفْتُوْحُوْنَ |
| Door | بَابٌ | أَبْوَابٌ |
| New | جَدِيْدٌ | جُدُدٌ |
| Table | طَاوِلَةٌ | طَاوِلَاتٌ |
| Hardworking | مُجْتَهِدٌ | مُجْتَهِدُوْنَ |
| Student | طَالِبٌ | طُلَّابٌ |
| Room | غُرْفَةٌ | غُرَفٌ |
| Car | سَيَّارَةٌ | سَيَّارَاتٌ |
| Long | طَوِيْلٌ | طِوَالٌ |
| Truthful | صَادِقٌ | صَادِقُوْنَ |

❖ Remember the predicate for negative sentences will be in the accusative state.

❖ Predicates for subjects that are plural non-intellectual beings will be ***SINGULAR FEMININE***.

## Negative sentences in a prepositional phrase

A prepositional phrase is made up by a preposition and a noun. As mentioned previously, a prepositional phrase can be an **acting predicate** of a sentence or an **Adverbial**. In English, sentences can be made negative by adding the particle '**NOT**' before the preposition. For instance,

'The girl is in the room.'

The negative particle will come before the preposition - in.

'The girl is **NOT** in the room.'

As we have seen previously, an appropriate predicate can be added in to the sentence. Hence, the prepositional phrase will act as an **Adverbial**.

'The girl is **NOT** sitting in the room.'

The negative particle will come before the predicate as stated in the previous section. The prepositional phrase is now an **Adverbial**.

1. Change the following sentences in to the **negative form** in English.

The first one has been done for you.

i. The men are with the teachers.

The men are **NOT** with the teachers.

ii. This pen is from you and this book is from me.

-----------------------------------------

iii. The girls from that school are sitting in their rooms.

-----------------------------------------

iv. The teacher is in the classroom.

-----------------------------------------

- The particle مَا **(NOT)** will come before the subject in Arabic to make the sentence negative. The subject will remain in the nominative state; which will be marked by a Dhamma (ُ). E.g.

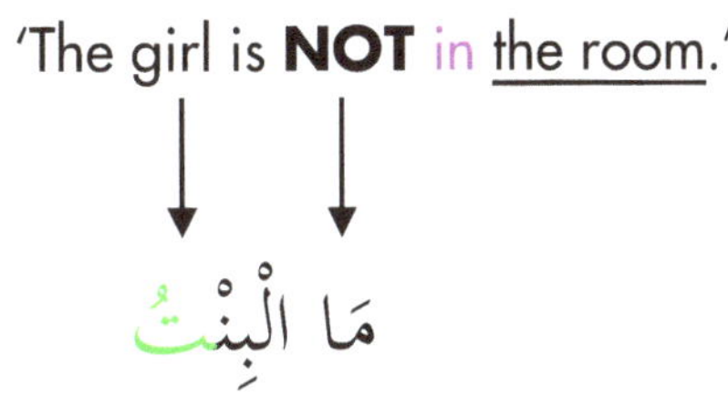


- In Arabic, prepositions will alter the noun in to the genitive state. This will be symbolised with a Kasra (ِ) or a Kasrataan (ٍ).

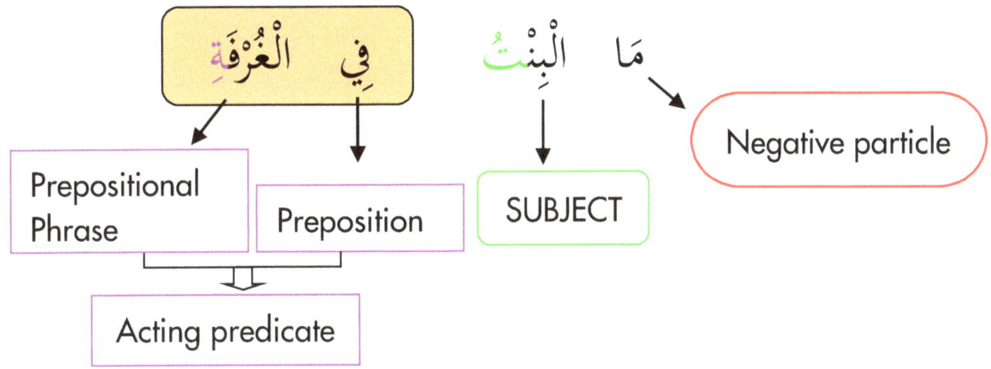


❖ The prepositional phrase in the above sentence is in the genitive state due to the preposition.

❖ The acting predicate will be assumed to be in the accusative state as a result of the effects of the negative particle مَا **(NOT)**. However, the noun will be written with a Kasra (ِ) or a Kasrataan (ٍ) as the preposition has a greater governing factor.

❖ The acting predicate will not have to agree with its subject in **gender** or **amount**.

- By adding a suitable *predicate*, the effects of the **negative particle** will take effect and the predicate will be in the accusative state. The prepositional phrase will be regarded as an **Adverbial**.

'The girl is **NOT** *sitting* in the room.'

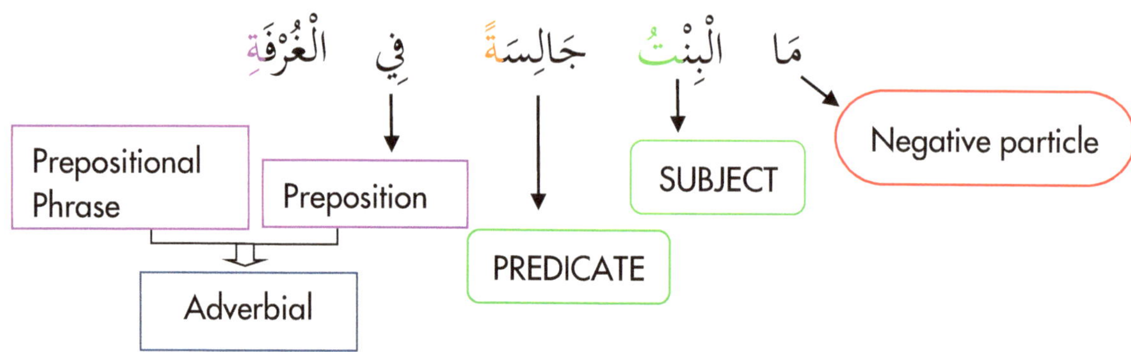


❖ The presence of a predicate will result in all the grammatical rules previously learnt to be applicable. Both subject and predicate will have to agree in **gender** and **amount**.

❖ The predicate will be in the accusative state due to the particle مَا **(NOT)**.

❖ The **Adverbial** will give further information to the sentence, although, without it the sentence will still be understood.

## 1. Translate the following English sentences in to Arabic using the words below.

The first one has been done for you.

1) The girls are **NOT** in the house.

---------------------------------

2) The men are **NOT** standing in the school.

---------------------------------

3) The two women are **NOT** in the car.

---------------------------------

4) The teacher is **NOT** in the office.

---------------------------------

5) The boys from the school are **NOT** going to the museum.

---------------------------------

6) The books are **NOT** on the table and the pens are **NOT** in the desk.

---------------------------------

---------------------------------

| | | | | | | | |
|---|---|---|---|---|---|---|---|
| مَدْرَسَةٌ | School | رِجَالٌ | Men | مَتْحَفٌ | Museum | كُتُبٌ | Books |
| مُعَلِّمٌ | Teacher | طَاوِلَةٌ | Table | قَائِمٌ | Standing | أَقْلَامٌ | Pens |
| مَكْتَبٌ | Office | بَنَاتٌ | Girls | سَيَّارَةٌ | Car | ذَاهِبٌ | Going |
| بَيْتٌ | House | مَرْأَتَانِ | Two women | أَوْلَادٌ | Boys | مَكْتَبٌ | Desk |

## 2. Break down the following sentences to its smallest units of subject and predicate.

The first one has been done for you.

*'The books are **NOT** from the school.'*

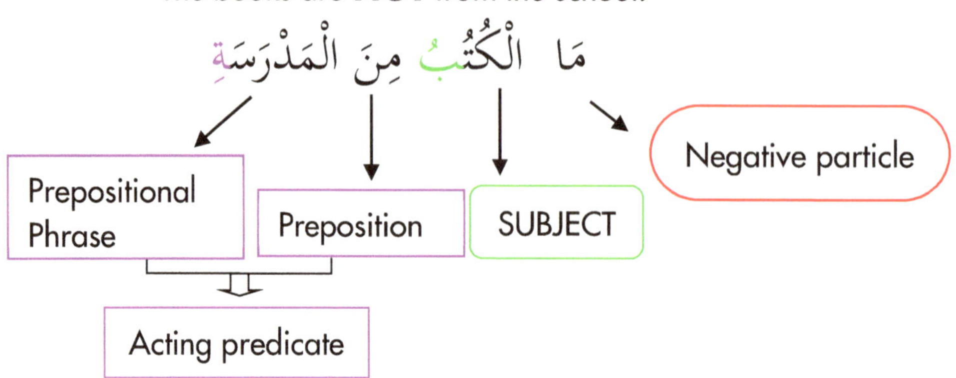


*'The men are **NOT** sitting in the cars.'*

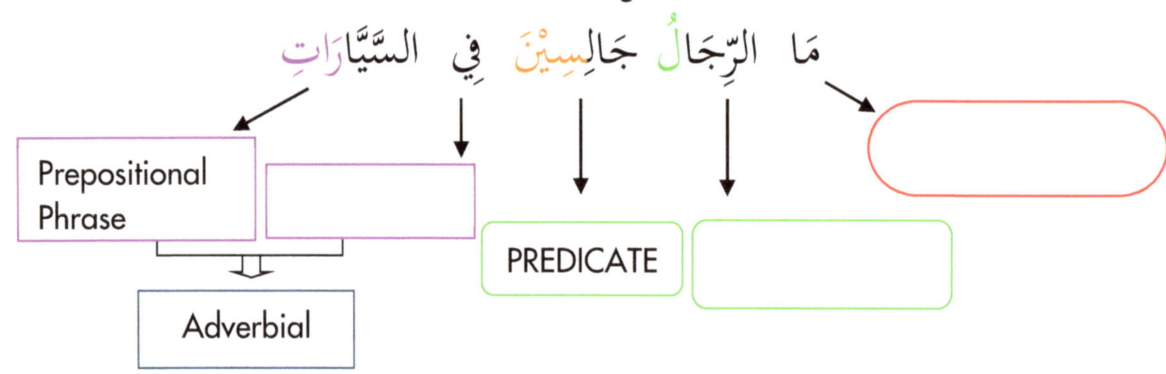


*'The two girls from the school are **NOT** going with the teacher.'*

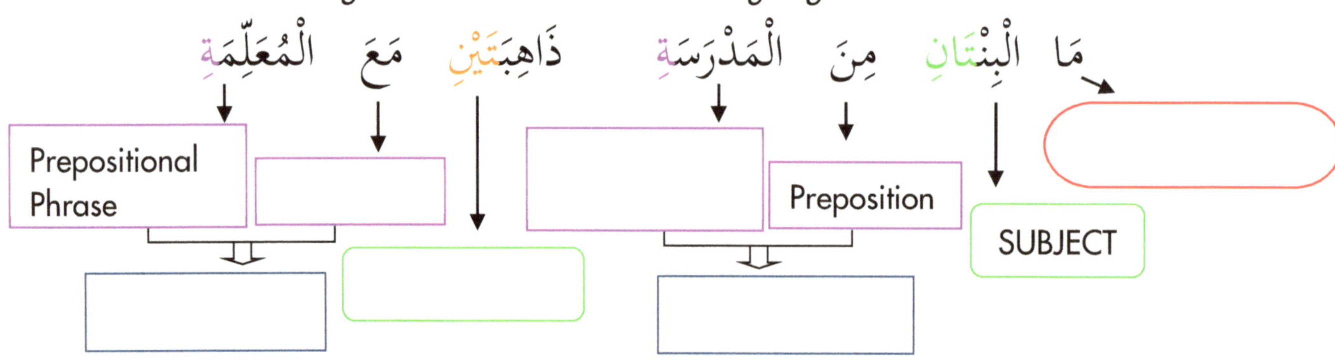

## Negative sentences in an advanced prepositional sentence

In an advanced prepositional sentence, the prepositional phrase is brought ahead of the subject. For instance,

Singular: 'In the house there is a man.' / 'There is a man in the house.'

Plural: 'In the house there are men.' / 'There are men in the house.'

The negative particle in an advanced prepositional sentence will negate the deferred subject from the rest of the sentence, e.g.

Singular: 'In the house there is**n't** a man.' / 'There is**n't** a man in the house.

Plural: 'In the house there are**n't** men.' / 'There are**n't** men in the house.'

### 1. Change the following sentences in to the **negative form** in English.

The first one has been done for you.

i. On the table there is a pen.

On the table there is**n't** a pen.

ii. In the room there are books and under the table is a box.

-------------------------------------------------------

iii. From the school there is a letter.

-------------------------------------------------------

iv. In the school there are children.

-------------------------------------------------------

v. Under the desk there are papers.

-------------------------------------------------------

- The particle مَا **(NOT)** will come before the advanced predicate. The advanced predicate will be in the genitive sate due to the preposition. E.g.

- The effect of the particle مَا **(NOT)** will negate the advanced predicate within the sentence. The advanced predicate is assumed to be in the accusative state, however, due to the effect of the preposition, the prepositional phrase will be in the genitive sate.

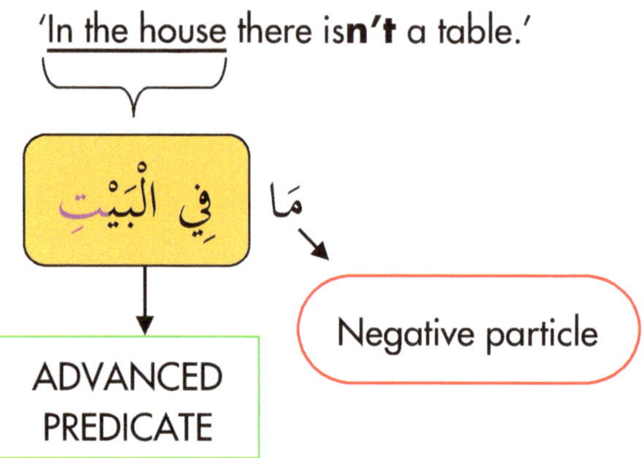


- The deferred subject within the sentence will **not** be rendered in to the accusative state as the governing effect of the **negative particle** is carried out on the advanced predicate. The deferred subject will be in the nominative state and will also be indefinite; in other words, the deferred subject will not have the article اَلْ and will be marked by a Dhammataan (ٌ).

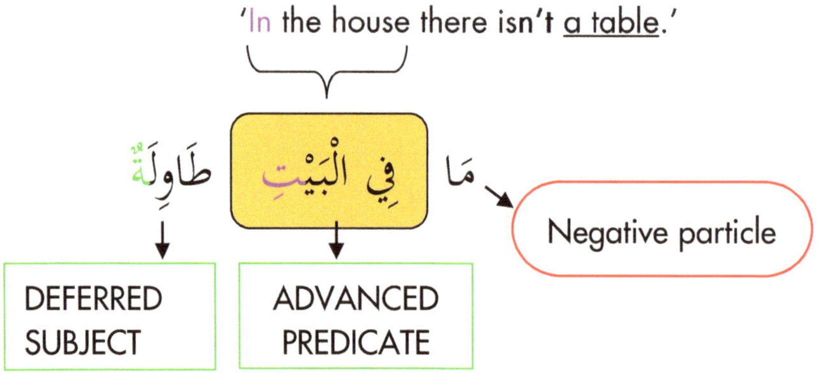

- Dual and plural sentences which are constructed with an advanced predicate will follow the same rules as previously mentioned.
  E.g.

*'In the two houses there aren't men.'*

مَا فِي الْبَيْتَيْنِ رِجَالٌ

*'In the cars there aren't two books.'*

مَا فِي السَّيَّارَاتِ كِتَابَانِ

## 1. Translate the following sentences in to Arabic using the words below.

The first one has been done for you.

a. In the room there is**n't** a bed.

مَا فِي الْغُرْفَةِ سَرِيْرٌ

b. On the two tables there are**n't** pens.

c. In the kitchen there are**n't** tables.

d. From the teachers there is**n't** a book.

e. In the two rooms there are**n't** two girls.

| مَطْبَخٌ | room | غُرْفَتَيْنِ | Two rooms |
|---|---|---|---|
| طَاوِلَتَيْنِ | two tables | طَاوِلَاتٌ | tables |
| كِتَابٌ | book | بِنْتَانِ | two girls |
| أَقْلَامٌ | pens | مُعَلِّمِيْنَ | teachers |

## 2. Break down the following sentences in to their simplest forms.

Some have been done for you.

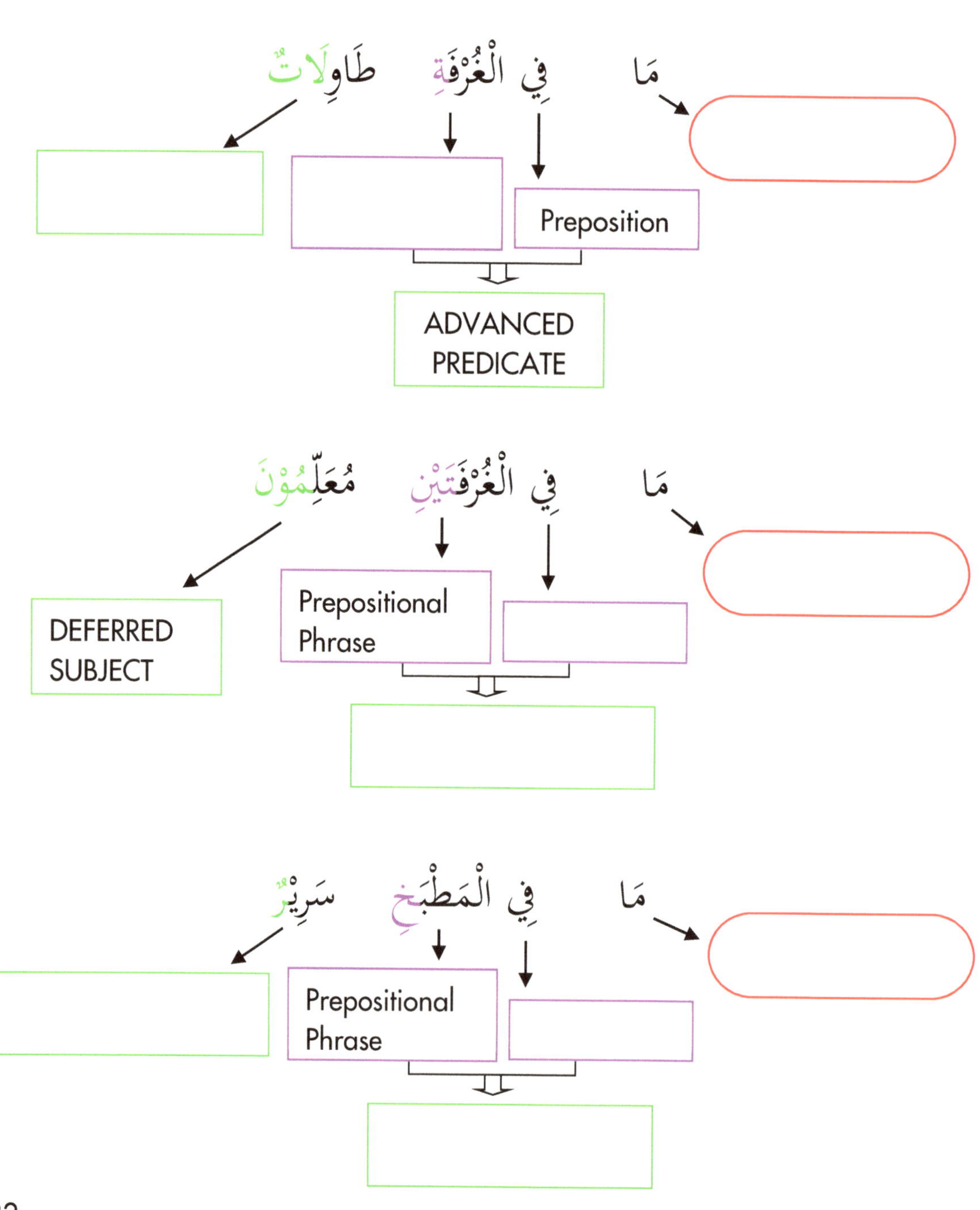

## Negative sentences with personal and possessive pronouns

Generally personal pronouns can replace nouns within a sentence. In English, the **negative particle** comes after the subject, in this same manner, the **negative particle** will come after the personal pronoun, for instance;

'The boy is **not** sleeping.'

The subject can be replaced by a personal pronoun

'He is **not** sleeping.'

As we have studied previously, possessive pronouns attach themselves to a noun. The **negative particle** in English will occur after the subject. E.g.

'Your car is **not** new.'

In English, applying the **negative particle** to a sentence is fairly simple. The negative particle will come after the complete subject and before the predicate.

### 1. Change the following sentences in to the negative form.

The first one has been done for you.

a. They are going to the school.

They are **not** going to the school.

b. Your house is old.

---

c. She is standing in front of the door.

---

d. My brother is coming to the park.

---

e. Our car is dirty.

---

f. I am going to the museum and your friend is going to the shop.

---

- In Arabic, the particle مَا **(NOT)** will come before the subject and the personal pronoun. Pronouns in Arabic are indeclinable and their structure will remain the same in all cases. Whereas in English, the structure of the pronoun will change due to its position in the sentences.

| | English | | |
|---|---|---|---|
| State | Nominative state | Accusative state | Genitive sate |
| Personal pronoun | We | Us | Our |

| | Arabic | | |
|---|---|---|---|
| State | Nominative state | Accusative state | Genitive sate |
| Personal pronoun | نَحْنُ | نَا | نَا |

- The personal pronouns for the nominative state are:

| 1st person Masculine/Feminine | | 2nd person Feminine | | | 2nd person Masculine | | | 3rd person Feminine | | | 3rd person Masculine | | |
|---|---|---|---|---|---|---|---|---|---|---|---|---|---|
| Dual/ Plural | singular | Plural | Dual | singular | Plural | Dual | singular | Plural | Dual | singular | Plural | Dual | singular |
| نَحْنُ | أَنَا | أَنْتُنَّ | أَنْتُمَا | أَنْتِ | أَنْتُمْ | أَنْتُمَا | أَنْتَ | هُنَّ | هُمَا | هِيَ | هُمْ | هُمَا | هُوَ |
| We | I | You | You | You | You | You | You | They | They | She/It | They | They | He/It |

- The particle مَا **(NOT)** will cause the predicate to be in the accusative state. The predicate will agree to the personal pronoun in **gender** and **amount**. E.g.

(Dual/Masculine)

'They are **not** sitting.'

1. Using the words below and the personal pronouns from the table above, translate the following sentences in to Arabic.

The first one has been done for you.

A. We are **not** going.

مَا نَحْنُ ذَاهِبِيْنَ

(Plural/Feminine)
B. They are **not** sleeping.

(Dual/Masculine)
C. You are **not** coming.

D. I am **not** tall and he is **not** small.

(Singular/Feminine)
E. You are **not** a teacher.

F. She is **not** standing.

(Singular/Masculine)
G. I am **not** going and you are **not** coming.

H. He is **not** a doctor.

(Plural/Masculine)
I. You are **not** sitting in the car.

| Going | ذَاهِبٌ | Doctor | طَبِيْبٌ |
|---|---|---|---|
| Coming | قَادِمٌ | Car | سَيَّارَةٌ |
| Standing | قَائِمٌ | Tall | طَوِيْلٌ |
| Sitting | جَالِسٌ | Sleeping | نَائِمٌ |
| Teacher | مُعَلِّمٌ | Small | صَغِيْرٌ |

- Possessive pronouns attach themselves to the end of a word in Arabic. Possessive pronouns are also indeclinable and their structure remains the same. The possessive pronouns for the nominative, accusative and genitive sate are:

| 1st person Masculine/Feminine | | 2nd person Feminine | | | 2nd person Masculine | | | 3rd person Feminine | | | 3rd person Masculine | | |
|---|---|---|---|---|---|---|---|---|---|---|---|---|---|
| Dual/ Plural | singular | Plural | Dual | singular | Plural | Dual | singular | Plural | Dual | singular | Plural | Dual | singular |
| ـنَا | ـي | ـكُنَّ | ـكُمَا | ـكِ | ـكُمْ | ـكُمَا | ـكَ | هُنَّ | هُمَا | هَا | هُمْ | هُمَا | هُ |
| Us/ Our | Me/ My | You/ Your | You/ Your | You/ Your | You/ Your | You/ Your | You/ Your | Them/ Their | Them/ Their | Her/ Her | Them/ Their | Them/ Their | Him/ His |

- The particle مَا **(NOT)** will come before the subject and the possessive pronoun. The **negative particle** will render the predicate in to the accusative state. The predicate will agree to the noun of possession in **gender** and **amount.**

*(Plural/Masculine)*

'Your house is **not** old.'

مَا بَيْتُكُمْ قَدِيمًا

- The predicate can also have a possessive pronoun attached to it. The predicate will be in the accusative state due to the negative particle. E.g.

*(Dual/Masculine)*

'He is **not** your friend.'

مَا هُوَ صَدِيْقَكُمَا

- Prepositions can be used before the predicate in a negative sentence. As mentioned previously, the predicate will be assumed to be in the accusative state, however, due to the effect of the preposition the noun will be in the genitive sate.

'Her pen is **not** on our table.'

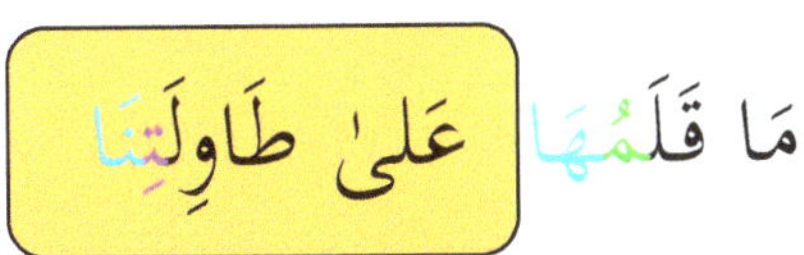


- Possessive pronouns can attach themselves to the end of prepositions, where the noun which is replaced by the pronoun is known in conversation.
  For instance, the noun – '**Desk**' can be replaced by a pronoun '**it**' in the sentence…

'Your pen is **not** on **it**.'

مَا قَلَمُكَ عَلَيْهِ

❖ The pronoun '**it**' is masculine as the noun '**desk**' is a masculine word in Arabic.

- Possessive pronouns can also be attached within an advanced predicate sentence. As a result of the positional changes of the nouns, the **negative particle** will not cause any changes to the state of the advanced predicate or the *deferred subject*.

'In your house there is **not** a kitchen.'

'In my house there is**n't** your book.'

- The grammatical construction above will also be intended for possessive pronouns that are attached to prepositions.

'There is**n't** a pen on **it** *(desk)*.'

مَا عَلَيْهِ قَلَمٌ

- Possessive pronouns can attach to nouns that are dual and plural. The construction of the dual and plural forms will alter due to the states in which they fall under. As mentioned previously, the ن will be omitted from the ***dual*** (masculine and feminine form), and ***plural masculine*** word and the pronoun will attach to the end of the word.

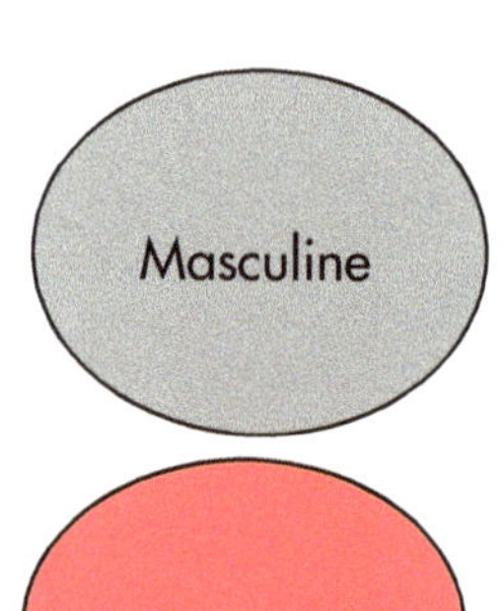


| Dual | Plural |
|---|---|
| 'Your books are **not** new.'<br>مَا كِتَابَاكُمَا جَدِيْدَيْنِ | 'Their teachers are **not** going.'<br>مَا مُعَلِّمُوْهُمْ ذَاهِبِيْنَ |
| 'Your cars are **not** new.'<br>مَا سَيَّارَتَاكُمَا جَدِيْدَتَيْنِ | 'Our teachers are **not** going.'<br>مَا مُعَلِّمَاتُنَا ذَاهِبَاتٍ |

- The *dual* and *plural* forms can be used in advanced predicate sentences with attached pronouns as well. The **negative particle** will not have an effect to the states of the words.

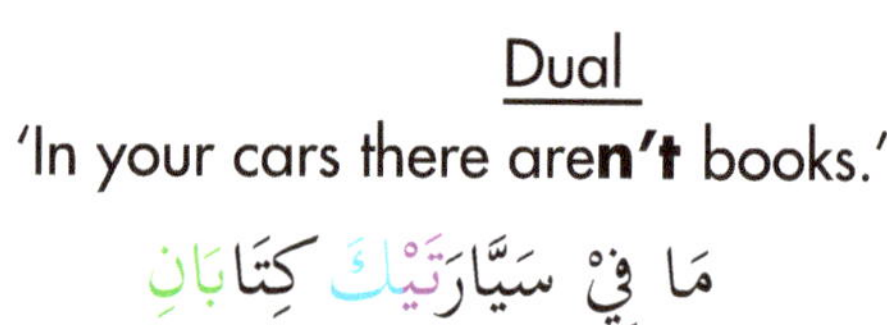

| Dual | Plural |
|---|---|
| 'In your cars there are**n't** books.'<br>مَا فِيْ سَيَّارَتَيْكَ كِتَابَانِ | 'On our tables there are**n't** pens.'<br>مَا عَلَى طَاوِلَاتِنَا اَقْلَامٌ |

- Possessive pronouns can be attached to an irregular plural noun within a negative sentence. E.g.

'Our children are **not** going.'

مَا اَطْفَالُنَا ذَاهِبِيْنَ

- The predicate for a plural non-intellectual being word will come as ***SINGULAR FEMININE***. E.g.

'Their houses are **not** new.'

مَا بُيُوْتُهُنَّ جَدِيْدَةً

## 1.Using the words below, translate the following sentences in to Arabic.

The first one has been done for you.

a. His pens are **not** new. مَا اَقْلَامُهُ جَدِيْدَةً

(Singular/Feminine)
b. Your cars*(two)* are **not** small.

(Dual/Masculine)
c. In your school there are**n't** books.

d. Our teachers are **not** old.

e. On their tables there are**n't** your pens.

f. My friends are **not** sitting in your house.

g. Her teachers*(dual)* are **not** going to the houses*(dual)*.

h. My books are **not** in his cars.

(Plural/Masculine)
i. Your houses are **not** far and my house is **not** close.

j. In his houses there are**n't** beds.

k. The men are **not** in the cars*(dual)*.

(Plural/Feminine)
l. They are **not** going.

| English | Singular | Plural |
|---|---|---|
| Car | سَيَّارَةٌ | سَيَّارَاتٌ |
| Small | صَغِيْرٌ | صِغَارٌ |
| School | مَدْرَسَةٌ | مَدَارِسُ |
| Pen | قَلَمٌ | اَقْلَامٌ |
| Old | قَدِيْمٌ | قُدَمَاءُ |
| Table | طَاوِلَةٌ | طَاوِلَاتٌ |
| Friend | صَدِيْقٌ | اَصْدِقَاءُ |
| Sitting | جَالِسٌ | جَالِسُوْنَ |

| English | Singular | Plural |
|---|---|---|
| Teacher | مُعَلِّمٌ | مُعَلِّمُوْنَ |
| Book | كِتَابٌ | كُتُبٌ |
| House | بَيْتٌ | بُيُوْتٌ |
| Bed | سَرِيْرٌ | سُرُرٌ |
| Close | قَرِيْبٌ | اَقْرِبَاءُ |
| Far | بَعِيْدٌ | بُعَدَاءُ |
| Men | رَجُلٌ | رِجَالٌ |
| Going | ذَاهِبٌ | ذَاهِبُوْنَ |

2. Break down the following Arabic sentences in to their simplest form.

Some have been done for you.

'Your friends*(dual)* are **not** sitting.'

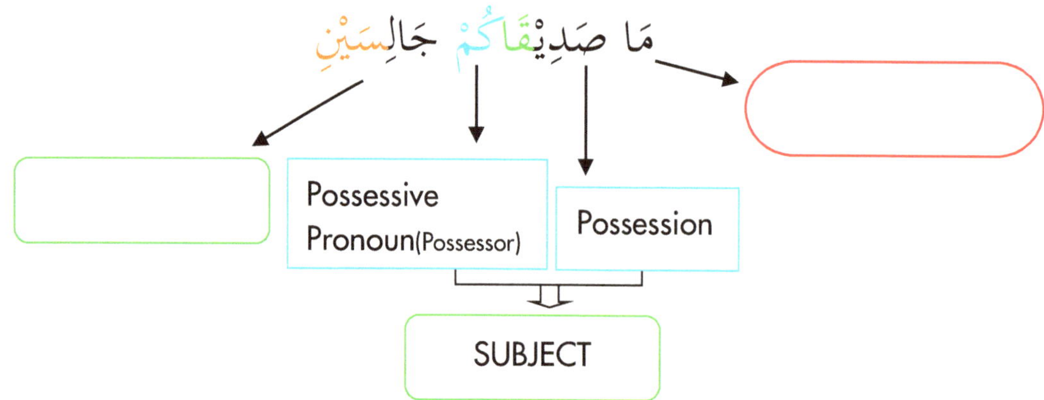

'In their car there is**n't** a man.'

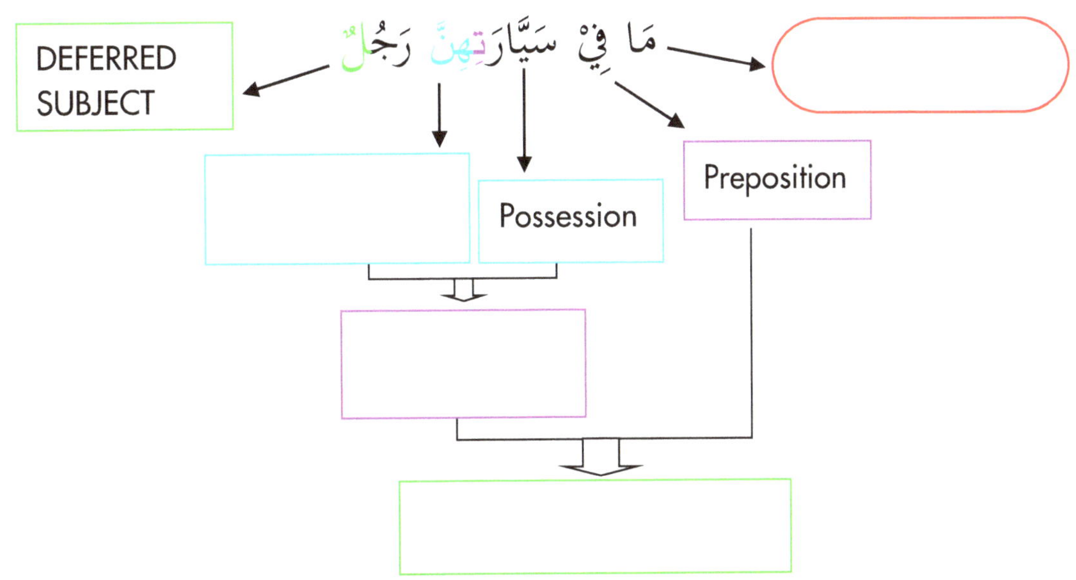


'Their pens are **not** in my school.'

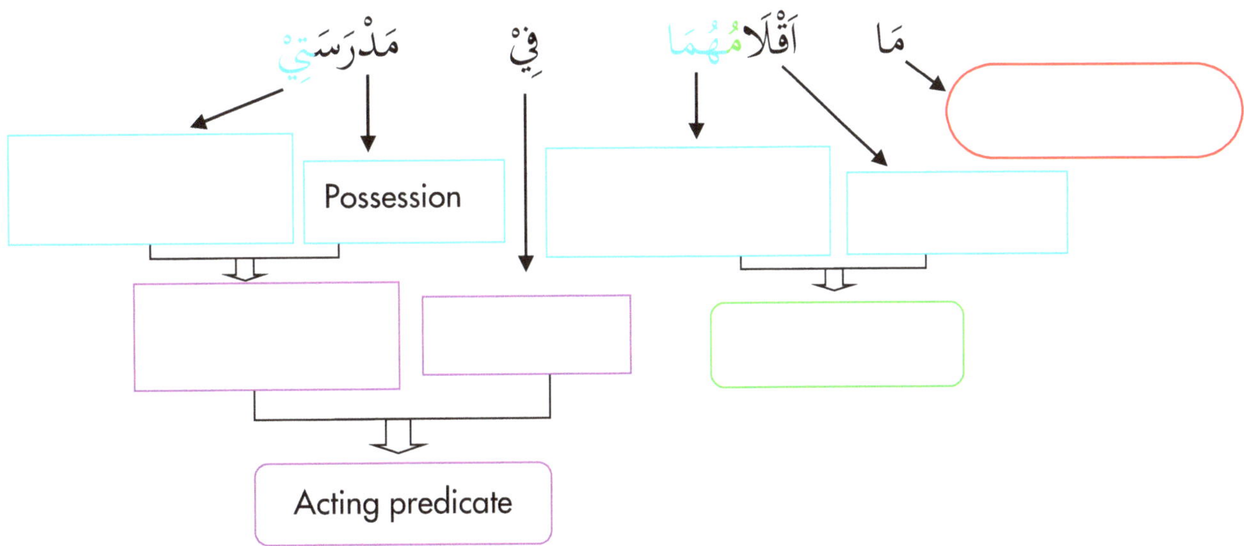

3. Re-write the Arabic sentences in to the negative form.

The first one has been done for you.

اَلْأَوْلَادُ جَالِسُوْنَ

The boys are sitting.

The boys are **not** sitting.

مَا الْأَوْلَادُ جَالِسِيْنَ

بَيْتُكَ كَبِيْرٌ

Your house is big.

Your house is **not** big.

اَقْلَامُنَا فِيْ الْمَدْرَسَةِ

Our pens are in the school.

Our pens are **not** in the school.

هُنَّ جَالِسَاتٌ فِيْ بَيْتِيْ

They are sitting in my house.

They are **not** sitting in my house.

## Negative sentences with demonstrative pronouns

Sentences with demonstrative pronouns can be made negative by adding the **negative particle** after the subject. The **negative particle** will be positioned after the demonstrative pronoun or the demonstrative phrase. E.g.

'This is new.' 'This house is new.'

'This is **not** new.' 'This house is **not** new.'

In English, the **negative particle** comes before the predicate. The ability of making sentences negative are much easier in English as they do not modify sentences to a great degree.

### 1. Change the following sentences in to the negative form.

The first one has been done for you.

a. This is big. This is **not** big.

b. That car is fast. ..................

c. Those are small. ..................

d. These houses are expensive and those schools are cheap.

..................

e. This boy is clever. ..................

f. That pen is on my desk. ..................

g. These books are in my house and that book is in our school.

..................

h. Those are from her doctor.

..................

- In Arabic, the particle مَا **(NOT)** will come ahead of the subject and demonstrative pronoun. Demonstrative pronouns in Arabic are indeclinable like pronouns. Their structure will remain the same in all cases except for the ***dual form***. The demonstrative pronouns are;

| Demonstrative pronouns | | | | | |
|---|---|---|---|---|---|
| English | Masculine | Feminine | English | Masculine | Feminine |
| This | هٰذَا | هٰذِهِ | That | ذَالِكَ | تِلْكَ |
| These<br>Nominative state<br><br>Accusative and Genitive state | هٰذَانِ<br><br>هٰذَيْنِ | هَاتَانِ<br><br>هَاتَيْنِ | Those<br>Nominative state<br><br>Accusative and Genitive state | ذَانِكَ<br><br>ذَيْنِكَ | تَانِكَ<br><br>تَيْنِكَ |
| These | هٰؤُلَاءِ | هٰؤُلَاءِ | Those | أُولٰئِكَ | أُولٰئِكَ |

- The particle مَا **(NOT)** will cause the predicate to be in the accusative state.

'This is **not** a pen.'

مَا هٰذَا قَلَمًا

- The predicate will agree to the personal pronoun in **gender** and **amount**. E.g.

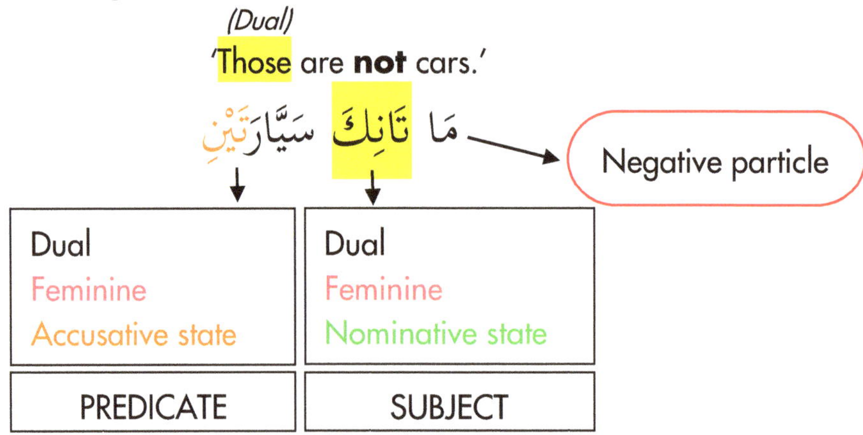

## 1. Change the following sentences in to the **dual form**.

The first one has been done for you.

a. This is **not** a door. مَا هٰذَا بَابًا

مَا هٰذَانِ بَابَيْنِ

---

b. This is **not** a tree.

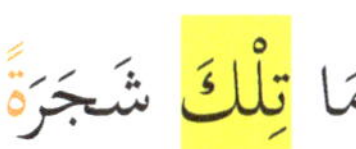


---

c. This is **not** a house. مَا ذَالِكَ بَيْتًا

---

d. This is **not** a table.

---

e. This is **not** a pen.

---

f. This is **not** a room.

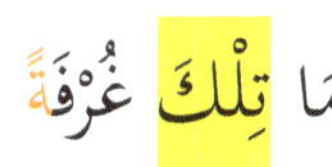


---

## 2. Using the words below write 5 negative sentences in the **plural form.**

The first one has been done for you.

**Nouns**

| مُعَلِّمُوْنَ | مُهَنْدِسُوْنَ | مُمَرِّضَاتٌ | نِسَاءٌ |
|---|---|---|---|
| Teachers | Engineers | Nurses | Women |
| رِجَالٌ | تِلْمِيْذَاتٌ | مُوَظَّفُوْنَ | سَارِقُوْنَ |
| Men | Students | Employees | Thieves |

i) مَا أُولٰئِكَ مُعَلِّمِيْنَ

ii)

iii)

iv)

v)

- As seen previously, plural non-intellectual being words will cause the **predicate** as well as the **demonstrative pronoun** to be in the ***SINGULAR FEMININE*** form. For instance,

'These *(houses)* are **not** new.'

مَا هٰذِهِ جَدِيْدَةً

❖ In the example above the subject *(houses)* is the noun which is being referred to. Due to the subject being a non-intellectual plural word, both the **demonstrative pronoun** and **predicate** are made ***SINGULAR FEMININE***.

- Prepositional phrases can be included within a demonstrative pronoun sentence. The particle مَا **(NOT)** will appear before the demonstrative pronoun. The preposition will result in changing its related noun in to the genitive sate. E.g.

'That is **not** in the book.'

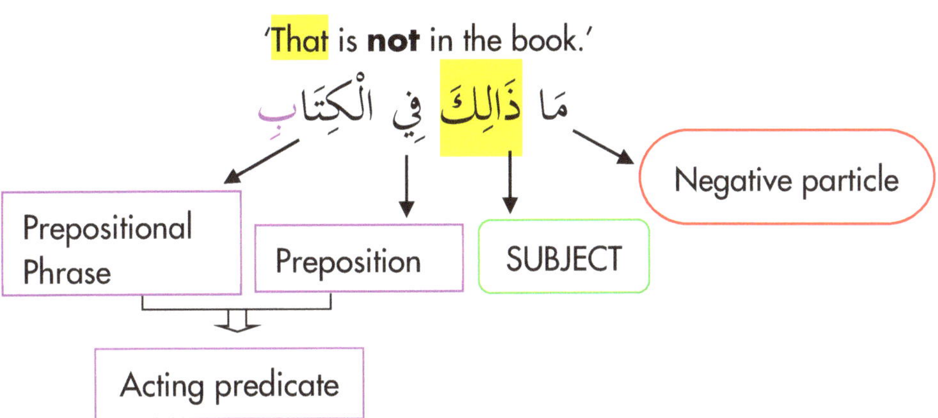


- In the same manner, advancing the prepositional phrase ahead of the demonstrative pronoun is also possible. E.g.

'In the book there is**n't** that.'

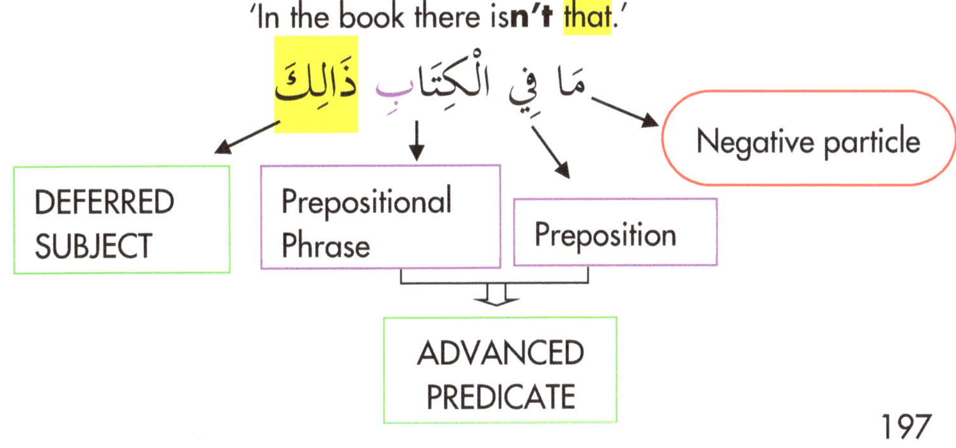

- Personal pronouns can replace the noun of the predicate in a demonstrative pronoun sentence. The effects of the **negative particle** will not affect the personal pronoun as personal pronouns are indeclinable.

| | Singular | Dual | Plural |
|---|---|---|---|
| Masculine | مَا هٰذَا هُوَ | مَا هٰذَانِ هُمَا | مَا هٰؤُلَاءِ هُمْ |
| | This is not it/him. | These are not them | These are not them. |
| Feminine | مَا تِلْكَ هِيَ | مَا تَانِكَ هُمَا | مَا أُولٰئِكَ هُنَّ |
| | That is not it/her. | Those are not them. | Those are not them. |

- Possessive pronouns can attach to the end of the noun within these types of sentences. The noun of the predicate will be in the accusative state due to the effect of the **negative particle**. As mentioned, the ن will be omitted from the ***dual*** (masculine and feminine) and ***plural masculine*** forms and the pronoun will be attached to the end of the word. E.g.

'This is not your house.'
مَا هٰذَا بَيْتَكَ

'Those are not your books*(dual)*.'
مَا هٰذَانِ كِتَابَيْكَ

'These are not my teachers.'
مَا هٰؤُلَاءِ مُعَلِّمِيَّ

## 1. Translate the following Arabic sentences in to **English**.

The first one has been done for you.

a. مَا هٰذِهِ سَيَّارَتِي

This is **not** my car.

b. مَا ذَالِكَ قَلَمَكَ

c. مَا فِي بَيْتِهَا أُولٰئِكَ

d. مَا تِلْكَ أَنَا

e. مَا أُولٰئِكَ مُعَلِّمِيْكُمْ وَ مَا هٰذِهِ كُتُبَنَا

f. مَا تَانِكَ فِي الْغُرْفَتَيْنِ

g. مَا هٰذَا هُوَ

| | |
|---|---|
| قَلَمٌ | Pen |
| بَيْتٌ | House |
| مُعَلِّمِيْنَ | Teachers |
| كُتُبٌ | Books |
| غُرْفَتَيْنِ | Two Rooms |

## 2. Break down the sentences below to their simplest grammatical form.

The first one has been done for you.

'These are **not** my books.'

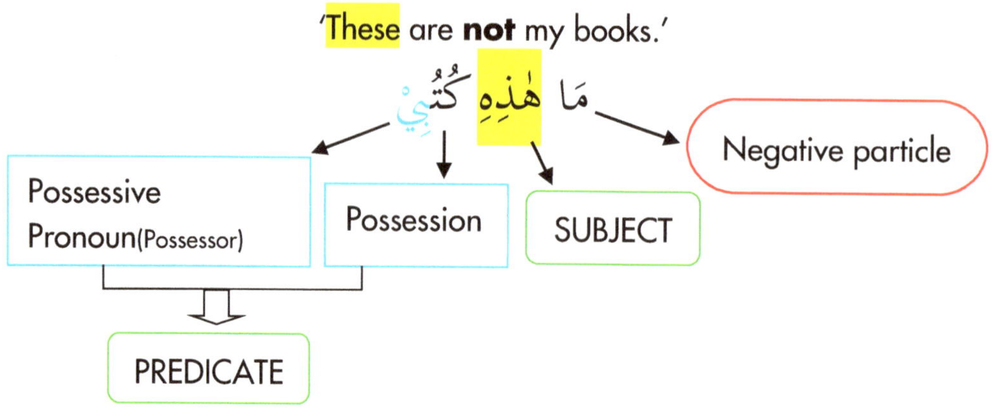


'That is **not** their cars.'

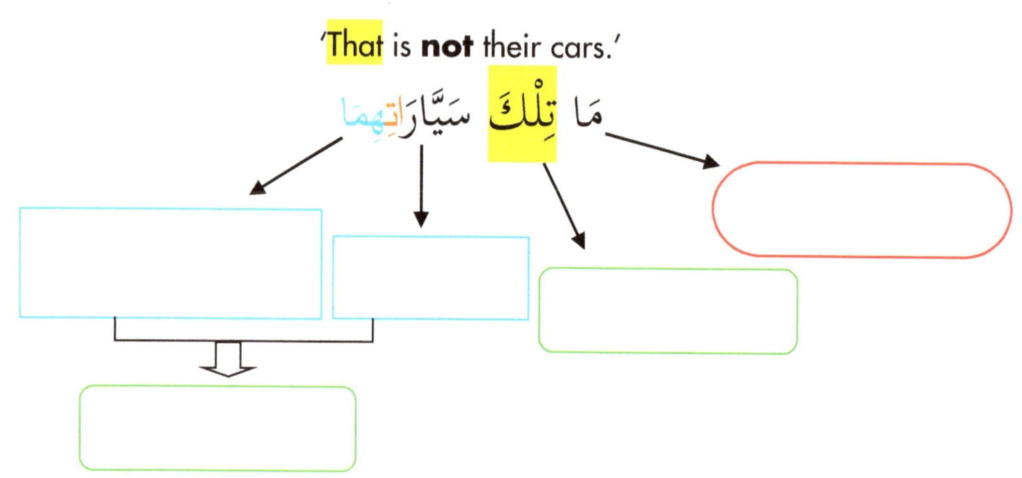


'This is **not** on your tables*(dual)*.'

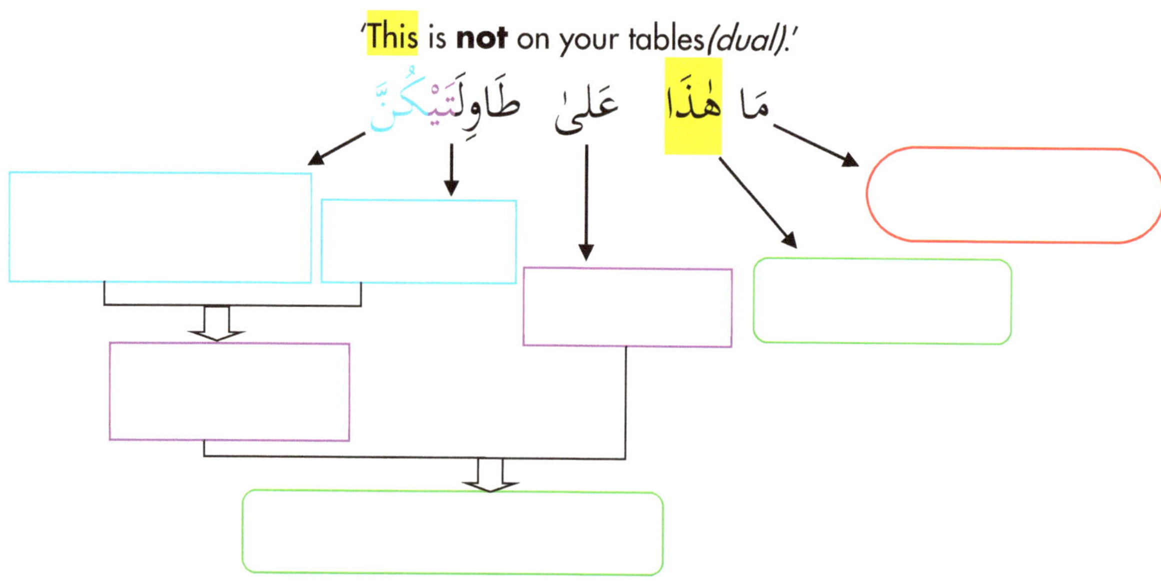

- Demonstrative pronouns can be made definitive by affixing the definite particle اَلْ to its corresponding noun. The **negative particle** مَا **(NOT)** will appear before the *demonstrative phrase*. The predicate of the *demonstrative phrase* will be in the accusative state. E.g.

'That boy is **not** hardworking.'

- The predicate will agree to its *demonstrative phrase* in **gender** and **amount**.

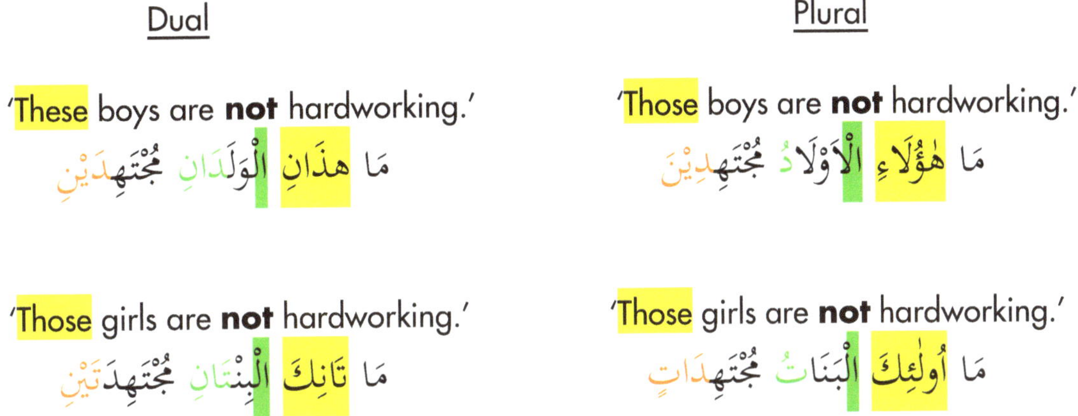


- Nouns that are a plural non-intellectual being will cause the demonstrative pronoun and subsequently its predicate to be ***SINGULAR FEMININE***. E.g.

'Those books are **not** open.'

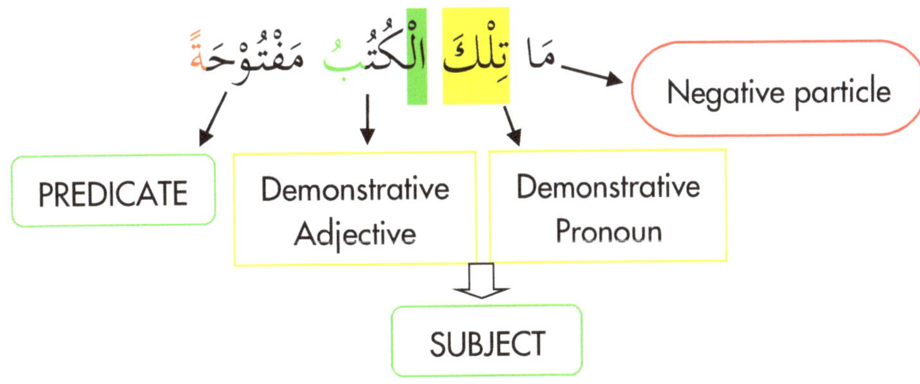

- Prepositional phrases can also be included in demonstrative phrasal sentences. The preposition will cause its relevant noun to be classed in to the genitive sate. E.g.

'This teacher is **not** in the school.'

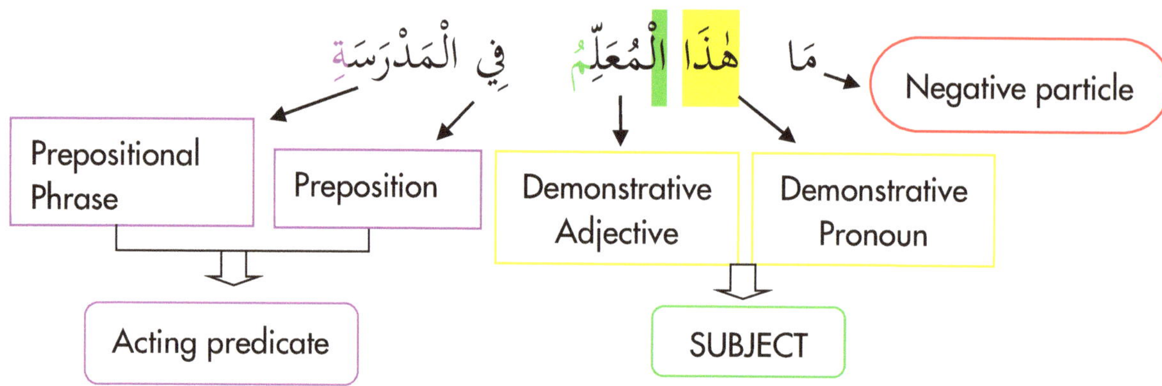


- Possessive pronouns can be connected to prepositional phrases in a negative sentence. E.g.

'This woman is **not** in our house.'

- As seen previously, possessive pronouns can be joined to the preposition. The negative particle will not cause any changes to the preposition. E.g.

'This is **not** mine.'

- Demonstrative phrases can be used in an advanced predicate sentences. The grammatical effects of the negative particle will not be in effect.

'In his room there is**n't** that book.'

- Possessive pronouns can be attached within the *demonstrative phrase* causing it to be an incomplete sentence. Due to the pronoun, the position of the demonstrative noun will come before the demonstrative pronoun. For instance,

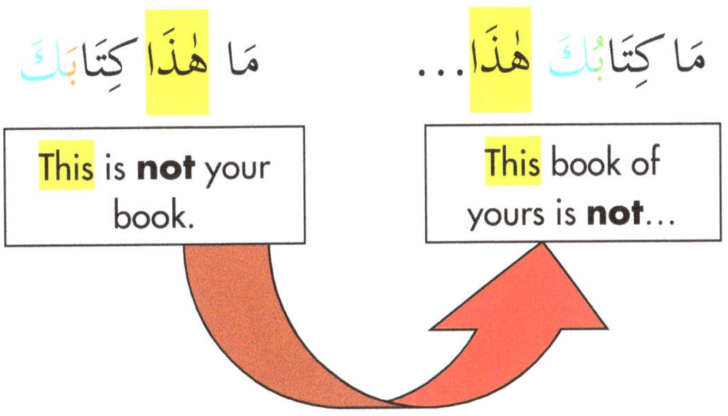


- The predicate for a sentence like the example above, will agree in **gender** and **amount** in relation to the possessional noun and will also be in the accusative state due to the **negative particle.**

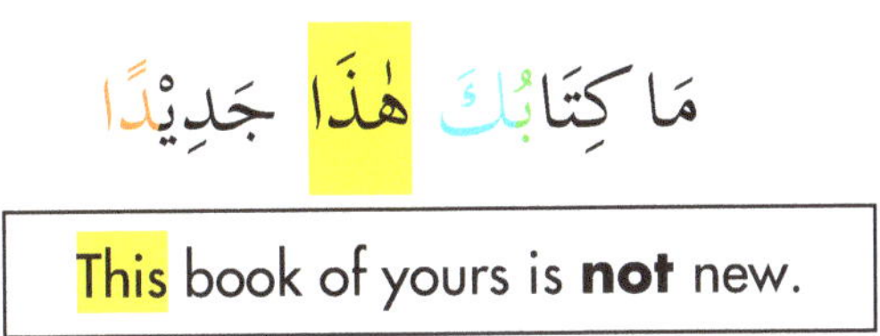


- A multiple amount of demonstrative pronouns can be used in negative sentences as well. For instance,

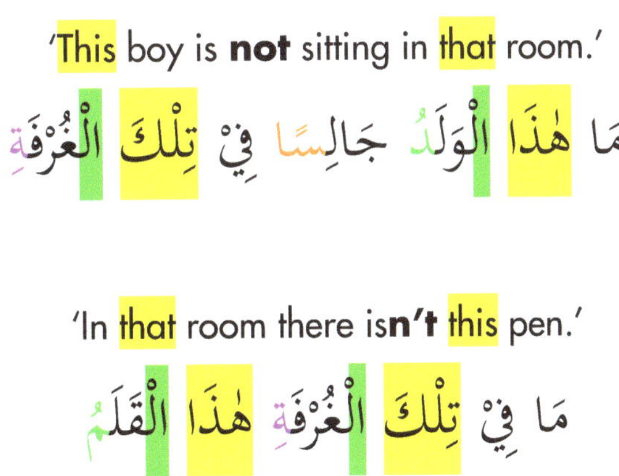

## 1. Translate the following sentences in to Arabic using the words below.

The first one has been done for you.

a) That boy is **not** sitting in my room.

مَا ذَالِكَ الْوَلَدُ جَالِسًا فِيْ غُرْفَتِيْ

b) Those books are **not** on that table.

c) This book of hers is **not** new.

d) That house is **not** far from this school.

e) Our pens are **not** in that car.

f) These girls are **not** standing in front of that school and those boys are **not** sitting in their rooms.

g) That car is **not** behind his house.

h) Our teachers are **not** in this school.

i) These girls are **not** going to that museum with their mothers.

j) This child is **not** coming from that school.

k) In your kitchen there is**n't** this knife.

l) That pen is **not** from your teacher.

m) Those pens*(dual)* (Dual/Masculine) of theirs are **not** new and these books are **not** small.

| مَدْرَسَةٌ | School | وَلَدٌ | Boy | مَتْحَفٌ | Museum | كُتُبٌ | Books |
|---|---|---|---|---|---|---|---|
| مُعَلِّمٌ | Teacher | طَاوِلَةٌ | Table | قَائِمٌ | Standing | أَقْلَامٌ | Pens |
| بَعِيْدٌ | Far | بَنَاتٌ | Girls | سَيَّارَةٌ | Car | ذَاهِبٌ | Going |
| بَيْتٌ | House | خَلْفَ | Behind | أَوْلَادٌ | Boys | مُعَلِّمُوْنَ | Teachers |
| جَالِسٌ | Sitting | جَدِيْدٌ | New | غُرَفٌ | Rooms | أُمَّهَاتٌ | Mothers |
| قَادِمٌ | Coming | طِفْلٌ | Child | مَطْبَخٌ | Kitchen | سِكِّيْنٌ | knife |
| صَغِيْرٌ | Small | كِتَابٌ | Book | قَلَمٌ | Pen | أَمَامَ | In front of |

## 2. Add the correct diacritical marks for the following sentences.

The first one has been done for you.

i. مَا هٰذَا الرَّجُلُ قَائِمًا

ii. مَا ذَانِكَ الْقَلَمان فِيْ بَيْتِها

iii. مَا تلك الْبُيُوْت كَبِيْرَة

iv. مَا هٰذَانِ الْوَلَدان ذَاهِبين وَ مَا تِلْكَ الْبِنْت قَادِمَة

v. مَا هذا الْكِتَاب مِنْ مُعَلِّماتكن

vi. مَا فِي بَيْتنا هٰذِهِ الطَّاوِلَة

vii. مَا قَلَمك هٰذَا مِنْ غُرْفَتنا

# Interrogative Sentences

# 11

The Arabic Sentence

# The Arabic Sentence
# Interrogative Sentences

Interrogative sentences pose questions and are used for requesting information from others. Interrogative sentences use interrogative pronouns ('who', 'whose', 'whom', 'what' and 'which') and finish with a question mark (?).

Sentences can be transformed in to a question by a number of ways;

1) Subject Auxiliary Inversion *(SAI)* - by moving the position of the **auxiliary** before its subject will cause the sentence to be a question.
   E.g.
   '*The boy **is** sitting.*'
   '***Is** the boy sitting?*'

   The auxiliary '**is**' has been positioned ahead of the subject 'The boy'.

2) Using an interrogative pronoun - by adding an **interrogative pronoun** at the beginning of a sentence.
   For example,
   '**Where** *did the boy sit?*

   The interrogative pronoun '**Where**' questions the entire sentence.

3) A part of the sentence is missing - sentences can be made into questions by removing either the **subject** or **predicate** from the sentence. For instance,
   '**Who** is sitting?'
   '**Where** is the boy?'

   In the first sentence the subject '**The boy'** is omitted and the predicate 'is sitting' is removed from the second sentence.

4) Declarative interrogatives - sentences can become interrogatives due to the change of the speaker's tone. The interrogative pronoun is not used and normally a question mark is written at the end of the sentence. E.g.
   '***The boy** is sitting?*

   The sentence has a subject '**The boy**' and a predicate 'sitting', the rising tone of the speaker would be the distinguishing factor in this sentence.

## 1. Change the following sentences in to questions.

The first one has been done for you.

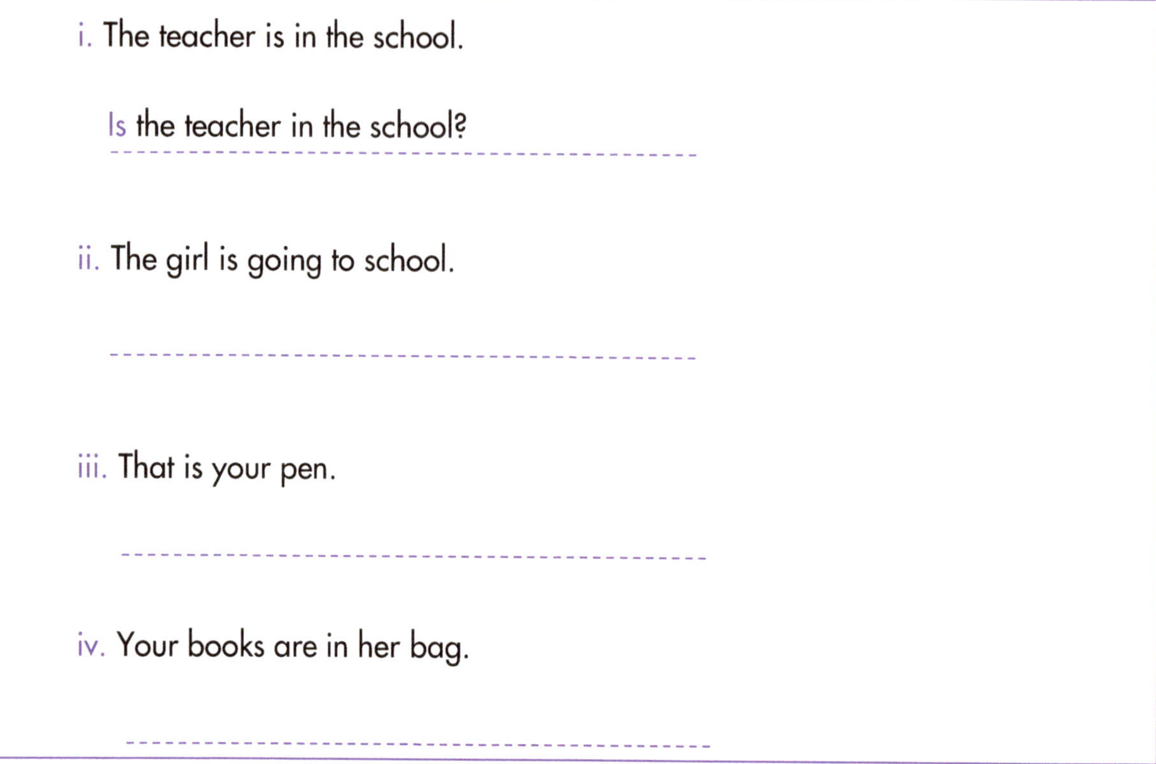

i. The teacher is in the school.

Is the teacher in the school?

ii. The girl is going to school.

---

iii. That is your pen.

---

iv. Your books are in her bag.

---

## 2. Circle the correct interrogative pronoun for each sentence.

The first one has been done for you.

i. Which / Where / Did…is the teacher?

ii. What / How / Who…is the time?

iii. When / How / Which…old are you?

iv. Whom / Who / What…is your name?

v. How / Where / When…is the weather?

vi. Whose / When / Which…are you going to sleep?

## Subject Auxiliary Inversion (*SAI)*

In English, sentences can be made in to a question by swapping the position of the subject with the auxiliary verb. For instance;

Nominal sentence - The boy is sitting.

Interrogative sentence - Is the boy sitting?

The sentence above demonstrates the inversion of the auxiliary verb 'is' with the subject 'The boy'.

In Arabic, sentences are transformed in to questions by the usage of interrogative pronouns.

- In Arabic, to make any nominal sentence in to an interrogative sentence the particle هَلْ is added at the beginning of the sentence. This particle does **not** affect the grammar of either the subject or the predicate. E.g.

Nominal sentence - '*The boy is* sitting.'

اَلْوَلَدُ جَالِسٌ

Interrogative sentence - '*Is the boy* sitting?'

هَلِ الْوَلَدُ جَالِسٌ؟

❖ In the example above, the particle هَلْ is written with a Kasra for ease in pronunciation when joining the words.

- Another particle that can be used at the start of an interrogative sentence is the letter أَ.

'*Are you going?*'

أَأَنْتُمْ ذَاهِبُوْنَ؟

## 1. Change the following Arabic sentences in to questions.

The first one has been done for you.

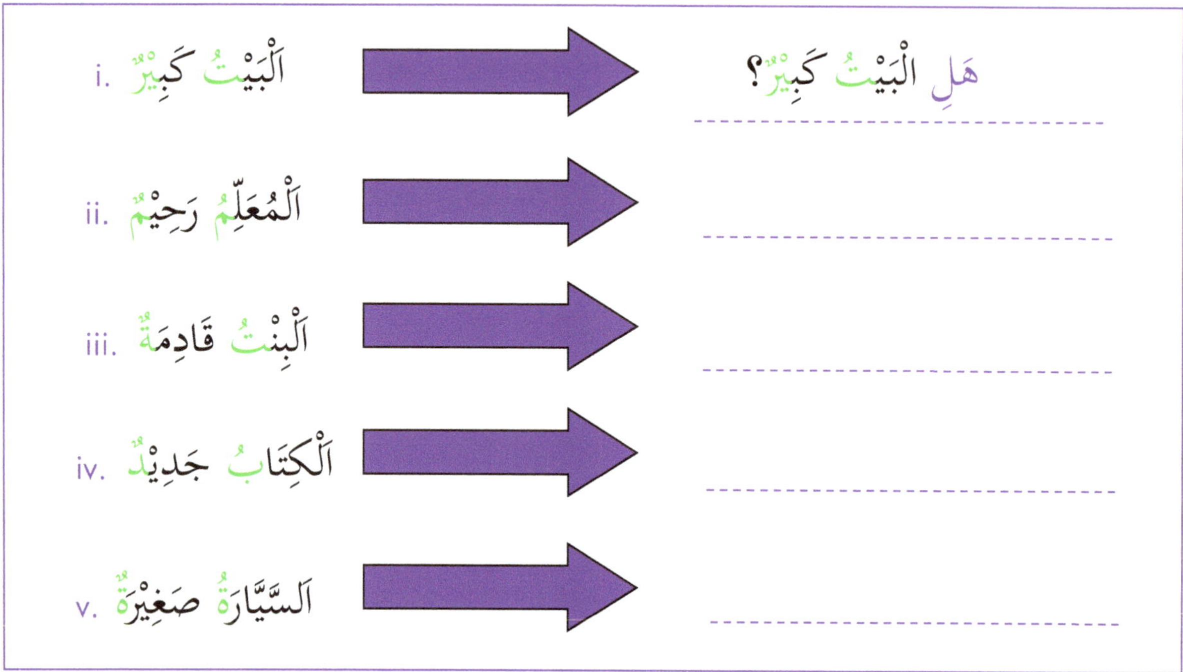


## 2. Translate the following sentences in to Arabic using the words provided.

The first one has been done for you.

a. Is the car new? هَلِ السَّيَّارَةُ جَدِيْدَةٌ؟

b. Is the teacher present? ------------------------------

c. Is the house small? ------------------------------

d. Is the man going? ------------------------------

e. Is the woman sitting? ------------------------------

| English | Arabic |
|---|---|
| Going | ذَاهِبٌ |
| Teacher | مُعَلِّمٌ |
| House | بَيْتٌ |
| Man | رَجُلٌ |
| Sitting | جَالِسٌ |
| Small | صَغِيْرٌ |
| Woman | اِمْرَأَةٌ |
| Present | حَاضِرٌ |

## The interrogative pronouns

Interrogative pronouns are pronouns that are used to ask questions. These pronouns are situated at the beginning of the sentence in English. All interrogative pronouns transform sentences in to questions, however, they differ due to their functional behaviour in meaning.

1. Who 
   - this pronoun is used in order to ask about human beings.
   - Who are you? مَنْ اَنْتَ؟

2. What 
   - this pronoun is used to ask about inanimate objects and animals.
   - What is your name? مَا اِسْمُكَ؟

3. Why 
   - this pronoun is used to request a reason for an action.
   - Why are you standing? لِمَ اَنْتَ قَائِمٌ؟

4. Where 
   - this pronoun is used in asking about the location or whereabouts.
   - Where is the Masjid? اَيْنَ الْمَسْجِدُ؟

5. When 
   - this pronoun is used to ask about the time an action takes place.
   - When is the test? مَتَى الْإِمْتِحَانُ؟

6. How 
   - this pronoun is used to ask about the condition and manner of a subject
   - How are you? كَيْفَ حَالُكَ؟

## 1. Fill in the missing gaps with the correct interrogative pronoun.

The first one has been done for you.

i. Where is your house?

اَيْنَ بَيْتُكَ؟

ii. Who is absent?

_______ غَائِبٌ؟

iii. Why are you going?

_______ اَنْتَ ذَاهِبٌ؟

iv. How is that?

_______ ذَالِكَ؟

v. When is it?

_______ هُوَ؟

vi. What is this?

_______ هٰذَا؟

## 2. Match the interrogative pronouns with their correct meanings.

The first one has been done for you.

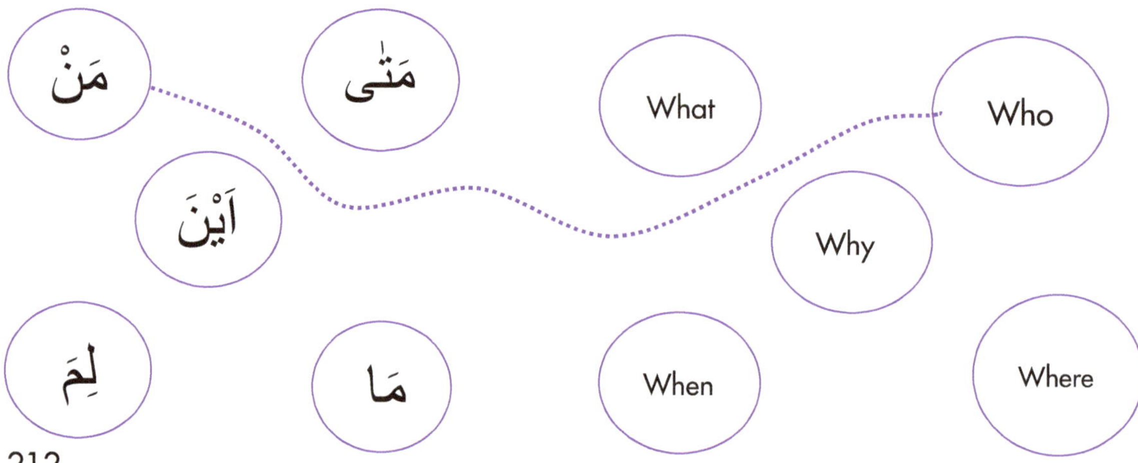

## Interrogative pronouns in dual and plural sentences.

Interrogative pronouns in English do not have a plural form. Rather, the subject is pluralised (s) and the auxiliary verb is changed in to its plural form (are). For instance;

| | Nominal sentence | Interrogative sentence |
|---|---|---|
| Singular: | The car is new. | Is the car new? |
| Plural: | The cars are new. | Are the cars new? |

- Just like English, interrogative pronouns in Arabic do not have a plural form. Sentences in the **dual** and **plural** form will be created using the structural changes at the end of the subject and predicate. The interrogative pronoun will be attached at the beginning of a **dual** and **plural** sentence. E.g. 'Where are the men?'

  أَيْنَ الرَّجُلَانِ؟

- The interrogative pronoun has no grammatical effects to the state of a word, therefore, the subject and predicate will be in the nominative state. For example,

Singular:

Dual:

Plural:

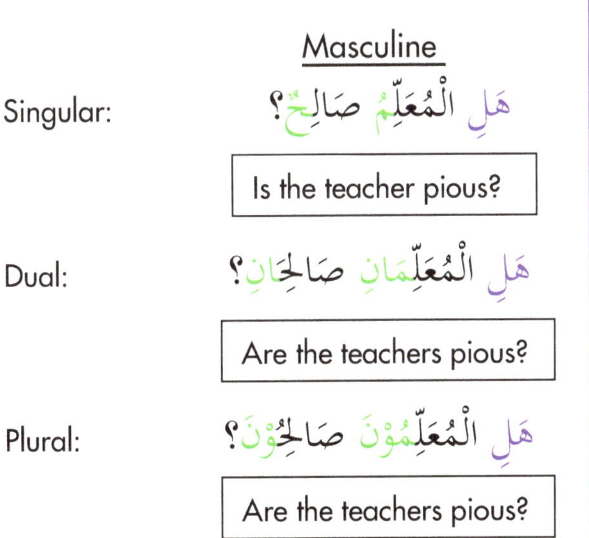


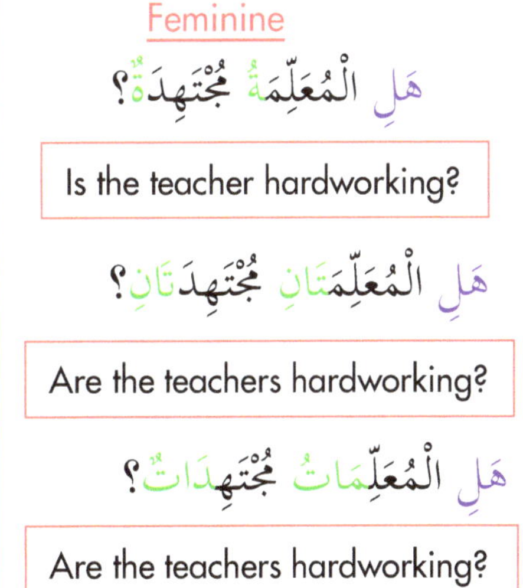


- Subjects that are plural non-intellectual will cause the predicate to be ***SINGULAR FEMININE*** as studied previously. E.g.

  'Are the houses new?'

  هَلِ الْبُيُوْتُ جَدِيْدَةٌ؟

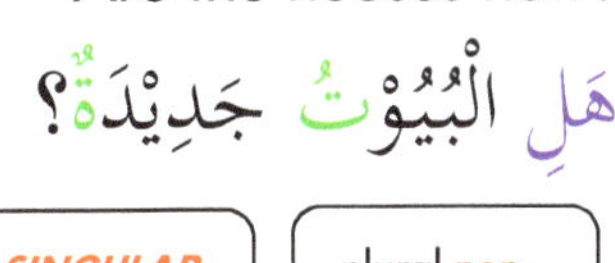

## 1. Change the following Arabic sentences in to the **dual form**.

The first one has been done for you.

i. هَلِ الْوَلَدُ جَالِسٌ؟ — هَلِ الْوَلَدَانِ جَالِسَانِ؟

ii. هَلِ الطَّاوِلَةُ صَغِيْرَةٌ؟ — ---------------------

iii. هَلِ الْعَالِمَةُ عَادِلَةٌ؟ — ---------------------

iv. هَلِ الْمَدْرَسَةُ جَدِيْدَةٌ؟ — ---------------------

v. هَلِ الْمُهَنْدِسُ ذَاهِبٌ؟ — ---------------------

## 2. Write the following sentences in Arabic.

The first one has been done for you.

a. Are the cars old? — هَلِ السَّيَّارَاتُ قَدِيْمَةٌ؟

b. Are the teachers absent? (Dual/Feminine) — ---------------------

c. Are the tables small? — ---------------------

d. Are the engineers hardworking? — ---------------------

e. Are the women coming? — ---------------------

| Arabic | مُعَلِّمَتَانِ | صَغِيْرٌ | مُجْتَهِدٌ | غَائِبٌ | نِسَاءٌ | قَادِمٌ | طَاوِلَاتٌ | مُهَنْدِسُوْنَ |
|---|---|---|---|---|---|---|---|---|
| English | Teachers | Small | Hardworking | Absent | Women | Coming | Tables | Engineers |

## Interrogative pronouns with prepositions

Prepositions can attach themselves to interrogative pronouns to vary the style of questioning. These affixation of prepositions in English can either be written by specific words or by combining the preposition with the interrogative pronoun.

The interrogative pronoun 'whose' is asking about the possessor of an item and its derivative form is produced from the phrase 'for who?'.
Some other interrogative pronouns that are combined with prepositions are:
'From who?'
'To where?'
'With what?'

- Prepositions can be attached before an interrogative pronoun in Arabic. The intended meaning will slightly alter due to the prepositions. For instance;

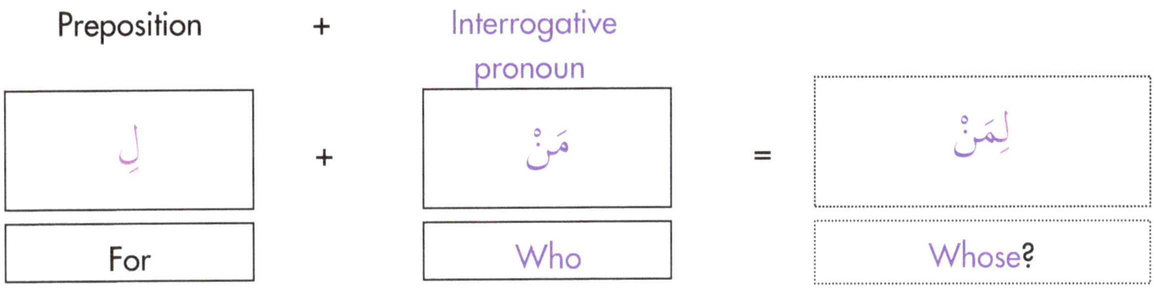


- Interrogative pronouns are indeclinable and therefore will not change in structure in all three cases. For this reason, prepositions will not affect the interrogative pronoun.

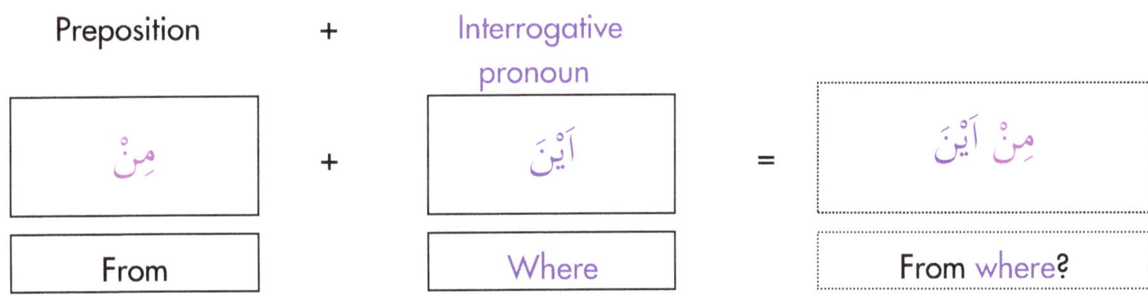

## 1. Join the prepositions to the interrogative pronouns below using the rules that have been explained.

The first one has been done for you.

| | Preposition | + | Interrogative pronoun | = | |
|---|---|---|---|---|---|
| 1. | From | | Who | | From Who? |
| | مِنْ | + | مَنْ | = | مِمَّنْ؟ |
| 2. | With | | What | | ______ |
| | بِ | + | مَا | = | |
| 3. | Regarding | | What | | ______ |
| | عَنْ | + | مَا | = | |
| 4. | To | | Where | | ______ |
| | إِلَى | + | أَيْنَ | = | |
| 5. | With | | Who | | ______ |
| | مَعَ | + | مَنْ | = | |

## Interrogative pronouns with prepositional phrases

Prepositional phrases in a sentence can be used in different ways. They may provide additional information regarding the **subject** and **predicate** or even replace the **predicate** within the sentence.

Interrogative sentences can be created by removing a part of the sentence. For instance, a questioner may inquire regarding the **subject** of an action or they may know the subject but need clarification regarding the **predicate**.

Interrogative pronouns can be in the position of the **subject** if the **subject** is not known. For instance, the question; 'Who is in the house?'
The interrogative pronoun is asking about the subject of the sentence.

- Interrogative pronouns can replace the **subject** if the inquirer is seeking information regarding the **subject**. In Arabic, interrogative pronouns are indeclinable therefore their structure will remain the same in all cases.

'Who is in the house?'

مَنْ فِي الْبَيْتِ؟

'What is in the room?'

مَا فِي الْغُرْفَةِ؟

- The interrogative particle هَلْ can be put at the beginning of a prepositional phrase sentence. This will alter the sentence in to an interrogative sentence.

| *'The boy is in the school'* | *'Is the boy in the school?'* |
|---|---|
| اَلْوَلَدُ فِي الْمَدْرَسَةِ | هَلِ الْوَلَدُ فِيْ الْمَدْرَسَةِ؟ |

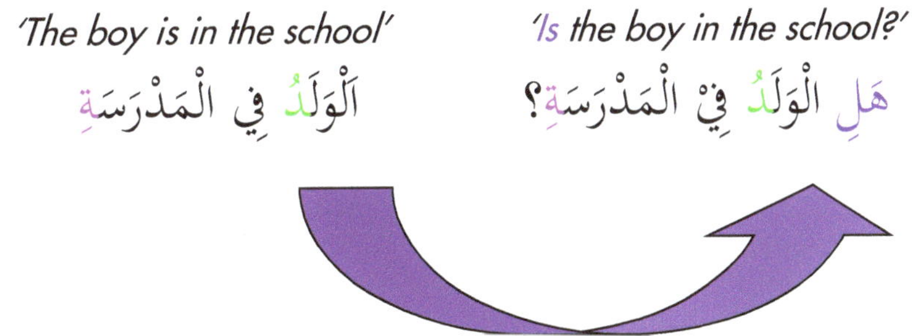

- Prepositional phrases that provide additional information can be turned in to a question in the same manner.

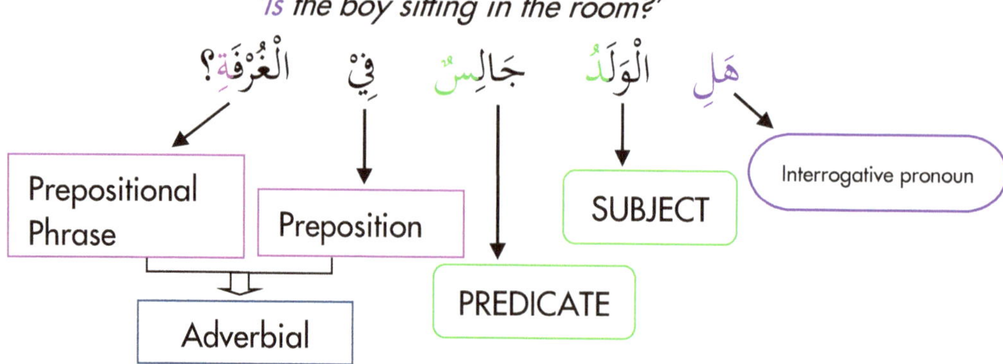


- An advanced predicate sentence can also be changed in to an interrogative sentence. The interrogative pronoun will come first in sequence followed by the advanced predicate. The deferred subject will be in the nominative state. E.g.

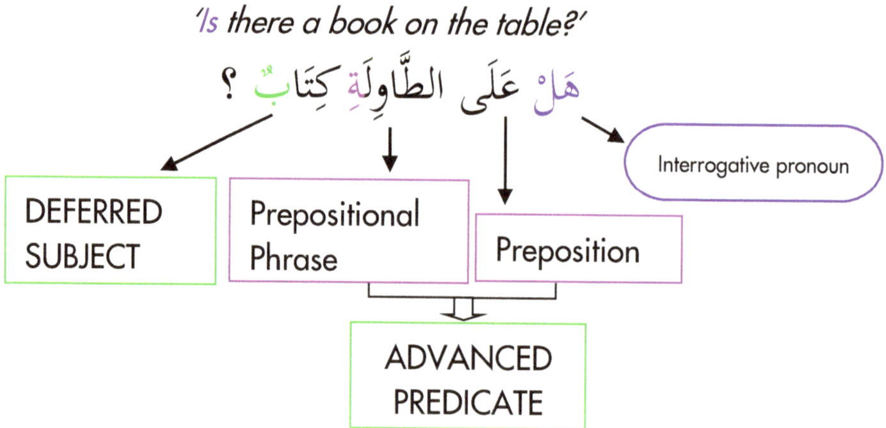


- All the rules of **gender** and **amount** that have been discussed previously will apply to interrogative sentences as well.

*'Are the girls sitting in the (two)rooms?'*

## 1. Change the following Arabic sentences in questions.

The first one has been done for you.

i. اَلرَّجُلُ فِي السَّيَّارَةِ — هَلِ الرَّجُلُ فِي السَّيَّارَةِ؟

ii. اَلْكِتَابَانِ عَلَى الطَّاوِلَتَيْنِ ------------------------------

iii. اَلْمَرْأَةُ قَائِمَةٌ فِي الْبَيْتِ ------------------------------

iv. فِي الْمَدْرَسَةِ اَقْلاَمٌ ------------------------------

v. اَلْمُهَنْدِسُ ذَاهِبٌ إِلَى الْمَكْتَبِ ------------------------------

## 2. Translate the following sentences in to **Arabic**.

The first one has been done for you.

a. Who is in the car? — مَنْ فِي السَّيَّارَةِ؟

b. What is on the table? ------------------------------

c. Are the teachers in the school? ------------------------------

d. Is the girl going to school? ------------------------------

e. Is there a book in the school? ------------------------------

| Arabic | مُعَلِّمُوْنَ | كِتَابٌ | مَدْرَسَةٌ | ذَاهِبٌ | بِنْتٌ | طَاوِلَةٌ |
|---|---|---|---|---|---|---|
| English | Teachers | Book | School | Going | Girl | Table |

## Interrogative pronouns with personal & possessive pronouns

Personal pronouns can be made in to a question by placing an interrogative pronoun before it. In English, personal pronouns that replace the subject within a sentence can be inverted with the auxiliary verb to form a question. The sentence - '**He** *is* the teacher.' can be made a question by swapping the **pronoun** with the *auxiliary verb*: '*Is* **he** the teacher?'

Possessive pronouns (attached pronouns) can be made in to an interrogative sentence by adding an interrogative pronoun before the possessional phrase. For instance, '**your** teacher' can be made in to a question by adding the interrogative pronoun 'where' as in 'where is **your** teacher?'

- The interrogative pronoun will come before the **personal** and **possessive pronoun** in Arabic. Both the interrogative pronoun and personal/pooseesive pronoun are indeclinable and there will be no change to the structure of both particles.

**Personal Pronoun**

**Possessive Pronoun**

- A nominal sentence that is using a pronoun in place of the subject can be made in to an interrogative sentence by using the particle هَلْ before the pronoun. E.g.

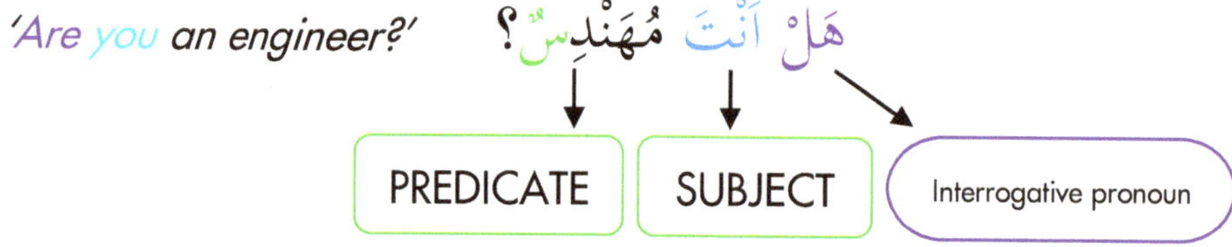

- Possessive pronouns can also be attached to nouns within an interrogative sentence.

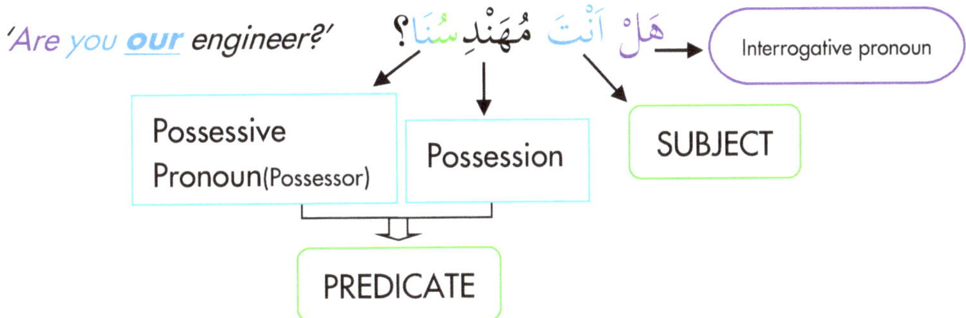


- Possessive pronouns can be attached to the subject as well as the predicate.

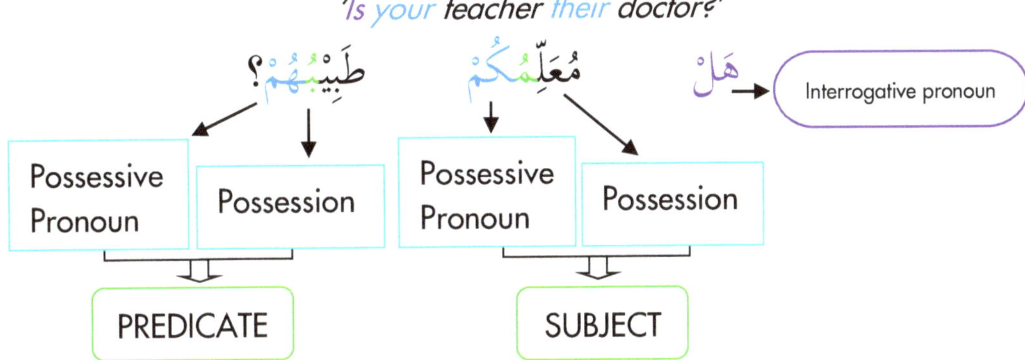


- A variety of Interrogative sentences can be made by using both pronouns and prepositions within a sentence. For instance,

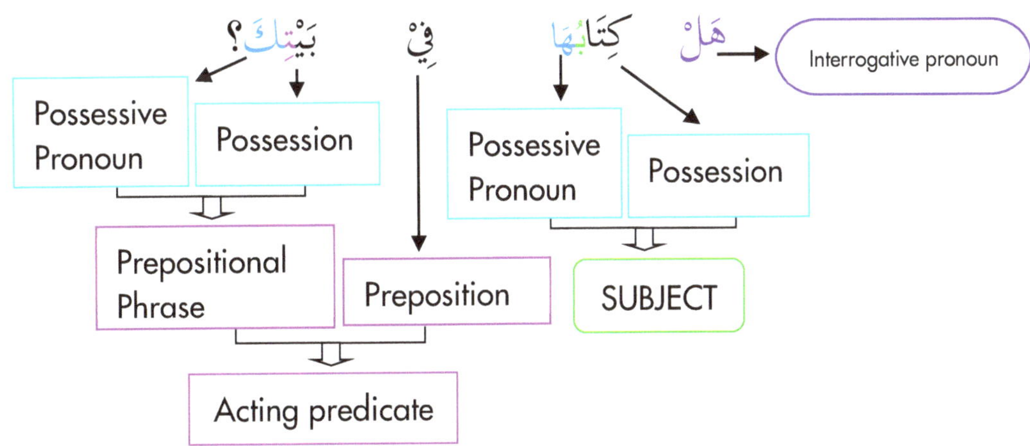


- All the rules of **gender** and **amount** which have been discussed previously will apply to interrogative sentences as well.

*'Are your teachers sitting in our (two)houses?'*

هَلْ مُعَلِّمُوكُمْ جَالِسُوْنَ فِيْ بَيْتَيْنَا؟

## 1. Change the following sentences in to **Arabic** using the table below.

The first one has been done for you.

a) Are your pens new?

هَلْ أَقْلَامُكَ جَدِيْدَةٌ؟

b) Is your book on my table?

c) Who is your doctor?

d) Where is your house?

e) Who is she?

f) Is his teacher from our school?

g) Are your books in the car?

h) Are your doctors(two) sitting in his car?

i) Why are you going?

j) Where are you?

k) Are the girls standing with their mothers?

l) Are the men going to your (two) offices?

m) Is she her doctor?

n) Is your house far?

o) Why is your teacher standing in our room?

| | | | | | | | |
|---|---|---|---|---|---|---|---|
| مَدْرَسَةٌ | School | وَلَدٌ | Boy | مَكْتَبٌ | Office | كُتُبٌ | Books |
| مُعَلِّمٌ | Teacher | طَاوِلَةٌ | Table | قَائِمٌ | Standing | أَقْلَامٌ | Pens |
| بَعِيْدٌ | Far | بَنَاتٌ | Girls | سَيَّارَةٌ | Car | ذَاهِبٌ | Going |
| بَيْتٌ | House | خَلْفَ | Behind | أَوْلَادٌ | Boys | مُعَلِّمَاتٌ | Teachers |
| جَالِسٌ | Sitting | جَدِيْدٌ | New | غُرْفَةٌ | Room | أُمَّهَاتٌ | Mothers |
| قَادِمٌ | Coming | طِفْلٌ | Child | مَطْبَخٌ | Kitchen | سِكِّيْنٌ | knife |
| طَبِيْبٌ | Doctor | كِتَابٌ | Book | قَلَمٌ | Pen | أَمَامَ | In front of |

2. Break down the sentences below to their simplest grammatical form and translate each sentence in to **English**.

The first one has been done for you.

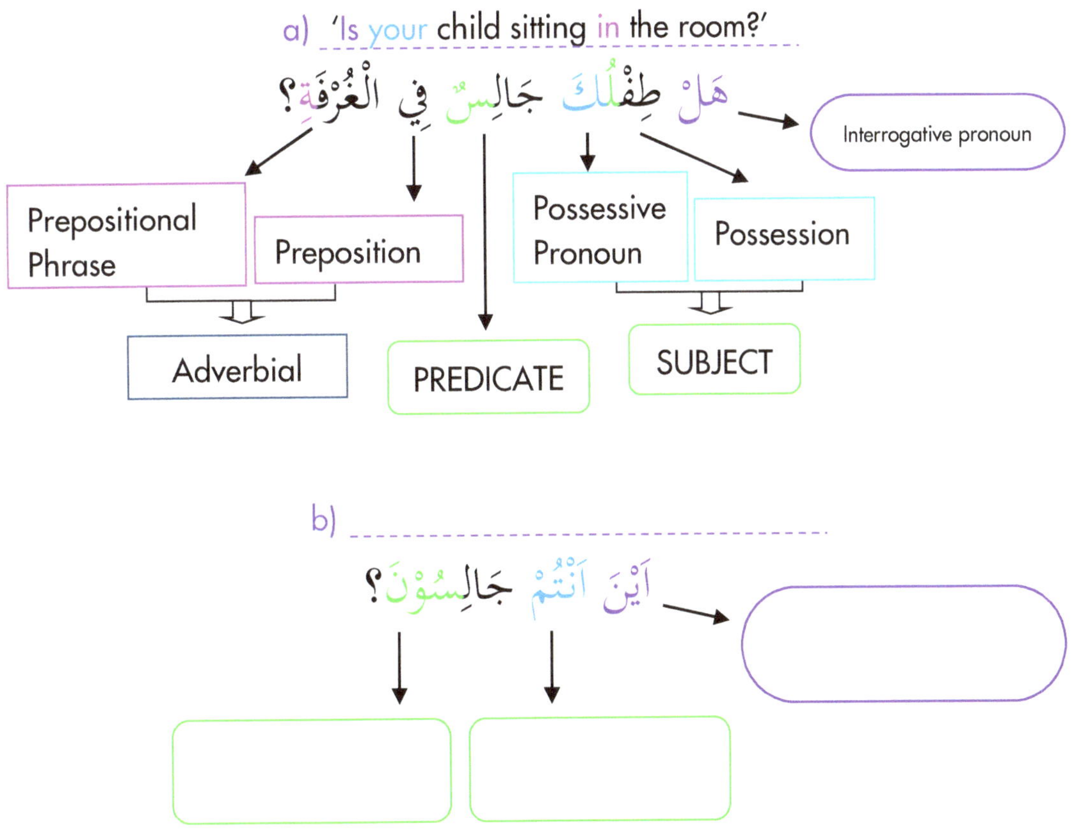

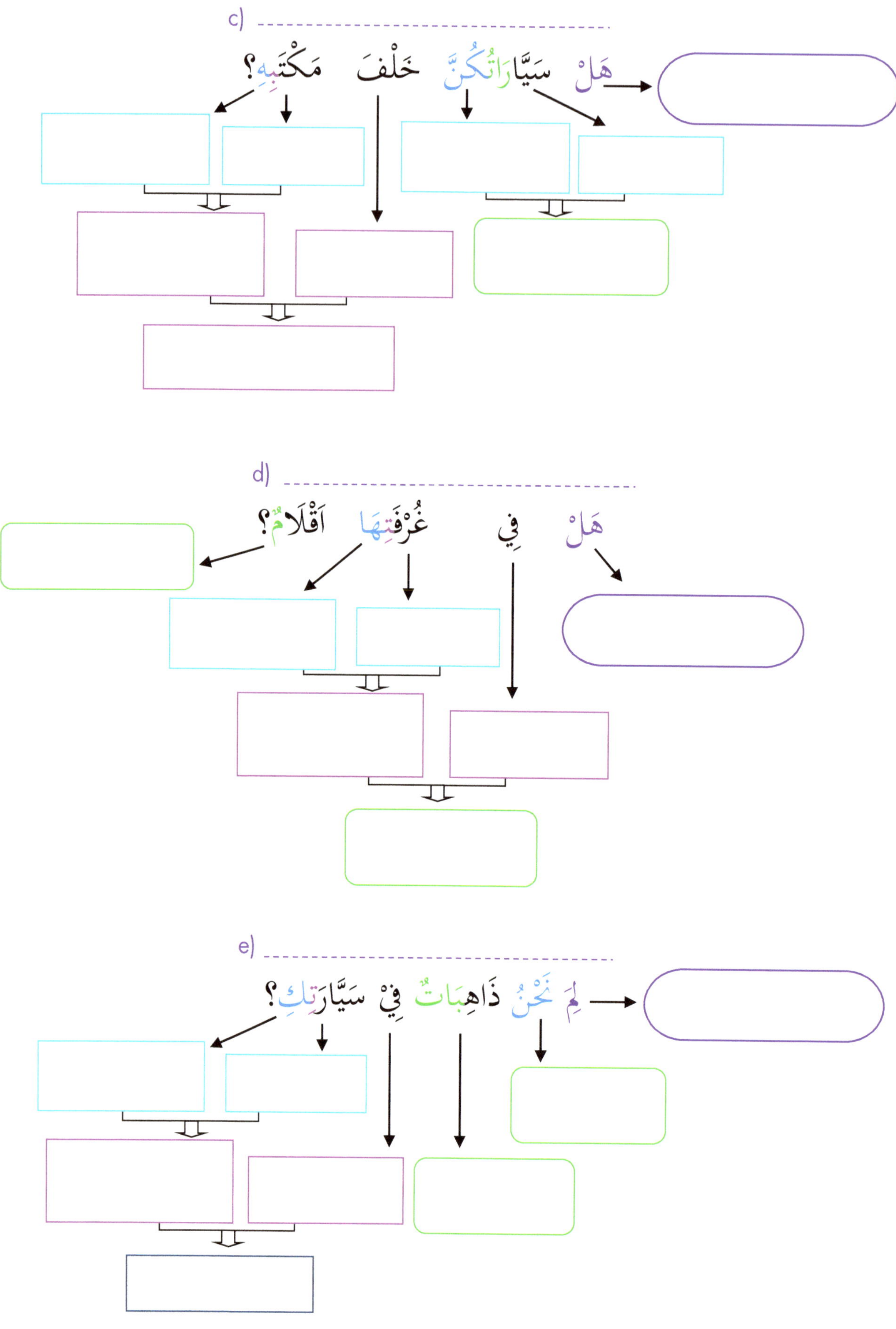
c)
هَلْ سَيَّارَاتُكُنَّ خَلْفَ مَكْتَبِهِ؟
d)
هَلْ فِي غُرْفَتِهَا أَقْلَامٌ؟
e)
لِمَ نَحْنُ ذَاهِبَاتٌ فِيْ سَيَّارَتِكِ؟

## Interrogative pronouns with demonstrative pronouns

Demonstrative pronouns by themselves can be turned in to a question by adding the appropriate interrogative pronoun before it. The demonstrative pronoun '*That*' can easily be changed in to a question; '**What** is *that?*', '**Who** is *that?*', '**Where** is *that?*' and '**When** is *that?*'

A demonstrative phrase, which is constructed by a demonstrative pronoun and its constituent noun, can be transformed in to an interrogative sentence by adding an appropriate pronoun. For instance, by attaching the interrogative pronoun - '**Where**' to the demonstrative phrase '*this* book' the question '**Where** is *this* book?' can be created.

In both circumstances where the demonstrative pronoun or the demonstrative phrase is in place of the subject, the inversion of the auxiliary verb with the subject of the sentence can take place. E.g.

| Nominal sentence | Interrogative sentence |
|---|---|
| '*This* is your pen.' | '**Is** *this* your pen?' |
| '*These* men are going.' | '**Are** *these* men going?' |

- In Arabic, the interrogative pronoun will come before the **demonstrative pronoun**. Both the interrogative pronoun and **demonstrative pronoun** are indeclinable and there will be no change to the structure of both particles.

| مَا هٰذَا؟ | مَنْ ذَالِكَ؟ | مَتَىٰ تِلْكَ؟ |
|---|---|---|
| What is **this**? | Who is **that**? | When is **that**? |

- Interrogative pronouns also come before the **demonstrative phrase** in place of the subject. For instance,

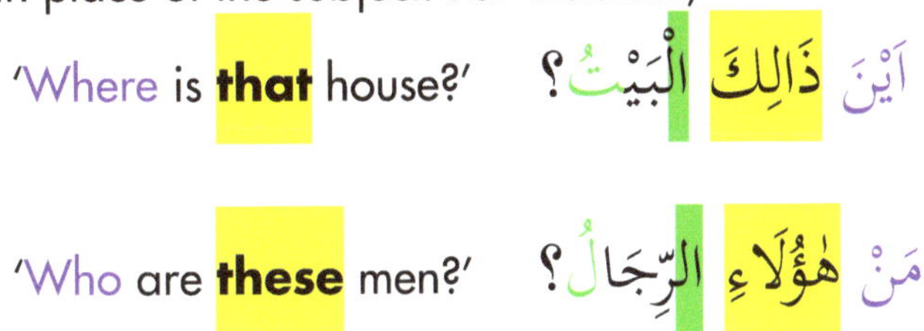

'Where is **that** house?' أَيْنَ ذَالِكَ الْبَيْتُ؟

'Who are **these** men?' مَنْ هٰؤُلَاءِ الرِّجَالُ؟

- The interrogative pronoun هَلْ can be added to sentences that contain a **demonstrative pronoun** to form questions. E.g.

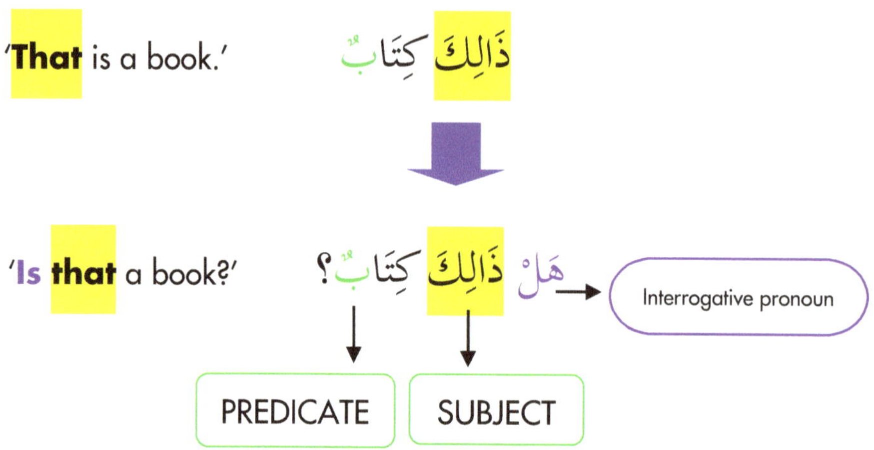


- Likewise, a **demonstrative phrase** can also be made in to a question by adding the particle هَلْ before the complete subject.

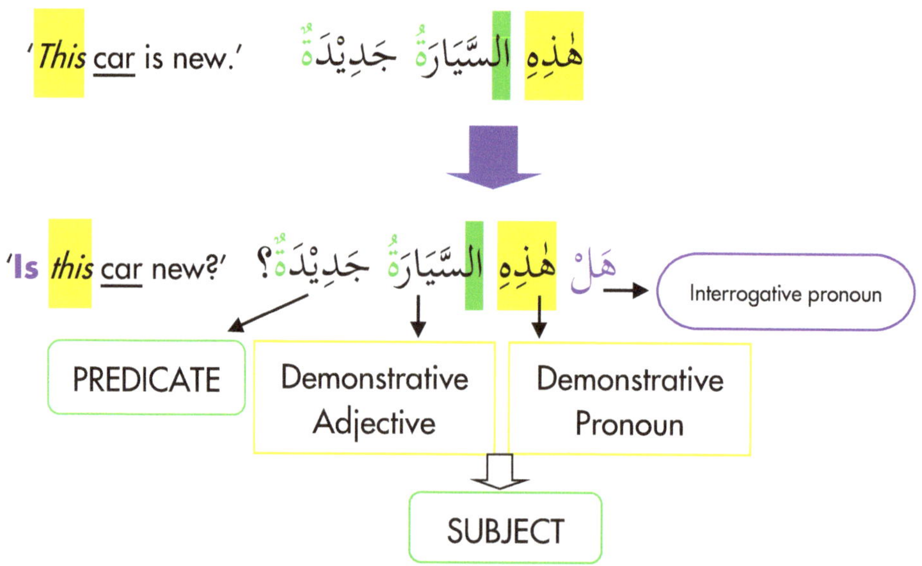


- All the rules of **gender** and **amount** which have been discussed previously will apply to interrogative sentences as well.

*'Are these (two)teachers sitting?'*

- Nouns that are a plural non-intellectual being will cause the demonstrative pronoun and subsequently its predicate to be ***SINGULAR FEMININE***. E.g.

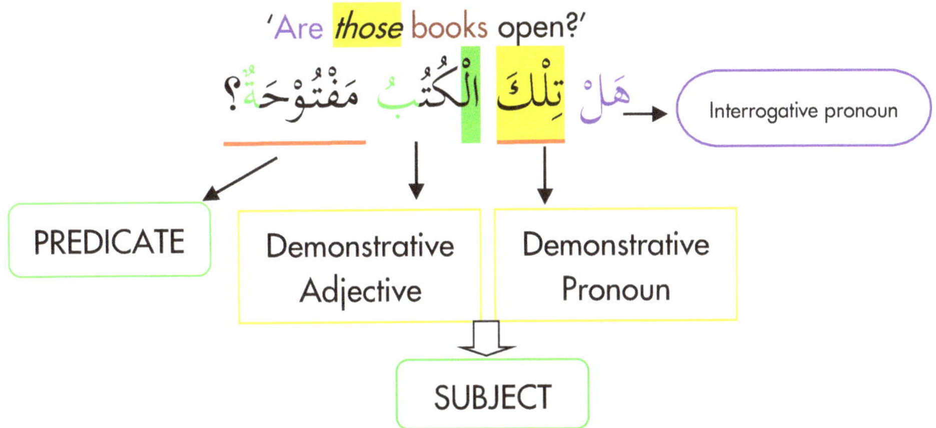


- Prepositions and prepositional phrases can be added in sentences containing a **demonstrative pronoun**. The interrogative pronoun will only result in changing the meaning of the sentence in to a question. E.g.

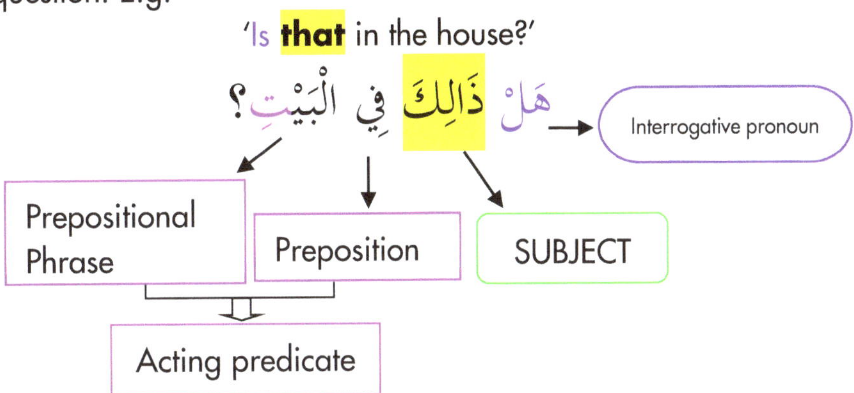


- In the same manner, an advanced predicate sentence can also be formed.

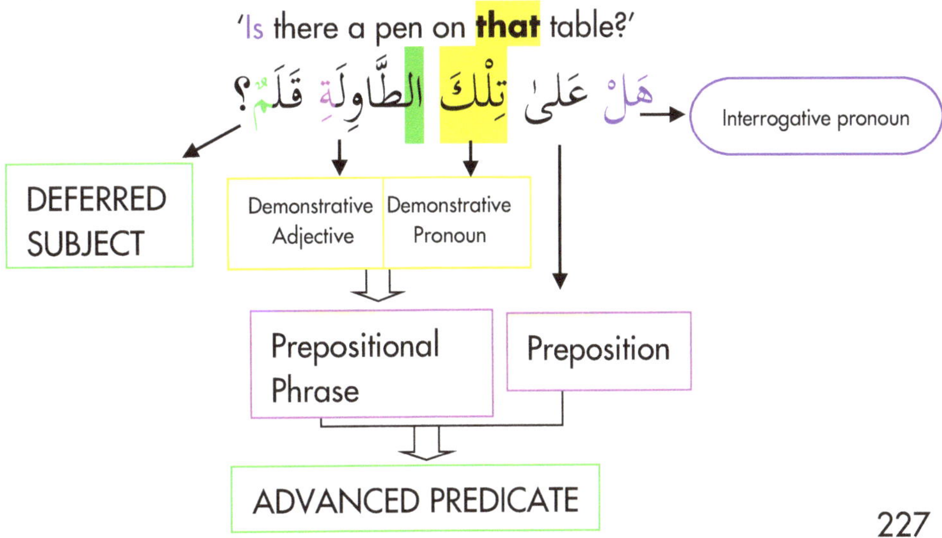

- Personal pronouns can be included in a demonstrative pronoun sentence. Both pronouns are indeclinable and their structure will not change. For instance;

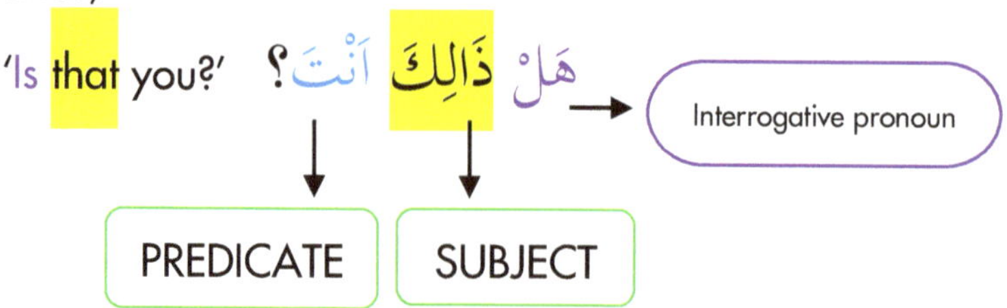


- Possessive pronouns can be attached to the demonstrative noun. As seen previously, the position of the **demonstrative pronoun** will come after the demonstrative noun in order to show possession.

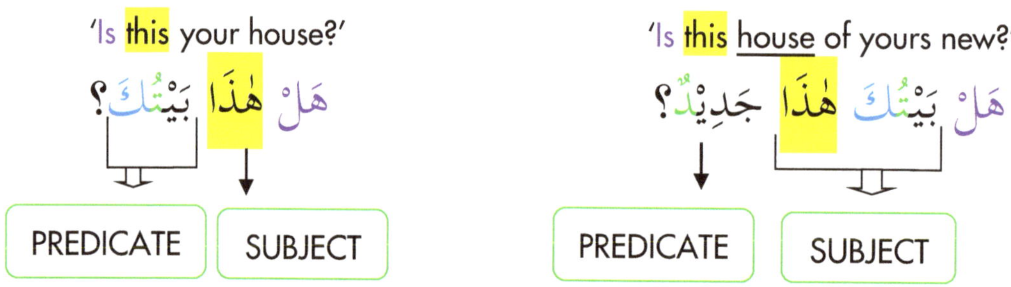


- More than one **demonstrative pronoun** can be used in an interrogative sentence. For instance,

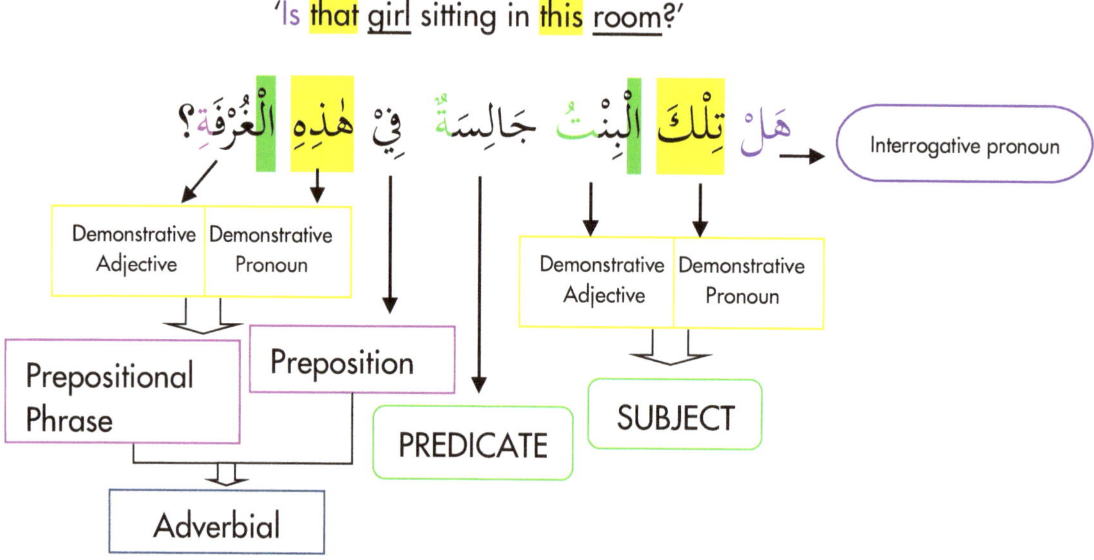

## 1. Translate the following sentences in to **Arabic** using the table below.

The first one has been done for you.

a) Is this her pen?

هَلْ هٰذَا قَلَمُهَا؟

b) Is that book of theirs new?

c) What are those?

d) When is that school open?

e) Is that girl standing in the house?

f) Are those teachers from this school sitting?

g) Why is this boy sitting on that table?

h) Are those books(two) in these cars(two)?

i) Who is this?

j) Are the boys in that room?

k) Is our doctor in that school?

l) Are these men going to that office?

m) Is this in that?

n) Where is that?

o) Are these boys coming with these teachers to that office?

| مَدْرَسَةٌ | School | وَلَدٌ | Boy | مَكْتَبٌ | Office | جَالِسٌ | Sitting |
|---|---|---|---|---|---|---|---|
| رِجَالٌ | Men | اَوْلَادٌ | Boys | قَائِمٌ | Standing | جَالِسُوْنَ | Sitting (plural) |
| مُعَلِّمُوْنَ | Teachers | بِنْتٌ | Girl | سَيَّارَةٌ | Car | قَادِمٌ | Coming |
| بَيْتٌ | House | قَلَمٌ | Pen | طَاوِلَةٌ | Table | قَادِمُوْنَ | Coming (plural) |
| طَبِيْبٌ | Doctor | جَدِيْدٌ | New | غُرْفَةٌ | Room | ذَاهِبٌ | Going |
| مَعَ | With | كِتَابٌ | Book | مَفْتُوْحٌ | Open | ذَاهِبُوْنَ | Going (plural) |

## 2. Break down the sentences below to their simplest grammatical form.

The first one has been done for you.

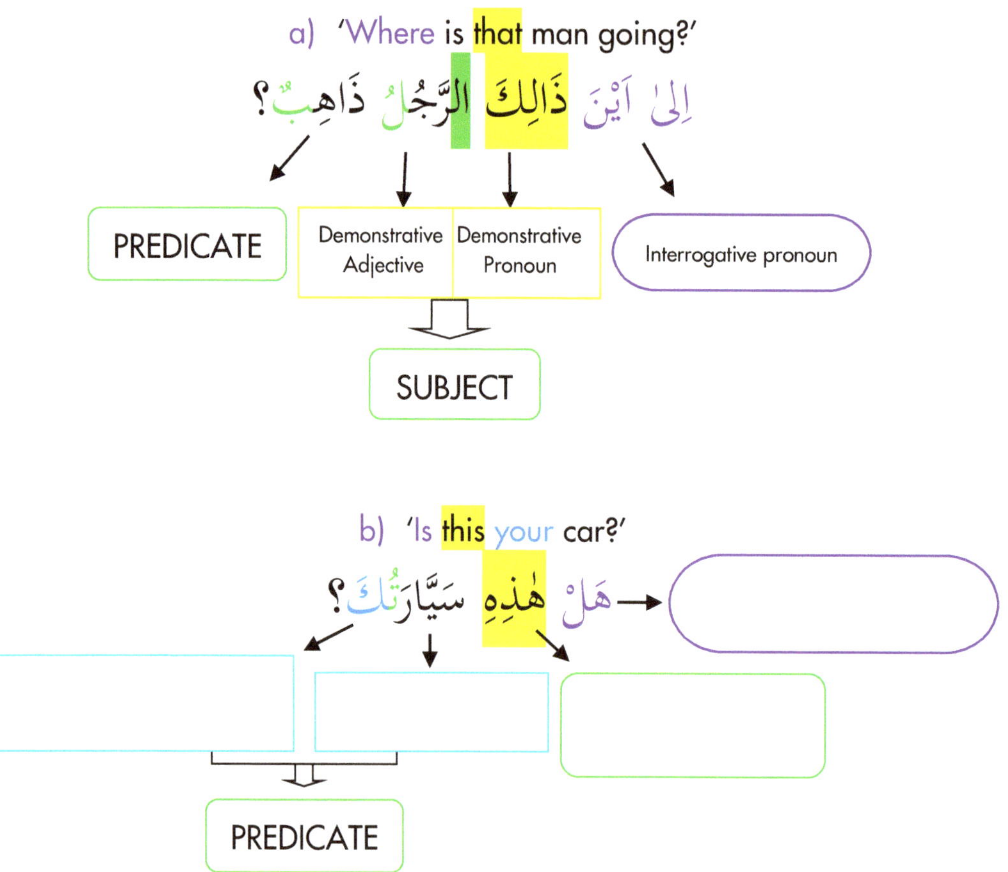

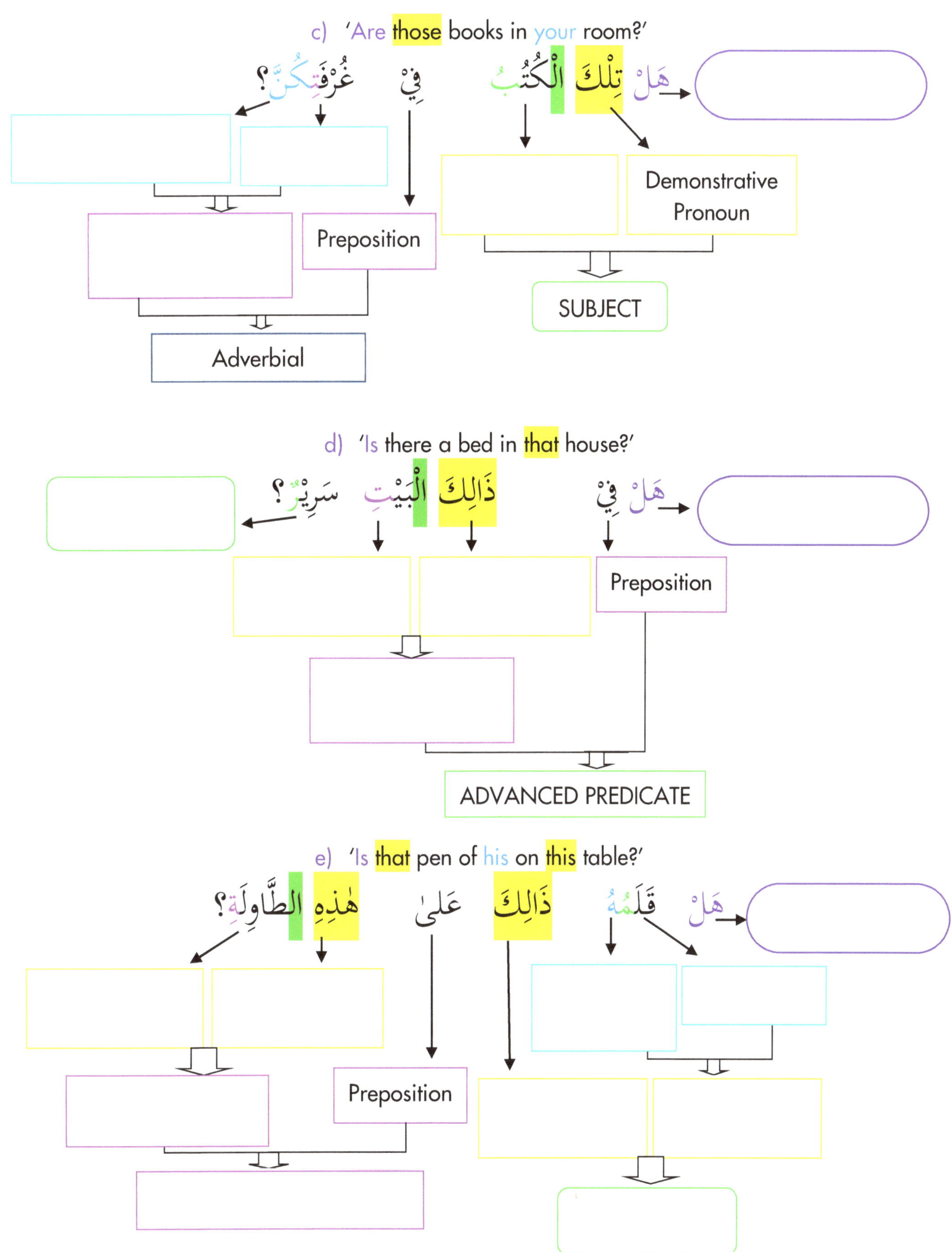
c) 'Are those books in your room?'
هَلْ تِلْكَ الْكُتُبُ فِيْ غُرْفَتِكُنَّ؟
Demonstrative Pronoun
SUBJECT
Preposition
Adverbial
d) 'Is there a bed in that house?'
هَلْ فِيْ ذَالِكَ الْبَيْتِ سَرِيْرٌ؟
Preposition
ADVANCED PREDICATE
e) 'Is that pen of his on this table?'
هَلْ قَلَمُهُ ذَالِكَ عَلَى هٰذِهِ الطَّاوِلَةِ؟
Preposition

## Interrogative pronouns in a negative sentence

Interrogative sentences can be made negative by adding the **negative particle**. The **negative particle** will come after the interrogative pronoun, for example - 'Is**n't** the boy sitting?'

The above example can be reverted to a nominal sentence by the Subject Auxiliary Inversion(SAI) method - '**The boy** *is* not sitting.'

- As seen from the previous sections, the interrogative particle هَلْ will be positioned at the beginning of the sentence.

- The **negative particle** مَا (NOT) will come after the interrogative pronoun. The predicate of a negative sentence will be in the accusative state. E.g.

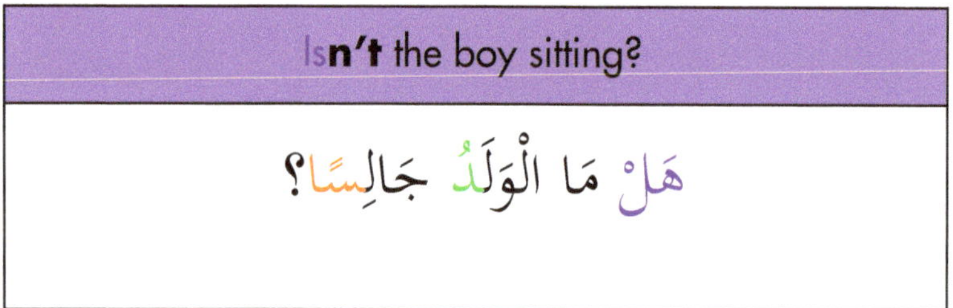

| Is**n't** the boy sitting? |
|---|
| هَلْ مَا الْوَلَدُ جَالِسًا؟ |

- **Negative** interrogative sentences with *prepositions...*

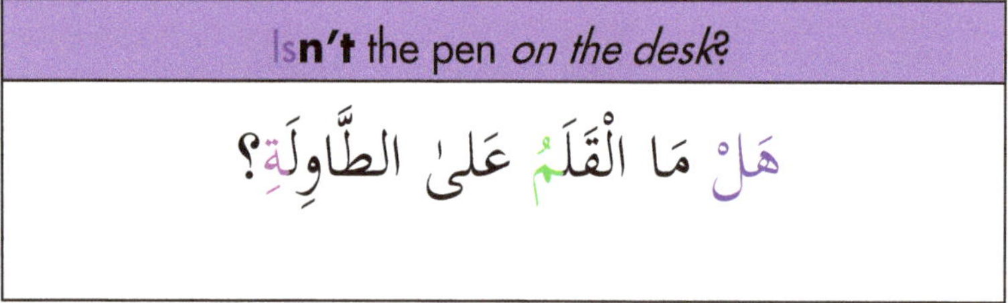

| Is**n't** the pen *on the desk*? |
|---|
| هَلْ مَا الْقَلَمُ عَلَى الطَّاوِلَةِ؟ |

- **Negative** interrogative sentences with an *advanced predicate...*

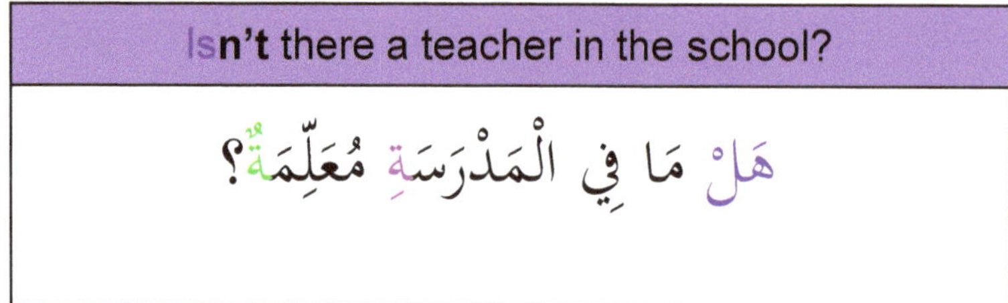

| Is**n't** there a teacher in the school? |
|---|
| هَلْ مَا فِي الْمَدْرَسَةِ مُعَلِّمَةٌ؟ |

- **Negative** interrogative sentences with *personal pronouns...*

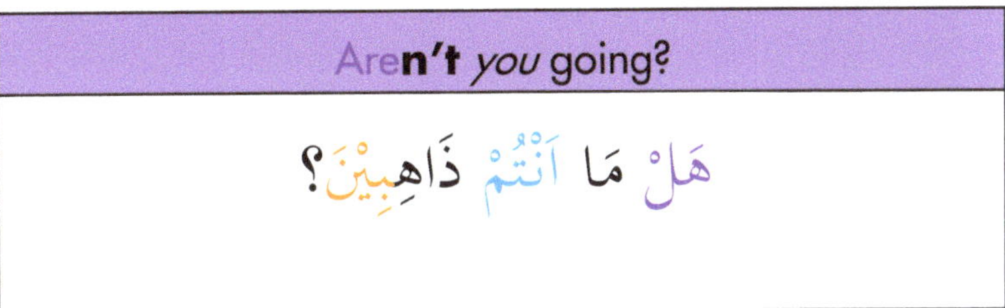


- **Negative** interrogative sentences with *possessive pronouns...*

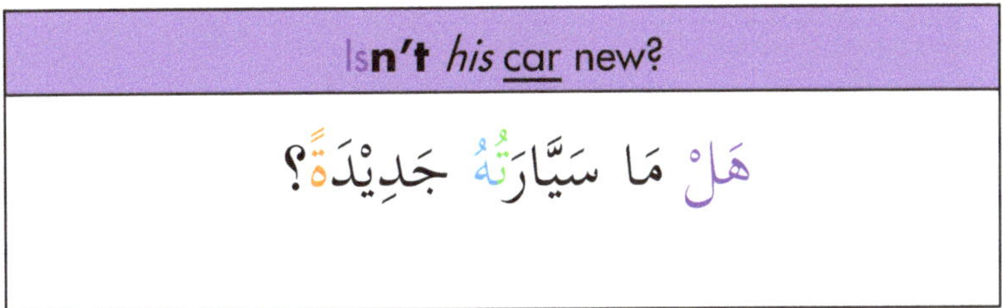


- **Negative** interrogative sentences with *demonstrative pronouns...*

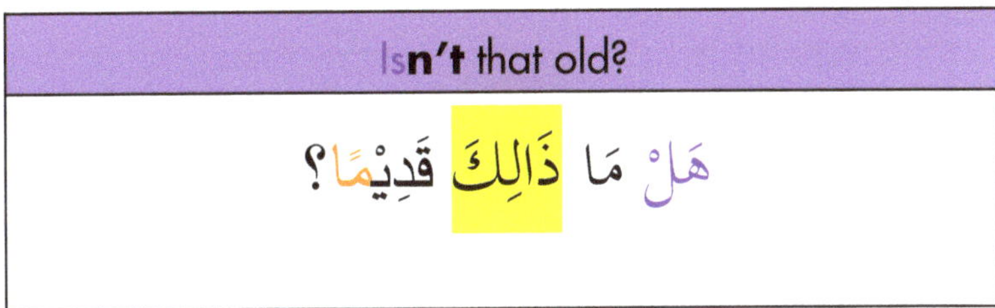


- **Negative** interrogative sentences with *demonstrative phrases...*

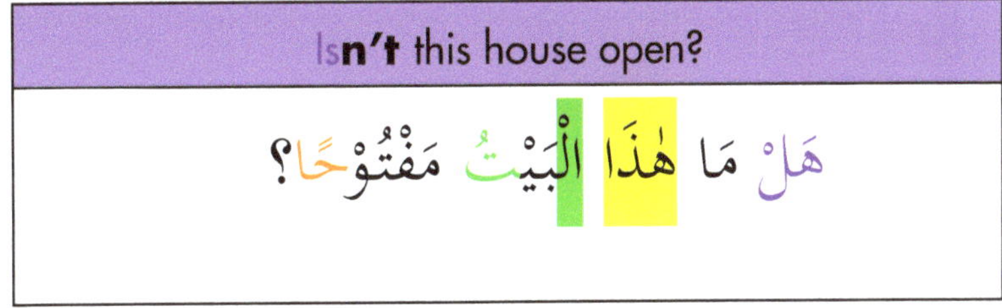

## 1. Translate the following sentences in to **Arabic** using the words below.

The first one has been done for you.

| Is**n't** your house new? |
| --- |
| هَلْ مَا بَيْتُكَ جدِيْدًا؟ |

Girl بِنْتٌ

Present حَاضِرٌ

| Is**n't** that girl present? |
| --- |
| |

| Are**n't** you in the room? |
| --- |
| |

You أَنْتُمْ

Room غُرْفَةٌ

Window شُبَّاكٌ

House بَيْتٌ

| Is**n't** there a window in that house? |
| --- |
| |

| Is**n't** the doctor in his office? |
| --- |
| |

Doctor طَبِيْبٌ

Office مَكْتَبٌ

2. Using the words from the table below create **5** sentences in **Arabic**.

| Nouns | |
|---|---|
| اَلسَّيَّارَةُ | اَلْبِنْتُ |
| The Car | The Girl |
| اَلْمَدْرَسَةُ | اَلْمُعَلِّمُ |
| The School | The Teacher |
| اَلرَّجُلُ | اَلطَّبِيْبُ |
| The Man | The Doctor |

| Adjectives | |
|---|---|
| جَدِيْدٌ | مَفْتُوْحٌ |
| New | Open |
| ذَاهِبٌ | جَالِسٌ |
| Going | Sitting |
| قَائِمٌ | نَائِمٌ |
| Standing | Sleeping |

(i

---

(ii

---

(iii

---

(iv

---

(v

---

3. Complete the table below by writing the correct form of the sentence in Arabic. Write the English translation for each sentence as well.

The first one has been done for you

| Affirmative | Interrogative | Negative |
|---|---|---|
| *E.g. The boy is sitting.*<br>اَلْوَلَدُ جَالِسٌ | *Is the boy sitting?*<br>هَلِ الْوَلَدُ جَالِسٌ؟ | *The boy is not sitting.*<br>مَا الْوَلَدُ جَالِسًا |
| | Is this your book?<br>هَلْ هٰذَا كِتَابُكَ؟ | |
| | | The engineer is not in his office.<br>مَا الْمُهَنْدِسُ فِيْ مَكْتَبِهِ |
| | Are we going to the museum?<br>هَلْ نَحْنُ ذَاهِبَاتٌ إِلَى الْمَتْحَفِ؟ | |
| The children from that house are sleeping.<br>اَلْأَطْفَالُ مِنْ ذَالِكَ الْبَيْتِ نَائِمُوْنَ | | |
| He is coming with my brother in your car.<br>هُوَ قَادِمٌ مَعَ اَخِيْ فِيْ سَيَّارَتِكَ | | |
| | | I am not going with you to that shop.<br>مَا اَنَاْ ذَاهِبًا مَعَكُمْ إِلَى ذَالِكَ الدُّكَّانِ |
| | Are the girls going with their mothers to that school?<br>هَلِ الْبَنَاتُ ذَاهِبَاتٌ مَعَ أُمَّهَاتِهِنَّ إِلَى تِلْكَ الْمَدْرَسَةِ | |

# 12 The Arabic Sentence

# Dialogue

# The Arabic Sentence Dialogue

Now that we have explored some basic elements of Arabic grammar, we can utilise what we have learnt and put it in to practice. The Arabic rulings that have been discussed from the previous chapters will enable us to converse in Arabic with limited and simple sentences.

Before looking at some dialogue there are two important particles of speech that need to be mentioned when answering questions. They are:

1) The particle of affirmation and
2) The particle of negation

In English, the particles of affirmation and negation are used to answer closed set questions; in which further information is not needed.
The particle for affirmation is '**YES**'.
And the particle for negation is '**NO**'.

These particles are not connected grammatically to sentences and therefore they can be used by themselves as a sentence.
For instance, if in conversation a questioner was to ask;
*"Is the teacher in school?"*
An answer could simply be; *"Yes, he is in school."*

Arabic is very similar to English in that both particles of affirmation and negation have no grammatical influence to the sentence.

## The particle of affirmation

- The particle for affirmation in Arabic is نَعَمْ (**YES**).
- This particle gives a positive meaning to the sentence.

## The particle of negation

- The particle for negation in Arabic is لَا (**NO**).
- This particle gives a negative meaning to the sentence.

## Arabic dialogue example

Below is a conversation in Arabic between a teacher and a student. Read the Arabic passage carefully, the translation has also been provided.

اَلْمُعَلِّمُ: اَلسَّلَامُ عَلَيْكُمْ

*Teacher: Peace be upon you.* (A traditional greeting phrase used in Arabic)

اَلطَّالِبُ: وَعَلَيْكُمُ السَّلَامُ

*Student: And peace be upon you.* (The customary response used in Arabic)

اَلْمُعَلِّمُ: مَنْ اَنْتَ؟

*Teacher: Who are you?*

اَلطَّالِبُ: اَنَا طَالِبٌ فِيْ هٰذِهِ الْمَدْرَسَةِ

*Student: I am a student in this school.*

اَلْمُعَلِّمُ: مَا اسْمُكَ؟

*Teacher: What is your name?*

اَلطَّالِبُ: اِسْمِيْ زَيْدٌ. هَلْ اَنْتَ مُدِيْرٌ؟

*Student: My name is Zaid. Are you the principal?*

اَلْمُعَلِّمُ: لَا، اَنَا مُعَلِّمٌ. أَاَنْتَ جَدِيْدٌ؟

*Teacher: No, I am a teacher. Are you new?*

اَلطَّالِبُ: نَعَمْ، اَنَا جَدِيْدٌ فِيْ هٰذِهِ الْمَدْرَسَةِ. هَلْ اَنْتَ مُعَلِّمِيْ؟

*Student: Yes, I am new in this school. Are you my teacher?*

اَلْمُعَلِّمُ: مَا اَنَا مُعَلِّمَكَ، مُعَلِّمُكَ فِي الْحَدِيْقَةِ وَهُوَ قَادِمٌ.

*Teacher: I am not your teacher; your teacher is in the garden and he is coming.*

اَلطَّالِبُ: شُكْرًا، مَعَ السَّلَامَةِ

*Student: Thank you, goodbye.* (The formal way of saying goodbye in Arabic)

## 1. Read the following dialogue and translate the text in to ENGLISH.

زَيْدٌ: اَلسَّلَامُ عَلَيْكُمْ
*Zaid:* ------------------------------------------------------------

اَلطَّالِبُ: وَعَلَيْكُمُ السَّلَامُ
*Student:* ------------------------------------------------------------

زَيْدٌ: اِسْمِي زَيْدٌ، وَ مَا اسْمُكَ؟
*Zaid:* ------------------------------------------------------------

اَلطَّالِبُ: اِسْمِيْ مَحْمُوْدٌ، هَلْ هٰذِهِ حَقِيْبَتُكَ؟
*Student:* ------------------------------------------------------------

زَيْدٌ: نَعَمْ، هٰذِهِ حَقِيْبَتِيْ وَ فِيْهَا كُتُبِيْ.
*Zaid:* ------------------------------------------------------------

اَلطَّالِبُ: اَيْنَ اَقْلَامُكَ؟
*Student:* ------------------------------------------------------------

زَيْدٌ: اَقْلَامِيْ عَلىٰ طَاوِلَتِيْ فِي الْمَدْرَسَةِ.
*Zaid:* ------------------------------------------------------------

اَلْمُعَلِّمُ: هَلْ اَنْتُمَا صَدِيْقَانِ؟
*Teacher:* ------------------------------------------------------------

اَلطَّالِبُ: نَعَمْ، هُوَ صَدِيْقِيْ وَ اَنَا صَدِيْقُهُ.
*Student:* ------------------------------------------------------------

| Bag | Pens | Books | Table | Friend |
|---|---|---|---|---|
| حَقِيْبَةٌ | اَقْلَامٌ | كُتُبٌ | طَاوِلَةٌ | صَدِيْقٌ |

2. Answer the following questions in **Arabic** from the dialogue below.

اَنَا: اَلسَّلَامُ عَلَيْكُمْ

Me

اَنْتَ:

You

اَنَا: مَا اسْمُكَ؟

Me

اَنْتَ:

You

اَنَا: هَلْ بَيْتُكَ كَبِيْرٌ؟

Me

اَنْتَ:

You

اَنَا: هَلْ عِنْدَكَ سَيَّارَةٌ؟

Me

اَنْتَ:

You

اَنَا: هَلْ لَكَ صَدِيْقٌ؟

Me

اَنْتَ:

You

# Review & Practice Test

# 13

The Arabic Sentence

# The Arabic Sentence Review

Points to remember

✓ The demonstrative pronouns are:

| هٰؤُلَاءِ | هَاتَانِ<br>هَاتَيْنِ | هٰذِهِ | هٰؤُلَاءِ | هٰذَانِ<br>هٰذَيْنِ | هٰذَا |
|---|---|---|---|---|---|
| أُولٰئِكَ | تَانِكَ<br>تَيْنِكَ | تِلْكَ | أُولٰئِكَ | ذَانِكَ<br>ذَيْنِكَ | ذَالِكَ |

✓ The demonstrative pronoun will agree to its predicate in **gender** and **amount**.

✓ Demonstrative pronouns can be made definitive by adding the particle اَلْ to its related noun. The demonstrative phrase will agree to its predicate in **gender** and **amount**.

✓ Prepositions can be attached before a demonstrative pronoun to create a linking phrase.

✓ When a possessive pronoun is attached to a demonstrative phrase the meaning and sentence changes.

| This is your book | هٰذَا كِتَابُكَ |
|---|---|
| This book of yours... | كِتَابُكَ هٰذَا... |

✓ To make a sentence negative the particle مَا **(NOT)** is added at the start of the sentence.

✓ The negative particle مَا **(NOT)** will cause the predicate to be in the accusative state. The accusative state for the dual and plural forms are:

| | Accusative and Genitive state (M) | Accusative and Genitive state (F) |
|---|---|---|
| Dual | ◌َ يْنِ | تَيْنِ |
| Plural | ◌ِيْنَ | ◌َاتٍ |

✓ Sentences can be made in to questions by adding the interrogative Particle at the beginning of a sentence.

✓ The particle for affirmation is نَعَمْ (**YES**).

✓ The particle for negation is لَا (**NO**).

* * *

Now see if you can complete this exam testing your knowledge on the rules of Arabic that you have studied so far.

## Practice Test

### SECTION A

1) In what state would a word be if it is preceded by a preposition?

2) How many types of pronouns are there? Explain how they are used and give an example in support of your answer.

3) What state would the predicate of a negative sentence be classified into?

4) Fill in the missing gaps from the demonstrative pronoun table.

| For Near | | | |
|---|---|---|---|
| Number | Gender | Translation | Pronoun |
| Singular | M | This | هٰذَا |
| Dual | M | These | |
| Plural | M | These | هٰؤُلَاءِ |
| Singular | F | This | |
| Dual | F | These | هَاتَانِ / هَاتَيْنِ |
| Plural | F | These | |

| For Far | | | |
|---|---|---|---|
| Number | Gender | Translation | Pronoun |
| Singular | M | That | |
| Dual | M | Those | ذَانِكَ/ ذَيْنِكَ |
| Plural | M | Those | |
| Singular | F | That | تِلْكَ |
| Dual | F | Those | |
| Plural | F | Those | |

5) Fill in the English and Arabic missing gaps from the pronoun table.

| | Personal pronouns | | Possessive pronouns | |
|---|---|---|---|---|
| | **Arabic** | **English** | **Arabic** | **English** |
| **Third person Masculine** | | | هُ | His |
| | هُمَا | They (Dual) | | |
| | هُمْ | They (Plural) | هُمْ | Their (Plural) |
| **Third person Feminine** | هِيَ | She | | |
| | | | | |
| | هُنَّ | They (plural) | | |
| **Second person Masculine** | | | كَ | Your |
| | | | كُمَا | Your (dual) |
| | أَنْتُمْ | You (Plural) | | |
| **Second person Feminine** | أَنْتِ | You | | |
| | | | | |
| | أَنْتُنَّ | You (Plural) | | |
| **First person** | أَنَا | I | | |
| | نَحْنُ | | نَا | Our |

## SECTION B

1) Translate the following sentences in to Arabic using the words from the glossary.

i. The girls are generous. ------------------------------------------

ii. The boy is in his school. ------------------------------------------

iii. The pen from that shop is old. ------------------------------------------

iv. The scholars are going to the museum.

------------------------------------------

(M. PL)

v. My car is on your street. ------------------------------------------

vi. The nurses (f) are in the pharmacy. ------------------------------------------

vii. The doctors from that school are hardworking.

(F. Dual) ------------------------------------------

viii. Their children are coming to the museum with me and my friend.

------------------------------------------

ix. My father is a merchant in that shop.

------------------------------------------

x. The shelf is broken. ------------------------------------------

xi. The flowers from this garden are beautiful.

------------------------------------------

xii. Her shirt is dirty.

------------------------------------------

xiii. This bed is new and that desk is not broken.

---------------------------------------------------------------------------

xiv. Are the knives on those tables are clean?

*(F. Dual)* ---------------------------------------------------------------

xv. Are we going to the museum?

------------------------------------------------------------------

xvi. The pages for that book are new.

---------------------------------------------------------------------------

## SECTION C

1) Break down the following sentences in to their simplest form

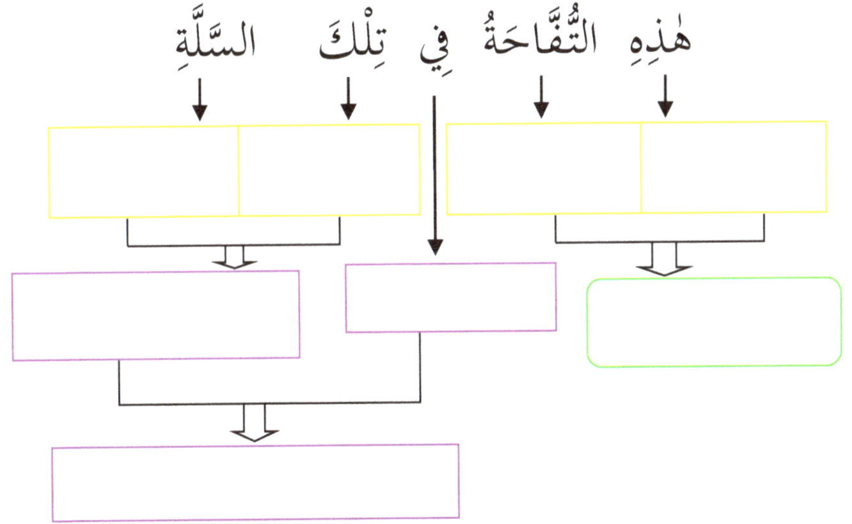

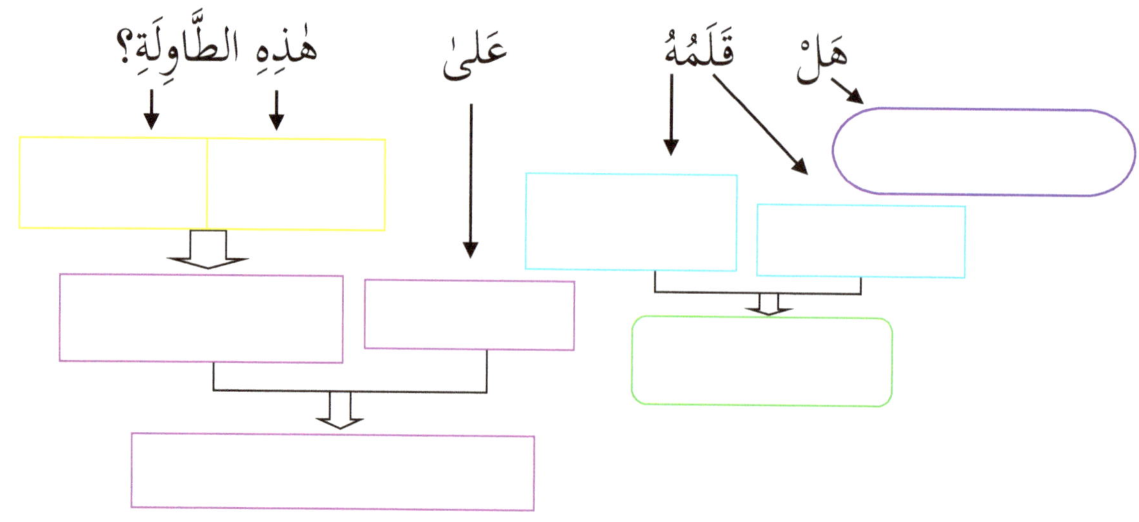
هَلْ
قَلَمُهُ
عَلىٰ
هٰذِهِ الطَّاوِلَةِ؟

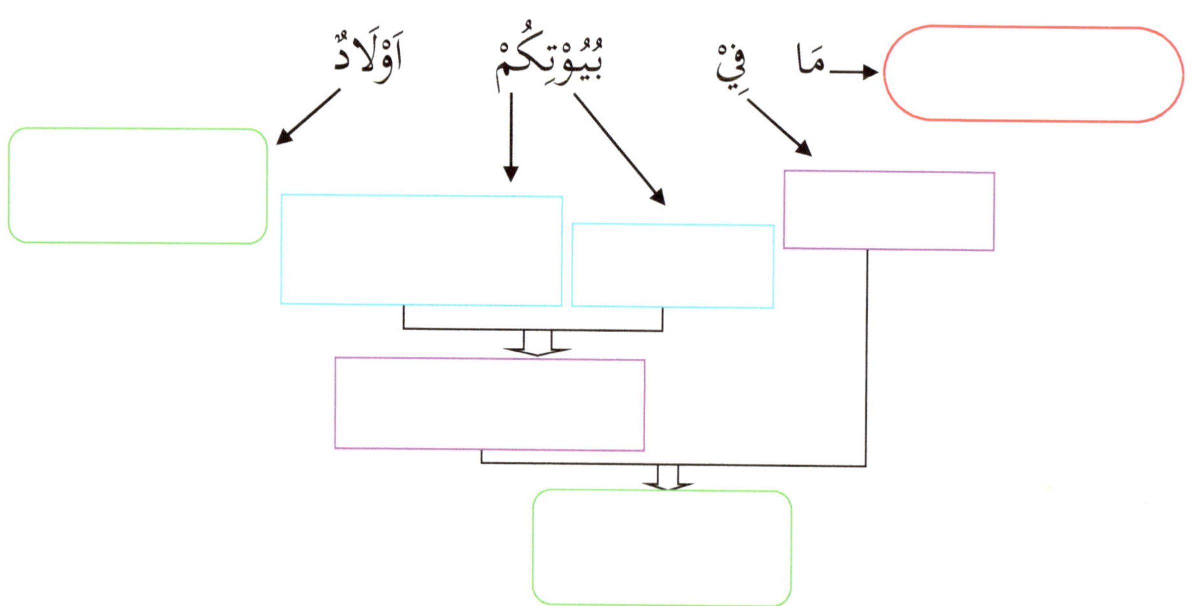
مَا
فِيْ
بُيُوْتِكُمْ
اَوْلَادٌ

**Key words**

صَدِيْقٌ – Friend
طَوِيْلٌ – Tall
ذَكِيٌّ – Clever
بَعِيْدٌ – Far
شَارِعٌ – Street
اَبُوْ – Father
خَبَّازٌ – Baker
عَامِلٌ – Worker
دُكَّانٌ – Shop
صَيْدَلِيَّةٌ – Pharmacy
اُخْتٌ – Sister
مُعَلِّمٌ – Teacher
فَصْلٌ – Class
دُرُوْسٌ – Lessons
رَحِيْمٌ – Merciful
ذَاهِبٌ – Going
مَتْحَفٌ – Museum
خَائِفٌ – Scared
بَلْ – But

2) Translate the following passage in to English and add the correct diacritical marks in the boxes provided (⬚).

لِيْ صَدِيْقَانِ، مِنْهُمَا صَدِيْقِيْ زَيْدٌ؛ هُوَ طَوِيْل⬚ وَ ذَكِيٌّ.

مَا بَيْتُهُ بَعِيْدا⬚ مِنْ بَيْتِيْ بَلْ هُوَ عَلَى شَارِعِيْ، اَبُوْهُ خَبَّاز⬚ وَ اَبِيْ

عَامِل⬚ فِي⬚ دُكَّانِه⬚؛ اُمُّهُ مُمَرِّضَة⬚ فِيْ صَيْدَلِيَّة⬚ ، لَهُ اُخْتَان⬚⬚ هُمَا

مُعَلِّمَتَان⬚⬚ فِيْ مَدْرَسَتِي⬚. صَدِيْقِيْ فِيْ فَصْلِيْ ، مُعَلِّمُنَا لِدُرُوْسِنَا

رَحِيْمٌ. اَنَاْ وَصَدِيْقِيْ ذَاهِبَانِ اِلَى الْمَتْحَف⬚ بِمَدْرَسَتِنَا⬚؛ مَا اَنَاْ خَائِفا⬚

بَلْ صَدِيْقِيْ خَائِف⬚.

---

---

---

---

---

---

---

---

---

---

* * *

# The Grammatical Case Ending Table

The Grammatical Case Ending Table will allow us to understand the state (nominative/accusative/genitive) of a word in a sentence.

By identifying the position and governing factors of a word within a sentence, we will be able to read the word with its correct vocalisation; also, the sentence will be connected in a manner by which its intended meaning will be understandable.

Depending on the functional behaviour of words within a sentence, a noun can be influenced to produce 22 variations of usability. These variations are split in to three case endings-

**8** variations for the Nominative case,

**12** variations for the Accusative case and

**2** variations for the Genitive case

Throughout the course of this book we have come across a few of these case endings (as can been seen from the tables below). The remaining variations will be added to these tables when discussed in their relevant chapters in the second and third volume of this series.

**Nominative (ـُ)**
**3/8**

1. Subject
اَلْبَيْتُ كَبِيْرٌ

2. Predicate
اَلسَّيَّارَةُ جَدِيْدَةٌ

3. Subject of the negative particle مَا
مَا الْوَلَدُ جَالِسًا

**Accusative (ـَ)**
**1/12**

1. Predicate of the negative particle مَا
مَا الرَّجُلُ طَوِيْلًا

**Genitive (ـِ)**
**1/2**

1. Prepositions
فِيْ مَدْرَسَةٍ

# Useful Tables

| | Masculine | | Feminine | |
|---|---|---|---|---|
| | Nominative state | Accusative and Genitive state | Nominative state | Accusative and Genitive state |
| Dual | ◌َانِ | ◌َ يْنِ | تَانِ | تَيْنِ |
| Plural | ◌ُ وْنَ | ◌ِيْنَ | ◌َاتٌ | ◌َاتٍ |

| Prepositions | | | |
|---|---|---|---|
| In | فِيْ | Under | تَحْتَ |
| On | عَلَى | Above | فَوْقَ |
| From | مِنْ | In front of | اَمَامَ |
| To, towards | اِلَى | Behind | خَلْفَ |
| For | لِ | Behind | وَرَاءَ |
| With | بِ | With | مَعَ |
| Like | كَ | By/with | عِنْدَ |

| Person | Amount | Personal | | Possessive |
|---|---|---|---|---|
| | | Nominative | Accusative | Genitive |
| 3rd | Singular | He, She, It | Him, Her, It | His, Hers, Its |
| | Plural | They | Them | Their |
| 2nd | Singular | You | You | Your |
| | Plural | You | You | Your |
| 1st | Singular | I | Me | My |
| | Plural | We | Us | Our |

| Personal pronouns | | |
|---|---|---|
| **Third person Masculine** | هُوَ | He/It (Singular) |
| | هُمَا | They (Dual) |
| | هُمْ | They (Plural) |
| **Third person Feminine** | هِيَ | She/ It (Singular) |
| | هُمَا | They (Dual) |
| | هُنَّ | They (Plural) |
| **Second person Masculine** | أَنْتَ | You (Singular) |
| | أَنْتُمَا | You (Dual) |
| | أَنْتُمْ | You (Plural) |
| **Second person Feminine** | أَنْتِ | You (Singular) |
| | أَنْتُمَا | You (Dual) |
| | أَنْتُنَّ | You (Plural) |
| **First person Masculine/ Feminine** | أَنَا | I (Singular) |
| | نَحْنُ | We (Dual/ Plural) |

| Possessive pronouns | | |
|---|---|---|
| **Third person Masculine** | ـهُ | His/ Its (Singula |
| | ـهُمَا | Their (Dual) |
| | ـهُمْ | Their (Plural) |
| **Third person Feminine** | ـهَا | Her/ Its (Singular) |
| | ـهُمَا | Their (Dual) |
| | ـهُنَّ | Their (Plural) |
| **Second person Masculine** | ـكَ | Your (Singular) |
| | ـكُمَا | Your (Dual) |
| | ـكُمْ | Your (Plural) |
| **Second person Feminine** | ـكِ | Your (Singular) |
| | ـكُمَا | Your(Dual) |
| | ـكُنَّ | Your (Plural) |
| **First person Masculine/ Feminine** | ـِي | My (Singular) |
| | ـنَا | Our (Dual/ plural) |

| Dual ◌َانِ | Dual ◌َيْنِ | Plural ◌ُوْنَ | Plural ◌ِيْنَ |
|---|---|---|---|
| كِتَابَاهُ | سَيَّارَتَيْهِ | مُعَلِّمُوْهُ | مُعَلِّمِيْهِ |
| كِتَابَاهُمَا | سَيَّارَتَيْهِمَا | مُعَلِّمُوْهُمَا | مُعَلِّمِيْهِمَا |
| كِتَابَاهُمْ | سَيَّارَتَيْهِمْ | مُعَلِّمُوْهُمْ | مُعَلِّمِيْهِمْ |
| كِتَابَاهَا | سَيَّارَتَيْهَا | مُعَلِّمُوْهَا | مُعَلِّمِيْهَا |
| كِتَابَاهُمَا | سَيَّارَتَيْهِمَا | مُعَلِّمُوْهُمَا | مُعَلِّمِيْهِمَا |
| كِتَابَاهُنَّ | سَيَّارَتَيْهِنَّ | مُعَلِّمُوْهُنَّ | مُعَلِّمِيْهِنَّ |
| كِتَابَاكَ | سَيَّارَتَيْكَ | مُعَلِّمُوْكَ | مُعَلِّمِيْكَ |
| كِتَابَاكُمَا | سَيَّارَتَيْكُمَا | مُعَلِّمُوْكُمَا | مُعَلِّمِيْكُمَا |
| كِتَابَاكُمْ | سَيَّارَتَيْكُمْ | مُعَلِّمُوْكُمْ | مُعَلِّمِيْكُمْ |
| كِتَابَاكِ | سَيَّارَتَيْكِ | مُعَلِّمُوْكِ | مُعَلِّمِيْكِ |
| كِتَابَاكُمَا | سَيَّارَتَيْكُمَا | مُعَلِّمُوْكُمَا | مُعَلِّمِيْكُمَا |
| كِتَابَاكُنَّ | سَيَّارَتَيْكُمْ | مُعَلِّمُوْكُنَّ | مُعَلِّمِيْكُنَّ |
| كِتَابَايَ | سَيَّارَتَيَّ | مُعَلِّمِيَّ | مُعَلِّمِيَّ |
| كِتَابَانَا | سَيَّارَتَيْنَا | مُعَلِّمُوْنَا | مُعَلِّمِيْنَا |

| | فِي | عَلَى | اِلَى | بِ | لِ |
|---|---|---|---|---|---|
| ـهُ | فِيْهِ | عَلَيْهِ | اِلَيْهِ | بِهِ | لَهُ |
| هُمَا | فِيْهِمَا | عَلَيْهِمَا | اِلَيْهِمَا | بِهِمَا | لَهُمَا |
| هُمْ | فِيْهِمْ | عَلَيْهِمْ | اِلَيْهِمْ | بِهِمْ | لَهُمْ |
| هَا | فِيْهَا | عَلَيْهَا | اِلَيْهَا | بِهَا | لَهَا |
| هُمَا | فِيْهِمَا | عَلَيْهِمَا | اِلَيْهِمَا | بِهِمَا | لَهُمَا |
| هُنَّ | فِيْهِنَّ | عَلَيْهِنَّ | اِلَيْهِنَّ | بِهِنَّ | لَهُنَّ |
| ـكَ | فِيْكَ | عَلَيْكَ | اِلَيْكَ | بِكَ | لَكَ |
| ـكُمَا | فِيْكُمَا | عَلَيْكُمَا | اِلَيْكُمَا | بِكُمَا | لَكُمَا |
| ـكُمْ | فِيْكُمْ | عَلَيْكُمْ | اِلَيْكُمْ | بِكُمْ | لَكُمْ |
| ـكِ | فِيْكِ | عَلَيْكِ | اِلَيْكِ | بِكِ | لَكِ |
| ـكُمَا | فِيْكُمَا | عَلَيْكُمَا | اِلَيْكُمَا | بِكُمَا | لَكُمَا |
| ـكُنَّ | فِيْكُنَّ | عَلَيْكُنَّ | اِلَيْكُنَّ | بِكُنَّ | لَكُنَّ |
| ـِـيْ | فِيَّ | عَلَيَّ | اِلَيَّ | بِيْ | لِيْ |
| ـنَا | فِيْنَا | عَلَيْنَا | اِلَيْنَا | بِنَا | لَنَا |

| | Demonstrative pronoun "This/These" | |
|---|---|---|
| | Masculine | Feminine |
| Singular | هٰذَا | هٰذِهِ |
| Dual (Nominative state) | هٰذَانِ | هَاتَانِ |
| (Accusative & Genitive state) | هٰذَيْنِ* | هَاتَيْنِ* |
| Plural | هٰؤُلَاءِ | هٰؤُلَاءِ |

| | Demonstrative pronoun "That/Those" | |
|---|---|---|
| | Masculine | Feminine |
| Singular | ذَالِكَ | تِلْكَ |
| Dual (Nominative state) | ذَانِكَ | تَانِكَ |
| (Accusative & Genitive state) | ذَيْنِكَ* | تَيْنِكَ* |
| Plural | أُولٰئِكَ | أُولٰئِكَ |

| English | Arabic gender classification. Masculine(M) Feminine(F) | Singular | Plural (Regular) | Plural (Irregular) |
|---|---|---|---|---|
| Apple | F | تُفَّاحَةٌ | تُفَّاحَاتٌ | |
| Bag | F | حَقِيْبَةٌ | | حَقَائِبُ |
| Basket | F | سَلَّةٌ | | سِلَالٌ |
| Bed | M | سَرِيْرٌ | | سُرُرٌ |
| Black-board | F | سَبُّوْرَةٌ | سَبُّوْرَاتٌ | |
| Book | M | كِتَابٌ | | كُتُبٌ |
| Booklet | F | كُرَّاسَةٌ | كُرَّاسَاتٌ | كَرَارِيْسُ |
| Box | F | عُلْبَةٌ | | عُلَبٌ |
| Boy | M | وَلَدٌ | | اَوْلَادٌ |
| Brother | M | اَخٌ | | اِخْوَةٌ |
| Bus | F | حَافِلَةٌ | | حَوَافِلُ |
| Car | F | سَيَّارَةٌ | سَيَّارَاتٌ | |
| Carpet | F | سَجَّادَةٌ | سَجَّادَاتٌ | |
| Child | M | طِفْلٌ | | اَطْفَالٌ |
| Companion | M | صَحَابِيٌّ | | اَصْحَابٌ |
| Cow | F | بَقَرَةٌ | بَقَرَاتٌ | |
| Curtain | M | سِتَارٌ | | سُتُرٌ |
| Desk | M | مَكْتَبٌ | | مَكَاتِبُ |
| Doctor | M | طَبِيْبٌ | | اَطِبَّاءُ |
| Door | M | بَابٌ | | اَبْوَابٌ |
| Earth | F | اَرْضٌ | | اَرَاضٍ |
| Employee | M | مُوَظَّفٌ | مُوَظَّفُوْنَ | |
| Engineer | M | مُهَنْدِسٌ | مُهَنْدِسُوْنَ | |
| Fan | F | مِرْوَحَةٌ | | مَرَاوِحُ |

| English | Arabic gender classification. Masculine(M) Feminine(F) | Singular | Plural (Regular) | Plural (Irregular) |
|---|---|---|---|---|
| Father | M | أَبٌ | | آبَاءٌ |
| Flower | F | زَهْرَةٌ | | أَزْهَارٌ |
| Friend | M | صَدِيْقٌ | | أَصْدِقَاءُ |
| Garden | M | حَدِيْقَةٌ | | حَدَائِقُ |
| Garden | F | بُسْتَانٌ | | بَسَاتِيْنُ |
| Girl | F | بِنْتٌ | | بَنَاتٌ |
| Glass | F | زُجَاجَةٌ | زُجَاجَاتٌ | |
| Governor | M | أَمِيْرٌ | | أُمَرَاءُ |
| Guard | M | حَارِسٌ | | حَرَسَةٌ |
| Hand | F | يَدٌ | | أَيْدٍ |
| Handkerchief | M | مِنْدِيْلٌ | | مَنَادِيْلُ |
| Head teacher | M | مُدِيْرٌ | | مُدَرَاءُ |
| House | M | بَيْتٌ | | بُيُوْتٌ |
| King | M | مَلِكٌ | | مُلُوْكٌ |
| Kitchen | M | مَطْبَخٌ | | مَطَابِخُ |
| Knife | F | سِكِّيْنٌ | | سَكَاكِيْنُ |
| Man | M | رَجُلٌ | | رِجَالٌ |
| Market | M | سُوْقٌ | | أَسْوَقٌ |
| Merchant | M | تَاجِرٌ | | تُجَّارٌ |
| Mosque | M | مَسْجِدٌ | | مَسَاجِدُ |
| Mother | F | أُمٌّ | | أُمَّهَاتٌ |
| Museum | M | مَتْحَفٌ | | مَتَاحِفُ |
| Nurse | F | مُمَرِّضَةٌ | مُمَرِّضَاتٌ | |
| Page | F | وَرَقَةٌ | | أَوْرَاقٌ |

| English | Arabic gender classification. Masculine(M) Feminine(F) | Singular | Plural (Regular) | Plural (Irregular) |
|---|---|---|---|---|
| Pen | M | قَلَمٌ | | اَقْلَامٌ |
| Pharmacy | F | صَيْدَلِيَّةٌ | | صَيْدَلِيَّاتٌ |
| Pupil | M | تِلْمِيْذٌ | | تَلَامِيْذُ |
| Room | F | غُرْفَةٌ | | غُرَفٌ |
| Scholar | M | عَالِمٌ | | عُلَمَاءُ |
| School | F | مَدْرَسَةٌ | | مَدَارِسُ |
| Servant | M | خَادِمٌ | | خُدَّامٌ |
| Shelf | M | رَفٌّ | | رُفُوْفٌ |
| Ship | F | فُلْكٌ | | |
| Shirt | M | قَمِيْصٌ | | قُمُصٌ |
| Sister | F | اُخْتٌ | | اَخَوَاتٌ |
| Sky | F | سَمَاءٌ | سَمَاوَاتٌ | |
| Son | M | اِبْنٌ | | اَبْنَاءٌ |
| Street | M | شَارِعٌ | | شَوَارِعُ |
| Student | M | طَالِبٌ | | طُلَّابٌ |
| Sun | F | شَمْسٌ | | شُمُوْسٌ |
| Table | F | طَاوِلَةٌ | طَاوِلَاتٌ | |
| Teacher | M | مُعَلِّمٌ | مُعَلِّمُوْنَ | |
| Thief | M | سَارِقٌ | سَارِقُوْنَ | |
| Tree | F | شَجَرَةٌ | | اَشْجَارٌ |
| Wall | M | جِدَارٌ | | جُدْرَانٌ |
| Window | M | شُبَّاكٌ | | شَبَابِيْكُ |
| Woman | F | اِمْرَأَةٌ | | نِسَاءٌ |
| | | | | |

| English | Arabic gender classification. Masculine(M) Feminine(F) | Singular | Plural (Regular) | Plural (Irregular) |
|---|---|---|---|---|
| Absent | M | غَائِبٌ | | غُيَّابٌ |
| Beautiful | M | جَمِيْلٌ | | |
| Believer | M | مُؤْمِنٌ | مُؤْمِنُوْنَ | |
| Big | M | كَبِيْرٌ | | كِبَارٌ |
| Broken | M | مَكْسُوْرٌ | | |
| Clean | M | نَظِيْفٌ | | نُظَفَاءُ |
| Clever | M | ذَكِيٌّ | | اَذْكِيَاءُ |
| Closed | M | مُغْلَقٌ | مُغْلَقُوْنَ | |
| Coming | M | قَادِمٌ | | قُدُوْمٌ |
| Dirty | M | وَسِخٌ | | |
| Far | M | بَعِيْدٌ | | بُعَدَاءُ |
| Generous | M | كَرِيْمٌ | | كِرَامٌ |
| Going | M | ذَاهِبٌ | ذَاهِبُوْنَ | |
| Good | M | جَيِّدٌ | | جِيَادٌ |
| Happy | M | سَعِيْدٌ | | سُعَدَاءُ |
| Happy | M | فَرِحٌ | فَرِحُوْنَ | |
| Hardworking | M | مُجْتَهِدٌ | مُجْتَهِدُوْنَ | |
| Honest | M | اَمِيْنٌ | | أُمَنَاءُ |
| Ignorant | M | جَاهِلٌ | | جُهَلَاءُ |
| Just | M | عَادِلٌ | عَادِلُوْنَ | |
| Lazy | M | كَسْلَانٌ | | كُسَالَى |
| Long | M | طَوِيْلٌ | | طِوَالٌ |
| Merciful | M | رَحِيْمٌ | | رُحَمَاءُ |
| Narrow | M | ضَيِّقٌ | | |

| English | Arabic gender classification. Masculine(M) Feminine(F) | Singular | Plural (Regular) | Plural (Irregular) |
|---|---|---|---|---|
| Naughty | M | شَقِيٌّ | | اَشْقِيَاءُ |
| Near | M | قَرِيْبٌ | | اَقْرِبَاءُ |
| New | M | جَدِيْدٌ | | جُدُدٌ |
| Old | M | قَدِيْمٌ | | قُدَمَاءُ |
| Open | M | مَفْتُوْحٌ | مَفْتُوْحُوْنَ | |
| Pious | M | صَالِحٌ | صَالِحُوْنَ | |
| Poor | M | فَقِيْرٌ | | فُقَرَاءُ |
| Present | M | حَاضِرٌ | حَاضِرُوْنَ | |
| Rich | M | غَنِيٌّ | | اَغْنِيَاءُ |
| Sad | M | حَزِيْنٌ | | حُزَنَاءُ |
| Short | M | قَصِيْرٌ | | قِصَارٌ |
| Sitting | M | جَالِسٌ | جَالِسُوْنَ | جُلُوْسٌ |
| Skilful | M | مَاهِرٌ | مَاهِرُوْنَ | مَهَرَةٌ |
| Sleeping | M | نَائِمٌ | نَائِمُوْنَ | |
| Small | M | صَغِيْرٌ | | صِغَارٌ |
| Standing | M | قَائِمٌ | قَائِمُوْنَ | |
| Stingy | M | بَخِيْلٌ | | بُخَلَاءُ |
| Strong | M | شَدِيْدٌ | | اَشِدَّاءُ |
| Sweet | M | حُلْوٌ | | |
| Thin | M | نَحِيْفٌ | | نِحَافٌ |
| Truthful | M | صَادِقٌ | صَادِقُوْنَ | |
| Unjust | M | ظَالِمٌ | ظَالِمُوْنَ | |
| Untruthful | M | كَاذِبٌ | كَاذِبُوْنَ | |
| Wide | M | وَاسِعٌ | | |

# Other Publications From Maktabatul-Hibr:

## AS SALAWAAT UL HUSNA WA TAZKIRATUL ULYA FI HUBIN NABIYI WA SIRATIHIL KUBRA

This small and concise book entails praises of the Prophet Muhammad ﷺ in a unique way, combining both the well-known Salawāt (salutations) and Sīrah (biography) of the Messenger ﷺ.

This book is written in the Arabic language containing the biography of the blessed life of the Prophet, peace be upon him. The first twenty-five salutations are written in a prosaic style containing memorable incidents and important individuals whose names and lives should be remembered and celebrated.

The last fifteen salutations are the conferring of peace (Salaam) upon the Prophet, peace be upon him, and they can be found from the books of Hadith.

ISBN -13: 978-1-9999760-0-2

**Coming soon**

## THE ARABIC SENTENCE PART 2: IDENTIFYING SENTENCE COMPOSITION

Image not available

Following on from the first part of The Arabic Sentence series, we continue the second part from where we left off. This book will contain similar tasks and activities as found in its previous publication.

The chapters will discuss phrases and their effects within a sentence. More intricate aspects of verbs and their conjugation will also be explored in detail.

Coming soon.

For more information and updates visit:

www.maktabatul-hibr.co.uk

www.ingramcontent.com/pod-product-compliance
Ingram Content Group UK Ltd.
Pitfield, Milton Keynes, MK11 3LW, UK
UKHW060024300726
14090UKWH00019B/1070